Wholly Round

Also by Rasa Gustaitis
TURNING ON

Wholly Round

RASA GUSTAITIS

HOLT, RINEHART AND WINSTON
New York   Chicago   San Francisco

For permission to quote from works, thanks to

BUCKMINSTER FULLER

KEITH LAMPE

LIL LECTRIC LULU

LEWIS MACADAMS

T. C. MCLUHAN
Touch the Earth, Outerbridge & Dienstfrey

JOHN NEIHARDT

PAUL SHEPARD
The Subversive Science
with Daniel McKinley, Houghton Mifflin Co.

PETER WARSHALL

PAUL WEISS
Rockefeller University Press

MANY OTHERS TO WHOM I AM GRATEFUL

COPYRIGHT © 1973 BY RASA GUSTAITIS
All rights reserved, including the right to reproduce this book or portions thereof in any form.

Published simultaneously in Canada by
HOLT, RINEHART AND WINSTON OF CANADA, LIMITED.

ISBN: 0-03-085524-1
Library of Congress Catalog Card Number: 72-78134

FIRST EDITION

Designer: Betty Binns
PRINTED IN THE UNITED STATES OF AMERICA

Portions of chapters II, IV, and X previously appeared in *West Magazine* of the Los Angeles *Times*.

You have noticed that everything an Indian does is in a circle, and that is because the Power of the World always works in circles, and everything tries to be round. In the old days when we were a strong and happy people, all our power came to us from the sacred hoop of the nation, and so long as the hoop was unbroken, the people flourished. The flowering tree was the living center of the hoop, and the circle of the four quarters nourished it. The east gave peace and light, the south gave warmth, the west gave rain, and the north with its cold and mighty wind gave strength and endurance. This knowledge came to us from the outer world with our religion. Everything the Power of the World does is done in a circle. The sky is round, and I have heard that the earth is round like a ball, and so are all the stars. The wind, in its greatest power, whirls. Birds make their nests in circles, for theirs is the same religion as ours. The sun comes forth and goes down again in a circle. The moon does the same, and both are round. Even the seasons form a great circle in their changing, and always come back again to where they were. The life of a man is a circle from childhood to childhood, and so it is in everything where power moves. Our tepees were round like the nests of birds, and these were always set in a circle, the nation's hoop, a nest of many nests. . . .

    BLACK ELK, as told through John Neihardt
    in *Black Elk Speaks, Being the Life Story of*
    a Holy Man of the Oglala Sioux

I know that the great tragedies of history often fascinate men with approaching horror. Paralyzed, they cannot make up their minds to do anything but wait. So they wait, and one day the Gorgon devours them. But I should like to convince you that the spell can be broken, that there is only an illusion of impotence, that strength of heart, intelligence and courage are enough to stop fate and sometimes reverse it. One has merely to will this, not blindly, but with a firm and reasoned will.

           ALBERT CAMUS

DEDICATED TO
THE SAN FRANCISCO GARTER SNAKE,
*Thamnophis sirtalis tetrataenia,
a vanishing creature known for the
beauty of its brilliant colors*

Contents

(W)rapper
1

1
Adam on the Mountain
7

2
Planet Alarm
28

3
People's Park
51

4
The Political Education
of Santa Barbara
75

5
Speed Fix
89

CONTENTS

6
Pollution of Ecology
99

7
Omni-Directional Bucky Fuller and His World Game
120

8
Dinosaurs out of the Ocean
165

9
The Last Place
182

10
Merchandizing a New Consciousness: Alvin Duskin
200

11
Nudging Along the Perceptual Shift: Ro-Non-So-Te
218

12
Holy Ground
265

(W)rap-up
280

Wholly Round

(W)rapper

This is a travel-log, of a sort. It's a journal(ism). But as there is, I now know, no way to separate looker from looked at, it's not an objective account.

When I started to write this book in autumn, 1969, I meant it to be about the ecology movement, to be titled "We Have Met the Enemy and He Is Us," quoting Walt Kelly's Pogo. But before I'd even started, after-dinner speakers everywhere were quoting him.

I read a pile of ecology books and journals, started a file on smog, water pollution, pesticides and war poisons, environmental law, alarmed scientists, maverick activists. I went to conferences, planned interviews and itineraries, revised my outline again and again as it became obsolete. Things kept changing and so did I.

During winter-spring, 1969-70 I was pregnant with our first child. My focus turned inward and connected in new ways to my surroundings. Meanwhile, billions of words were being expended to spread the news that humanity seemed doom-bound. The message was so overwhelming and was repeated so often that we never took it in. We just got word poisoning.

Words treated reverently can be magic. As Lama Anagarika Govinda wrote at the start of his *Foundations of Tibetan Mysticism*, they are "seals of the mind, results—or more correctly, stations—of an infinite series of experiences which reach from an unimaginably distant past into the present, and which feel their way into an equally unimaginably distant future."

But we are word consumers—using, discarding. By the time our daughter Usha was born, July, 1970, ecology had been adapted to the selling of soap suds. A Northern California developer billed his new "planned community" as "surrounded by five acres of ecology."

The doom message drifted through our minds as a vague anxiety while pesticide residues settled in our livers, asbestos dust in our lungs, radioactive particles in our bones. We were forced to respond to some of the information. Each time we did, we experienced a slight perceptual shift.

At a restaurant one evening, I found myself looking at a menu in a new way. Chicken liver contains antibiotics and maybe speed. Fish may carry mercury. I wasn't going to become one of those food neurotics who travel with little jars of sprouts, ginseng root, and brewer's yeast. But the nasty news had intruded into my dining pleasure. I had to face the fact that plain good food was now largely obsolete.

Each additional news fragment—about eagles shot, pines dying of smog, plastics oozing poison into fresh orange juice—brought on a faint nausea. I didn't want to hear any more. What could I do with the information that my government now used plastic fragmentation bombs that send out shards, which, unlike the old steel ones, can't be detected by X-ray? How could I accept being part of horrors that rank with those perpetrated by Stalin and Hitler? A paralysis of the soul began to set in.

Then, in the cold pre-dawn fog of January 18, 1971, two oil

tankers collided under the Golden Gate Bridge and jarred me back to life. Suddenly, verbal matter was transmuted into sense reality. The word oil no longer referred to data yellowing in my files. It meant a seabird gasping for breath.

"Why don't you call the book *Ecology to Epiphany?*" my friend Keith Lampe suggested.

Epiphany, according to Webster's *Third International Dictionary*: ". . . a usually sudden manifestation of the essential meaning of something ["its soul, its whatness leaps to us from the vestment of its appearance . . . the object achieves its epiphany" —Joyce]: an intuitive grasp of reality through something usually simple or striking."

The Bay oil spill was certainly an epiphany. Through it, anxiety condensed into a liberating new understanding. I saw how pollution and social injustice were inseparable; how the Indian, the black welfare mother, the junkie soldier and the blue heron were all suffering for the same reason: as a society, we have no sense of wholeness or holiness. We have forgotten that we cannot be whole except as part of a whole.

"Ecological thinking," wrote Paul Shepard in *The Subversive Science*, "requires a kind of vision across boundaries. The epidermis of the skin is ecologically like a pond surface or a forest soil, not a shell so much as a delicate interpenetration. . . . Although ecology may be treated as a science, its greater and overriding wisdom is universal."

People on this continent had this wisdom while North America was still Turtle Island, before the Europeans. We are now slowly beginning to rediscover it through seed experiences such as our own special oil spills.

"Why not *Freedom of Species?*" suggested Paul Krassner, as we watched two chained mountain lions at a press conference.

"*Mo(u)rning Sickness?*" offered Margot Patterson Doss, conservationist and writer.

It's a lift-off we're talking about. Three two one zero lift-off—

the flame explodes and licks the earth. The rocket thrusts out into space with two astronauts in the nose cone, to be freed of gravity, to view the great ball of Earth as just that, one single ball, oceans land mountains all together, joined by a shifting layer of clouds. Why not *Lifting Off?*

>   becoming
>   airborne
> unstuck
>   Flying turning
>   whole earth world-around
>   together.

Sit comfortably, straight-backed, preferably in lotus for that is a position most conducive to lift-off. Count your exhalations. One two three . . . to ten and then backward, nine eight seven . . . one. Again. Again. Just watch your breath; relax. Let everything flow; be an observer of your own thoughts, like a person watching a river. When you fly don't get excited. Visions are nothing special.

*It's all one
constantly changing
whole
holy.*

In the early 1960s, Timothy Leary gave his vision: turn on, tune in, drop out. I wrote a book in 1967, titled *Turning On*, describing what I learned and saw of the new lifeways sparked by psychedelic epiphanies. There followed a tuning in to the universal harmonics which, we know now, do not sound like Newtonian physics.

But the third step must be bigger than the one Leary taught. Dropping out of the American Way is not enough. Where do you go then—and how? Leary smiled feebly at Cleaver and retired to rest, like so many other deposed princes, in Switzerland.

But Leary went a good distance. One of the first things we

(W)RAPPER

learned in turning on was that everyone has his own quota of stamina and must not be judged if it falters. Also that it's no use getting fixed on anything. Buddhists talk of "not clinging."

After turning on and tuning in, it seems to me that we must find our place within the whole. That requires frequent lift-offs because we don't yet have the spiritual technology to stay high for long. It's important to stay high so positive energy will be generated.

Some ecologists now talk of multi-loop feedback systems to try to convey, in language usually reserved for the inanimate, that there is no clear separation between life and non-life, the natural and the artificial. The spiderweb is technology; the nest is technology; the mantra is technology. Also the spaceship, the bulldozer, and the bomb. Man, according to R. Buckminster Fuller, is technology of the universe, with evolutionary function. Uni-vers means "toward one."

To see man wholly is to know that he is inseparable from the whale, the snake, and the forest; that the answers to all questions are inside but that to search inside is not enough because there is no in-out separation and "the rubber glove stripped inside-outingly from off the left hand now fits only the right hand," to quote Fuller again.

The earth, seen wholly, is holy ground. There is no waste, only matter-energy, all transformable into life and life support.

Because wherever you are is the center of the universe, all change must begin within yourself. Myself. And my child is my teacher.

When my little daughter falls she sometimes does not get up right away and walk on. She looks around and gets involved where she unexpectedly landed. Watching her, I see that as adults we forget that sort of fluidity. My child and I together are enclosed in the round of the learning process.

A child's vision expands from his mother's breast to her eyes, to other people, to the walls of the room and beyond. According to Sterling Bunnell, psychiatrist and ecologist, man evolves in a similar way: from ego-centricity to ethno-centricity to anthropo-centricity to bio-centricity or life-centeredness.

In the 1950s, decade of the psychoanalyst, we sought to heal our individual minds. In the '60s, psychedelics showed there is no mind-body, us-them division. The concept of self expanded, for many, to a vision of all mankind together. But now, in the '70s, humanism seems parochial as we begin to recognize that we are members of one interdependent family of living creatures sharing one fragile sky ocean earth.

More and more, scientists and poets help us to perceive the wholeness of all life. Familiar categories keep crumbling and we feel compelled to change.

Well, that's all very fine, you might say, but what good is it to the starving Bengali or a man looking into the barrel of a gun?

I don't have an answer. I don't know what it's like to be a starving Bengali or a beggar in Calcutta or a mother of ten in strip-mined Appalachia. I cannot talk in any meaningful way about what it's like to be black in America, or old, or fatally sick. I'm a white woman, gladly married, a mother, a person of middle income, with a set of experiences in diverse places and contexts. What I perceive is limited by what I am. But this shift toward the wholly round view seems to me the most significant and joyous movement now in America.

In doing these notes on that shift I did not use much of the carefully gathered file on pollution, etc. It became more important to try to show how things meshed than to get a smattering of news bulletins from across the country. There's a Tantric saying: "What is here is elsewhere. What is not here is nowhere." I kept it in mind, together with Carl Rogers's discovery that "what is most personal is most general."

1

Adam on the Mountain

❦

It's mid-August and we're on the road, with six-week-old Usha asleep on the back seat of the Volkswagen, the maps and instructions for getting to Adam's place tucked into the glove compartment. The car is stuffed with gear for camping in mountains and deserts.

Compact and self-sufficient we hum northeastward along Route 50, passing hundreds of trailers all equally self-sufficient, each a snail shell for some family on the road. You could take all those wagons and make them units for the plug-in city some architects see in our future: skeleton towers equipped with water, sewer, and electrical outlets, with slots for the mobile homes. You could stop anywhere at any level and never have to pack or unpack.

Surely such tower towns would be more pleasing than these drab trailer parks—an astonishing number of them—that we pass in our ride across Nevada and Utah. They are nothing but parking lots on the fringes of town, equipped with toilets, showers, laundromats, and maybe a small general store.

But why are all these people on the road in their ugly aluminum boxes? Are they all on vacation or are some of them (how many?) nomads of no fixed address, invisible to pollsters and census takers, hooked on the freeway, and driving forever with no destination in mind?

(Why not have trailer schools moving across the plains mountains deserts with children watching the history geography geology ecology their books and teachers tell about?)

We don't have a trailer and don't want one. But we have all the necessities for stopping anywhere to enjoy nights full of stars. I'm looking forward to camping in some of those places I saw in cowboy movies and Marlboro ads, just me and Mel and Usha.

But I'm in for a shock. All along Nevada and Utah, a wire fence runs along both sides of the highway. The countryside is vast and devoid of human habitations. Yet nowhere do we see occasion to pull off and enjoy our self-sufficiency. We are confined to a narrow passage, compelled to race through the landscape, seeing it unreel like a travelogue outside our windows. The campgrounds are designed almost exclusively for trailers. You smell your neighbor's bacon, blink at the brightness of his lights, try to avoid hearing his talk.

On the third day out we reach Colorado—enormous flat-top mountains, the most beautiful cumulus clouds I have ever seen. The state where land has been destroyed by years of careless coal mining, and where, more recently, thousands of buildings, including schools, have been built on uranium mine wastes contaminated with radon gas, which has been linked with lung cancer among miners. We continue through the Beautiful Southwest. Late one afternoon we come to the grocery–gas station corner near which Adam lives. We find the dirt road our directions describe. It's a fire road, rough and rutty, winding along slopes covered with sage and slowly climbing higher. The tracks we see are old. When we have gone the seven miles we were told to go, we arrive at a cattle-drinking trough. Water trickles into it from a spigot, apparently from a spring. Here the road forks into three barely visible trails. And here, in the midst of these sage-covered mountains, our directions end.

We decide to head to our right along the trail that seems to lead toward a clump of trees on a peak, figuring that anyone choosing to live in so lonely a landscape would surely settle near what trees he found. Storm clouds are moving in from the southwest, a strong wind is blowing. I glance at the gas gauge and see we only have a quarter tank left. Lucky we had the car checked thoroughly before leaving San Francisco. If it broke down here we'd have to walk down the mountain. But at least—at last—we'd have found a wilderness to camp in.

Nobody lives by the trees. But Mel spots fresh car tracks leading off toward the south. He follows them over a knoll and around a bend and behold—there's Adam's old white truck, facing us, piled high with firewood. The brakes must be gone because logs prop the wheels into place. The passenger side door is open and there—in case we could possibly have a doubt—is that chrome emblem from a wood-burning stove Adam found somewhere, reading: "The Great Majestic." A black dog barks. "Pluto!" shouts Adam.

A ray of sun that has burst through the storm clouds has caught our friend's woolly hair and turns it into a red-gold halo. Standing there against the trembling leaves of some aspen trees, in this dramatic light, he is more than ever an elfin wizard. His pale, fine-featured face looks even finer and paler than I remember it because his hair is longer, fuzzing—Afro-style—several inches around his head. The oversized sweater, with broad horizontal stripes of green-blue and light green, emphasizes the thinness of his legs in their narrow corduroys. And the somber figure of his companion—a dark, dour-looking man standing a few paces behind, stiff-armed in a gray raincoat—heightens Adam's fragility.

He smiles but shows no surprise. The other man stares at us without expression.

"Good," says Adam. "You're in time to help us load some wood."

But of course. For him, magic is part of everyday life. There is nothing surprising to him in the fact that we're here, unannounced, or that we found him here—miles from his home, where he just happened to be, today of all days, gathering firewood.

"What makes Adam a wizard?" my little stepdaughter Tara once asked.

"The fact that people believe he's a wizard," Mel had answered. Now Mel is delighted but also unsurprised. He gets out to help the others while I roll up the car windows and tuck netting around Usha's bed. The first raindrops are falling and mosquitoes whine around us.

A half-hour later, with the truck bed towering with firewood, Adam removes the props from under the Great Majestic's wheels. The dark man gets into the passenger side, then leans back to stare at us above his heavy mustache and pronounces: "The mosquitoes are out." They're the first words I hear from him.

"Yes," says Adam.

Slowly, the Majestic bumps and rolls downhill. But a couple of hundred feet later it stops. Adam gets out to inspect a clutch of mushrooms, gets back in, rolls another few hundred feet, gets out again, walks over and invites Mel to come with him to look at a spring. I see that to Adam this isn't the monotonous wilderness it is to us. He knows it intimately and to him it is full of life. At the cattle-watering trough he stops to get a drink. This is where he gets his water, to carry two miles to home in fifty-gallon barrels. At a pond he cuts a huge bundle of willows, to be used as lath for adobe plastering inside the dome of his house.

Slowly, we make our way toward Adam's home. We come to a gate and Adam stops. It's just a gate across the road—there's no fence. You could easily drive around it. The dark man opens it, we pass; he closes it. The storm clouds have moved on and the mountains are once more aglow in the late sun as we arrive on the crest of Adam's mountain and stop at his establishment.

I was expecting something special but nothing this exquisite. Adam has built a little adobe castle here that looks as though it grew straight out of the ground. It is a mound—a dome, actually, built low for protection against snow and wind—with a little tower on one side, sun sparkling in a narrow, leaded, stained-glass window. There's a little rock garden by the door, with steps leading across. The dome is shingled with flattened cans. The turreted addition is roofed with slabs of sandstone and can tops. So finely wrought is this little home that it is absolutely Adam's. A wizard's castle.

Near the tower-dome I see a couple of tepees built with dry aspen and a small adobe shelter from which comes the cackling of chickens.

To all sides of this castle kingdom the lonely country stretches out and down toward broad valleys, then rises again to more rounded peaks. There is not a tree or large bush within miles. Only the knee-high clumps of sage and, in the valley below, green meadows.

Adam has been a filmmaker, ceramicist, sculptor. (Adam isn't the name he's known by, but I must guard his privacy.) A few years ago, before I knew him, he worked in plastics, allowing their fumes to eat away his lungs. His last and most ingenious piece was a figure of himself in a plastic bathtub, buried in plastic ice cubes with only the head, toes, and penis exposed. He buried himself as plastics-sculptor in that piece.

Abandoning art, he set out in pursuit of commercial success. He designed some purple glue-on psychedelic fingernails (it being the height of the LSD era) and packaged them mandala-like in transparent plastic. But he never tried to market them. He made a few samples, gave them away to friends and left San Francisco for this mountaintop, a few miles from where he was born.

He spent one summer here and began to build his house. In the fall he returned to the Bay area and settled down at the ranch where we have our cabin. That's where I first met him. One afternoon there he was, sitting on the stump of a tree near the main house, grinning at me from under the brim of a huge brown hat. He was thin, almost transparent, and his teeth were somewhat yellow. I sensed right away he wasn't just another stoner. Only at first I didn't think "magical." I thought "weird."

Next I thought "flipped out, acid freaked," because he was fascinated by astrology and was always scribbling horoscopes in mandala pattern.

These horoscopes took about three hours to explain. He would sit crosslegged in the middle of a carpet on an evening, a candle in front of him, a few sticks of incense on either side, astrology books and papers before him. The person whose chart was about to be explained sat opposite. It was all very solemn and ritualistic.

He read Mel's chart and I listened, struggling to stay awake. I didn't understand it at all. So I never did find the time to hear mine (and later was sorry).

But once I learned to know Adam a little better I observed that to him astrology was not at all what it was to all those kids who ask "What's your sign?" all the time and then, when you tell them, inevitably exclaim: "Far out!" In some way beyond my grasp, Adam was transforming the rituals and symbols of astrology into a magical art experience. In some complex, convoluted way he was transporting himself to another level of consciousness via astrology.

Art and magic are the same thing in societies we call primitive. Shamans are artists, poets, and healers all at once. Many of the artifacts in art museums are magical in their home context. And Adam, dropped-out sculptor, had become a shaman. That fact came through to me most clearly one warm autumn day when Mel and I, celebrating the beginning of our life together, took mescaline at the ranch.

ADAM ON THE MOUNTAIN

We swallowed the capsules at the main house and, when we began to feel them, walked out. Adam was squatting on a fallen log, grinning at us. He beckoned. We followed. He'd walk awhile, stop, and wait for us to get closer—but never really close—and move on.

After a while we decided we didn't want to follow. So we called to him and all three of us strolled together a while. Then Mel took Adam's wide hat, placed it on his own head, and asked if he could borrow it. Adam said yes and we went separate ways.

After a while Mel hung Adam's hat on a tree. We lost ourselves in the woods, transformed now into a magical garden. We climbed rocks, dipped our feet into a mountain stream and, toward midday, came upon the broken-down dance pavilion—built some fifty years ago, when the ranch was a resort—where Adam, at that time, was camping. There we saw him again.

Drug experiences don't translate into words and I can't really describe the moment. But there was Adam, sitting on the floor with a pad of paper on his drawn-up knees, sketching something. Think of Antoine de St. Exupery's *Little Prince*, of the birthday party in Alain Fournier's *The Wanderer* (*Le Grand Meulnes*), and of the little tune played by Fellini's clown as he dances, laughing, across an empty movie lot at the very end of 8½. There was that sort of aura.

"Would you like some tea?" Adam asked.

As soon as he said it we knew that tea was what we most wanted in the world.

He brought it to us in two tiny Italian demitasse cups. As I lifted mine the liquid shimmered, alive with reflections. It was a potion, not tea, and its taste was new and strange.

Then Mel, who had taken off his shirt, began to shiver in the pavilion's shade. Adam produced from somewhere an ancient torn satin quilt and placed it over Mel's shoulders.

"The cloak of many colors," I exclaimed. "You must be the king."

And then we both laughed. For at the same time that this was, indeed, the cloak of many colors, it was also a torn ancient quilt, hanging over the bony shoulders of a man in his mid-thirties who sat on a broken bench in a decaying pavilion on one of the last warm autumn days. We laughed because "What is life? It is the flash of a firefly in the night. It is the breath of a buffalo in winter time. It is the little shadow which runs across the grass and loses itself in the Sunset." (The words of Crawfoot, orator of the Blackfeet Confederacy, on his deathbed.) Adam, meanwhile, had disappeared into the woods.

He stayed at the ranch about a year and we saw him there often. He grew more frail and transparent, on his diet of brown rice, tea, vegetables, and hand-rolled cigarettes with Bugler tobacco. Sometime that fall he acquired a goat named Raga.

When it was too cold to continue camping in the pavilion, Adam moved into the cabin where two young people from New York were spending a quiet year reading, writing, and meditating. He spread his astrology books on the kitchen table, befriended a nervous cat nobody liked, and went into near-seclusion.

By now he only had energy for chores like woodchopping in the morning. Afternoons he had to rest and stay with his charts. At times I thought he had entirely left the wavelengths most of us moved on. He would sit silent, make only a few slow, deliberate remarks, and slip away if any sort of heavy discussion or argument developed.

But at other times I was astounded how, despite all that, he was aware of the nuances and subtleties of nearly everything transpiring around him.

Around Easter time, a girl came to visit at the ranch during her vacation from one of the best small colleges in the East. When it was time for her to go back to finish her senior semester, she sent for her luggage instead. It seemed an odd combination—the bright, quick, urban girl and Adam.

In June Adam decided it was too jangly at the ranch. Too

many city vibes, he said. He built a plywood shelter on the Great Majestic truck, made a place for the goat Raga and the girl Monica, for their trunk, their few books, and their pots and pans. Nobody could believe that vehicle would make it beyond the first mountain. But they headed for Colorado.

"We'll come to visit you," I said.

"Anyone who comes will have to stay three days without speaking to get cooled out," he replied.

That didn't sound particularly inviting.

"One day," Mel said, "Adam will just disappear in the clouds above that mountain of his."

But now that we were here it was quite apparent that Adam was much more rooted in the soil than he had been when we last saw him. He had reestablished his connections with the earth.

Inside the house, a central space with a table, benches, a rocker, a sewing machine, a bookshelf. In the turreted alcove, the big wood-burning cast-iron stove, some shelves and cabinets. In another alcove a bedstead built three feet above ground, where it's warmer. Monica descends heavily. She's almost due to deliver their baby.

Her hair is long now—I remember it clipped just below the ears and neatly pinned down, but now it falls rich and dark over her shoulders. Her features are softer, rounder, her movements sensuous and slow. She is wearing a long Indian cotton print dress and heavy boots. The bright young college girl has blossomed into earth mother and pioneer wife.

We sit on benches by the table, drinking tea and telling our news to each other. Outside the arched windows the landscape falls away and the sunlight fades. Slowly, Monica cooks dinner on the wood stove, helped by Julia, the rather high-pitched young wife of the man in the raincoat. Richard sips his tea in silence, scowling.

The truck had made it without trouble to Colorado. Adam and Monica spent the summer working on the house, planting, and getting settled. But they did not manage to weatherproof it before winter, so at the first snow they took Raga and drove to a commune in New Mexico. In the spring they returned. This year they would spend the eight months of winter right here.

"Must be terribly cold here. Isn't this one of the coldest places in the whole country?"

"Doesn't often get colder than thirty below," Adam says.

"The road must be impassable."

"We don't use it. You can walk down to the highway on snowshoes. It's only two miles if you go straight down, not following the road. This is the last year for the truck anyway, I guess. After that the road will wash out. With nobody driving on it it will get real bad and that will be good. We'll get a burro then for water hauling."

"But with the little baby?"

"It will be warm in the house."

He tells us about the hole he is digging beside the house to catch rain water. He will line it with paraffin-covered canvas and it should hold enough water for household use. The burro will bring drinking water from the spring. And he talks of other plans: to expand the chicken house and build a wall with bottles which the hens could perch on; to make shakes for shingling the dome's roof. The tin cans are too noisy when it rains.

"Do you still do horoscopes?" I ask.

"No. I'll do the baby's and that will be the last one."

Over the slow dinner of brown rice, carrots, tomatoes, sesame seeds, and tea we learn that Richard and his lady have just bought land in British Columbia back country and plan to move there next spring to start what they hope will be a self-sufficient life. He's a filmmaker, she a public-school teacher in San Francisco. Both are sick of air pollution, freeways, the tragedy of school children who never get a chance.

Their life is likely to be even more rugged than Adam and Monica's. It gets even colder than here in that part of British

Columbia. The nearest town is seventy miles away. I wonder, watching Julia wash dishes with long rubber gloves. But they're determined.

Richard is one of those doom-minded ecology types. He reels out statistics on pollution. He mentions the beer cans in the deepest trench of the Pacific. He harangues against the diversion of rivers, the warming of oceans, the poisoning of souls. He's angry. "I give it all twenty years. Mother Earth just won't take anymore," he says.

"So you're giving up on Western civilization?" I ask.

"No, man. I just want to live right in the time I've got."

But his resignation to doom is not complete, it turns out. He's making a movie about animals. "All the films I've done so far have been for me," he says. "This one is for the animals. People have to know those animals."

He's been around, Richard. Collected a college degree that, he says, was nothing but a worthless piece of paper; made the trek to Nepal, before it became a must on the head tripper's world tour. Knows a lot of hip scenes. Glowers with a gloomy air of misanthropy.

Julia's very different—full of energy and enthusiasm, but rather middle-class proper, it seems to me. She'll either go back to the city after one of those bitter winters or she'll turn into a superbreadbaker and gardener, will put up shelves and shelves of wild berry preserves every year, and raise a family (ecologically correct: no more than two kids). Adam doesn't say much while Richard does his apocalyptic litany. He uses speech now as economically as he does the rice and the hauled-in spring water. But unlike the rest of us, he always seems to hear what is being said.

I remember how once, last year at the ranch, we were talking about some social crisis and it turned out Adam knew nothing about it. I was shocked and accused him of indifference. He told me there was no point in cluttering his mind with things he couldn't do anything about.

"You have to be informed. You're just escaping," I argued. But now I understand what he meant. I've stopped reading about Vietnam. No Vietnamese will be saved because we have all diligently memorized the grim data about their slaughter. Only by affirming life can we overcome the forces of death.

When Richard has finished his ego-doom monologue, Adam remarks that he might build another house in a year or two, a stone house higher up than this, just for him, Monica, and the child.

"The pollution will get up there too," Richard says.

"Then we'll just keep going up."

"Into the clouds?" I ask.

"Not yet."

He sits with his elbows on the table, right arm across his chest, a cigarette between yellow-stained fingers. Monica is slightly behind him, with her arms around his shoulders, leaning against him. In the light of the single kerosene lamp her face glows with a joyous serenity she did not have last year. How she cares for him. You can see it in the way she moves his arm when, forgetful, he lets the cigarette burn close to his left sleeve. He needs caring for and she does it without dominating or patronizing, while retiring into his will like the most demure old-time country wife.

Richard talks of the addictiveness of speed. "After that long drive from British Columbia," he says, "I thought I'd have to taper off by driving three hundred miles one day, a hundred, fifty, ten."

Sure. Yesterday we veered off the highway to look at the Black Canyon. There's a road all around the rim, with lookout points. So we drove a stretch, stopped, walked to the edge, peered down hundreds of feet, past layers of rock and trees clinging to cracks, to the stream way below which over centuries had created this great cleft. We looked a few moments, got back into the car and continued. After a while we began skipping lookouts because no view was more spectacular than the next. At the end of the sightseeing trail, hungry, we stopped to picnic—and found everyone else had too. The tables under the piñon pines were mostly occupied. As we settled at one, the measured cadences of some midwestern mama intruded into our lunch. We rushed to finish, get back into the car, and go on.

Since leaving San Francisco we had been traveling about 500 miles a day, passing towns and cities so fast we don't even remember their names. Now we couldn't slow down, so we saw of the canyon only what automotive speed would allow. To get a sense of it, really, required a slowing down that would permit us to watch the cactus grow. We would have had to spend at least a day there, watch the light change, listen to the sounds. But it would have taken us at least a day to wind ourselves down.

Of course on the other hand there was this: by moving so fast we got, though only dimly, a glimpse of the grand sweep of time, of the way the water and wind had worn the rocks in the course of millions of years and gouged this giant cleft in the earth. A glimpse came through. But we were geared for relentless forward motion. We were agitated, off balance, straining out of the present, unable to yield to the moment. Tensely we pressed on, anxious to "make good time." We were locked in transit, prisoners of speed. Only now, for the first time since we left San Francisco, do we have the sense of actually being in a place.

Late in the night, Adam lights a Coleman lantern and escorts us to a little one-room house a couple of hundred feet down from his. It is empty now, while the couple who built it is away earning food money by picking peaches. The wall next to the bed is covered with a large quilt that must have taken at least two months to make. The girl living here made it. Outside is the slow grass. The moon is just rising, casting an opalescent light through the huge window at the foot of the bed. It has grown cold and I bundle up Usha and slip into the sleeping bag next to Mel.

WHOLLY ROUND

In the morning we build a little wood fire outside on a barren spot of ground, make coffee and fry some eggs. It's the most delicious breakfast ever.

The landscape stretches out in front of us, vast. It's disorienting. There is a foreground—where we are—and a background—the distant mountains—but no in-between. In between there is only air. The effect is both exhilarating and dizzying. Everything is constantly larger than life, written against the sky.

And the joy of the simple breakfast, the simplicity of life here, is exciting. What would living here be like, I wonder. Unrealistic, impossible, I tell myself, scared. Irresponsible, escapist. But another part of me says: why is that?

No, I wouldn't want this. This is the hard life that our grandmothers wanted to get away from. What, then, is the temptation?

During the day we wander. Others have been here with the idea of establishing a home. Some writer has almost finished building a cave dwelling, expanding a cave dug by prospectors years ago. He's away now too, picking peaches. A few old notebooks, *National Geographic*s, some candles, a few clothes are all we find of his presence.

Further on, another dome has been begun by someone. In it there's a bookshelf: a book by Krishnamurti, a dictionary, some Hesse, and—strange in context—*A Short Guide to Writing About Literature*.

In our own cabin I had found Thoreau, the Bible, the *Bhagavad-Gita*, the *Teachings of Don Juan* by Carlos Castaneda, *How to Survive in the Woods*, Hesse's *Magister Ludi*, *The Herbalist*, and a photograph book—*Children and Their Fathers*—full of wonderful and amusing pictures of infants and men.

In Adam's house I saw some science fiction, a big book on Indian dance, the biography of Madame Blavatsky, an atlas, Andreas Feininger's elegant book on trees.

And what would I take to my mountaintop? Not Shakespeare,

maybe Lama Govinda's *Foundations of Tibetan Mysticism*, a book of Tantric art and some handbooks on herbs, food, emergency medical aid. Probably I'd bring some carefully chosen reading matter and some that happened into the baggage by accident, as no doubt these people did.

Toward evening, Adam takes a clay pitcher and goes to milk Raga in her pen, which he has built of aspen trees. He stuck them into the ground, untrimmed and of various lengths, so that it seems almost as though they grew there. Inside is a smaller pen, divided in half and patched with animal skins to shelter the burro, Raga, and Raga's kid from the elements. Last year, when it began to freeze, the goat had to be brought into the kitchen. This year Adam hopes to make her place livable with a canvas covering.

The highway is only two miles away, if you go straight down. We stand beside the pen and look down at the corner with the gas station. But this is another country.

"Adam lives as close as he can to what nature allows," Mel says. He makes no compromises. He's as pure and passionate on this mountaintop as he was as a sculptor working with plastics. No detail is too small for his attention.

There is no visible plastic in the house because plastic is hard to dispose of, may leech out a toxin, and takes more energy to manufacture than other materials that can be substituted. Monica won't even use plastic panties for the baby. She will knit woolen soakers. I, on the other hand, came with plastic-covered paper diapers.

Adam and Monica have cut their needs to what seems to me a minimum but they hope to cut them even more. Last year, Monica met a couple who owned only two household objects: one cup and one spoon. She admires that.

When I offer her some things for her baby she refuses. "I have extra receiving blankets. You can always use more of those in the beginning," I say.

"No, thanks. I have some flannel I can cut up. Everyone is always trying to give us things. My sister wanted to give us a ham radio. But we decided we don't need it."

"And what if there's an emergency? If someone gets sick? You won't have a car or a road or a telephone."

"The only time a doctor would come up is if you were dying," she says.

"And if you're dying, you don't need a doctor," says Adam.

I've met many young people who have tried to go back to the land and live on it. But most of them playact. They're serious the way children in a game are serious, but at the same time they know that back there, somewhere, in a suburb or city, the conveniences remain available the moment they want them. And they draw on them. They need them. Many rural communes are depopulated in winter months.

Many talk of "liberating" a piece of Mother Earth. But in one of the southwestern communes where this is supposed to be happening, I saw little awareness of what living with nature means. At the gate was a junkyard of cars. The inner road was rutted by trucks hauling water from the spring to dwellings—though a pipeline could very easily have been installed, preventing erosion. The commune had been in existence for two years. Many substantial and interesting homes had been constructed. But there was not even one outhouse. People used little pits, the kind you'd dig beside a temporary backpacking camp. There was an organic garden but no chickens or other animals. Few people seemed to know much about the local herbs and wild edibles.

But here with Adam and Monica, everything feels harmonious. They've made a place for themselves within this landscape and accepted its demands. I believe they can survive here.

"Don't you get lonely up here?" I ask.

"When you've seen how people live it's nice to come up here and see how animals live," he says. "The more you get to know them, the more company you have."

The following evening, Mel tells about the developer from Orange County who came to look at land adjoining the ranch, with a trailer park in mind.

"If that happens it's all ruined," I say.

"Then it will be time for you to move on," says Adam.

"We can't. We have to be near the city," I protest.

"Then you're not really committed to the ranch, you're committed to the city," he says.

"To *both*."

"You can't be to both."

"The trouble is," I say, "that I like a lot of the very things that are causing the trouble."

"No you don't," Adam says. "I've heard you speak against them."

He's scaring me, the way he makes those statements so quietly and flatly, without trying to persuade yet with a conviction that makes them undeniable.

"Look," I say, "if Mel quit teaching and I stopped writing we'd be poor. We've been poor—both of us—and there's no freedom in that. Living like this, with all that work—making your own flour, hauling water—you don't have time for the other things you want to do."

"I have plenty of time," Adam says. "I *want* to build this house. I *want* to visit with the animals. In the winter I'll have even more time than I want for drawing pictures. What don't I have time for?"

His face floats in the dusk. Mine, I know, is tense. I know I have a stiff half-smile on because he scares me. What exactly is it I'm so attached to? I think of the profusion of moments I squander because I live in the city—getting places, waiting, entertaining, shopping. Always desiring quiet moments, making them impossible by the clutter of events and activities of my daily life.

Up here at Adam's there is no clutter. Only the essentials are here and a simplicity as pure as the mountain air. There is no small talk. Nothing is extraneous. The dilemmas of our life become silly, in this landscape with only foreground and background, no in-between.

As we leave, I want to ask if there's anything they miss. But I don't ask because I know they don't miss anything. I remember how years ago, I was puzzled by what to choose as a parting gift for the Greek fisherman's family I had stayed with on the island of Aegina. Everything that occurred would have been an intrusion in their lovely little house. I settled, finally, on some yards of black wool for the long black dresses the lady of the house always wore.

We leave in the morning. They watch us go, standing in the wind on the peak, larger than life against the sky, in front of their fantasy castle.

The road down doesn't seem quite so long. We stop to wash at the spring by the cattle trough. Already we are beginning to feel rushed. Autopace is getting us again.

"We'll be back," says Mel.

What does he mean, I wonder anxiously. "You never know where and when we'll return," I say, covering with a generality.

Down the bumpy road, the castle momentarily visible as a mound far away, then gone.

"You know, Adam is right about a lot of things," says Mel.

"Like what?" I ask, knowing full well what he's thinking.

"Wouldn't you like to have a burro? And Usha could milk the goat," he says. "We wouldn't send her to school. We'd get her books and we'd send her to other people to live and learn. She could spend a summer at Adam's. She wouldn't have to stand in line or sit still in a classroom. We should be raising people who know how to see the possibilities in this contracting world."

We open the gate across the road—the gate without a fence—and close it again behind us. At the bottom of the hill, where this dirt road meets the paved one, there's a sign: "Public access." Adam told us that quite a few people had come up to look around, having heard of the existence of freaks in a dome up there. That's why he put up that gate in the middle of nowhere. Beyond, it's his land.

"We should blow that sign up," says Mel.

"You sound like any landowner. But soon there won't be any wilderness mountaintops left to build separate worlds on."

Below, the grocery store sells powdered mashed potatoes, candy, the essentials. We stop for coffee and rolls at the adjacent lunch counter. Coffee in paper cups with plastic holders. A powder in aluminum envelope instead of cream; a paper envelope of salt, one of pepper, one of sugar. Sticky sweet rolls in cellophane.

I leaf through some magazines on the rack. Trivia. Just words.

"What's your book about?" Adam had asked.

"The ecology movement."

"Ecology! Everyone wants to talk about it, write about it, but nobody wants to do anything about it," he said. I didn't mention my writing again.

One thing is clear: Adam is living what he believes while we are addicted to the very things we are so—in the abstract—against: waste of energy, consumption of goods, speed.

The visit to Adam's mountain was to have been merely a prelude to a tour of southwestern communes and communities for us. But it proves to be the high point.

After a few more stops I conclude that life in the lap of Mother Nature is not for me. Right now I'm more inclined to fantasize about jetting around the world with a light suitcase—flash flash—feeding the eyes ears mind on changes, afterward retiring to the ranch—for a spell only—to hear the wind blow Spanish moss around.

R. Buckminster Fuller says that if Einstein is more correct than Newton in his perception of the nature of the universe, then its natural for the mind to move at the speed of light. He thinks there's no need to give up such space trips and the other wonders of Western technology. He thinks they can all be made to harmonize with the laws of the universe. Must check into Fuller further. He's been on my mind because all these communes seem to have geodesic domes.

We take the southern route back toward home, stopping in Las Vegas for dinner at a casino. I nurse Usha under a shawl as we eat and observe the ladies from the special flight from Los Angeles parade, two by two, clutching their purses, to and fro between drinks and gambling tables. They won't let me gamble with Usha.

The road toward Reno is arrow-straight. Behind us the pathetic Gomorrah recedes like a toy city drawn in lights on two-dimensional black. We want to drive as far as we can during the night, to avoid the desert's daytime heat. About 1 A.M., we stop at a motel in Tonapah. The next day it's Yosemite, the Great Central Valley, then home.

Our first morning home, we're eating breakfast when the phone rings. It's our friend Ted Streshinsky, the photographer, about to leave for Nevada with Roger Rappaport, to do a story for *West* on the world's largest nuclear wasteland.

"We'll go as fast as we can," he says. "You know, some scientists won't even drive that road between Reno and Las Vegas any more."

"Why?" That's the way we came back yesterday.

He says some recent "safety experiments" by the Atomic Energy Commission had, accidentally, contaminated 250 square miles of Nevada with plutonium 239 particles, a hot isotope with a radioactive half-life of 24,400 years. Once inhaled, these particles deliver intense alpha radiation to lung tissues and increase the chance of lung cancer. In the past nineteen years, 399 *announced* nuclear tests have been detonated in the Nevada test site. Complete data on their by-products have not been publicly available.

"They told us especially not to stay at Tonapah," says Ted.

"We stayed there the night before last," I tell him, my heart sinking at the thought of tiny Usha exposed so early in life to an overdose of radiation.

"They've been trying to keep it quiet," says Ted.

But the people who live in Tonapah surely knew. Yet they did not move away. How extraordinary. The Golem is at large but they won't recognize it.

There are several versions of the legend of the Golem. In the one I heard, the ruler of a certain city ordered the Jews to pack up and leave town. No pleas would dissuade him. So the rabbi resorted to magic. He used an alchemical symbol to call to life a clay giant that stood inert in a locked compartment of his cellar. The Golem now was at the rabbi's command. It was so strong and terrifying that the ruler wisely revoked his eviction order.

But before the rabbi had a chance to turn the Golem back to clay by removing the magic symbol from its forehead, a servant got to it and tried to make it serve his personal and selfish desires. The Golem went out of control, proceeded to stomp through town and to throw people around as though they were rag dolls. It was finally felled by a little girl who looked it straight in the eye and removed the alchemical symbol from its forehead.

This Golem can be odorless, soundless, invisible. It threatens the entire planet. No mountaintop is high enough for safety.

2

Planet Alarm

❧

Plaque for the moonlanding, suggested by I. F. Stone:

> Here Men First Set Foot Outside The Earth On Their Way To The Far Stars. They Speak Of Peace But Wherever They Go They Bring War. The Rockets On Which They Arrived Were Developed To Carry Instant Death And Can Within A Few Minutes Turn Their Green Planet Into Another Lifeless Moon. Their Destructive Ingenuity Knows No Limits And Their Wanton Pollution No Restraint. Let The Rest Of The Universe Beware.

It's autumn, 1969, and people are beginning to save bottles in recycling bins. It's bad form to fail to separate newspapers from the rest of your trash or to put vegetable peels anywhere but in a compost pile. Nobody will own up any more to spraying roses with chemicals. The most unlikely folks are making their own yogurt and following Adelle Davis's nutrition advice.

Women pregnant with their third or fourth child feel they must explain or even apologize. "The Population Bomb Is Everybody's Baby," I read on bumper stickers. And "Ecology—The Last Fad." Everyone is talking ecology—from Governor Reagan to the ex-nun I know who's now into women's liberation, yoga, and macrobiotics. More and more people are aware of the rampaging Golem.

Some scientists had been trying to tell us about it for years, but now they are so alarmed they've grown shrill and command our attention. Take, for instance, Dr. Kenneth E. F. Watt, head of the Environmental Systems Group, Institute of Ecology, at the University of California, Davis. At a recent congressional hearing he predicted that in the year 2000, great numbers of U.S. citizens would be starving, crowds of them would die of pollution-connected diseases, few would be able to afford medical care. Civil insurrection would be extensive. All that seemed inevitable, he said, unless drastic steps were taken right away to reverse alarming trends.

It was from Dr. Watt that I first heard an explanation of the intricate way the many aspects of "environmental crisis" interconnected. (Actually, the term "environmental crisis" is misleading. It implies that we're somehow apart from our environment and that, of course, is far from being the case.)

Dr. Watt's predictions derive from information gathered in an effort to build a mathematical model of California that could serve as a catastrophe warning device by projecting the social costs of the anticipated increase in population density.

First, he said, is the question of land use. Right now the state has more than enough first- and second-degree agricultural land (.34 acre per person) to raise the food the population needs to stay healthy. But each year, .2 acre is taken out of farming for every person added to the population. By 2000, there will be only .14 acre per person—about half of what will be needed.

"Can't the state import from underpopulated areas?" I asked.

Not for long, he said. The same process—population increase coupled with urbanization of good agricultural land—is happening elsewhere, though perhaps not as rapidly. "Every region in the country is essentially planning to get out of agriculture on the assumption that someone else will supply the food.

"The basic problem is that it's not in the local or regional interest of any part of the country to do what's of interest to the whole."

"Well, there's still the ocean."

"I don't know of a major oceanic stock that's not close to what it can produce," he replied. "Besides—we're poisoning a lot of marine life with toxic substances."

"Can't we manufacture food somehow? I've heard of experiments in that direction."

"It takes energy and we're not in that good shape on energy. It has yet to be demonstrated that all fossil fuel can be replaced by other fuel, like solar or nuclear. We're learning that there are some problems that technology can't solve. But I haven't told you the worst of it."

That's his vision of the icy apocalypse. Within the past thirty years, the average global temperature has fallen about .5 degrees Fahrenheit. Frost and ice boundaries have been shifting to the south. It's possible that air pollution is changing the climate. Small particles (aerosols) emitted into the atmosphere could be keeping out solar radiation. It's known that volcanic eruptions, which released fine ash into the atmosphere, affected the weather for up to ten years afterward. In 1916, following the eruption of Mount Tomboro in the Dutch East Indies, during the "summer that never was," a dry haze was observed over much of this continent and Europe. Crops failed on both continents.

Now, said Dr. Watt, we may be doing gradually the same thing the volcanoes did suddenly—cooling the earth. If temperatures were to drop above 7 degrees Fahrenheit—and there is evidence to suggest they might—conditions would be just about right for another ice age.

We were talking at a table on the outdoor terrace of the

student cafeteria on the peaceful rural campus of UC–Davis. In the sun, with the smell of new-mown grass around us, such predictions could not help but sound abstract. And yet even here, there was some smog. In the city this morning it was really awful. I had coffee with my friend Lil Lectric Lulu on the roof of our Russian Hill apartment house, where you can usually enjoy a fine view of the Golden Gate Bridge. But this morning the bridge was barely visible though there didn't seem to be any fog. It was shrouded in the thick brownish murk we get during a temperature inversion. Lulu was quite upset. She had just arrived from New York where, she said, she had stopped doing yoga because it made her too conscious of the danger in breathing.

"It's everywhere," she said with resignation. "Man's cosmic fart."

"Emphysema, lung cancer, cancer of the liver, and strokes can, it seems, be related to pollution," Dr. Watt continued. "The emphysema mortality rate has risen by about 12 percent a year during the past twenty years. In 1950, it was 1.5 per 100,000 in California. By 1968 it had jumped to 14.1—and in Riverside County to 26.4.

"If pollution keeps building up in the Los Angeles basin, by the winter of 1975-76 it will be at levels where we can expect mass mortality incidents. The weaker ones will go during an inversion."

Pollution has risen despite anti-smog devices on cars. "New smog control devices are only effective for the first eight thousand miles. Then their effectiveness drops sharply. Also, it now appears there are two compounds of smog that are vastly more lethal than the others—sulphur dioxide and nitrogen dioxide. There's strong circumstantial evidence they may be factors in causing gastrointestinal cancer. And smog control devices cause a fifty percent increase in nitrogen dioxide as a by-product of hydrocarbon combustion.

"The most deadly stuff in the air is what you can't see—sulphur dioxide, nitrogen dioxide, and heavy metals like cadmium and lead which have an irritating effect in exceedingly small quantities."

So, if present trends continue, there will be more people getting sick from smog—but fewer doctors to treat them. The percentage of young and old people—who don't pay taxes but require services—is rising, putting an ever heavier burden on the taxpayer. The taxpayer rebels. Result: cutbacks in many things, including medical education. By 2000, Dr. Watt predicted, the state would have only half the MDs it will need by current standards.

Perhaps the most disturbing aspect of this many faceted crisis is that "very large numbers of people may have been committed to die long before the first evidence shows up that something is going wrong," because it takes time for the damage to build up and for the facts to be gathered and interpreted.

Therefore, according to Dr. Watt, the entire catastrophe brought on by overpopulation and pollution may crash in on us suddenly—when it's too late to do much about it.

"The options are birth control or death control. That's what the public must be made to see," he concluded. If the birthrate does not fall, massive die-offs will be inevitable.

But if the news is that bad, why not just forget it and get all you can of life while it lasts? Some people, my friend Lulu for instance, are trying just that. But others will try to head off the apocalypse.

The planetary alarm is meeting two types of responses: a demand for more centralized controls aimed at everyone's benefit, and an effort at cultural change that begins with personal change and may eventually affect society's power structures.

Representing the first viewpoint would be *Time* Magazine's editorial statement February 2, 1970: "Ideally, the entire environment should be subjected to computer analysis and systems control"; also Dr. Richard A. Falk, interviewed by *The New York Times* while at work on the future's world order at Stanford University. "The only hopeful alternative is some kind of central framework of control to define community interests and to impose them on a global basis," he was quoted as saying.

The second viewpoint can be found in the second issue of *Root, Branch and Mammal*, "a monthly bulletin of animal discourse," in a commentary signed "A Holocene Gazetteer":

> The whole question of "survival" must be kept squarely in the context of liberation. The ecological crisis is essentially the result of authoritarian mystical civilization; the domestication and colonization of everyday life; the separation of man from his imagination and his own deepest resources which included ecological awareness in the first instance. Survival, then, does not lie in more control and in the final humiliation of the instincts but in the liberation of the body and the imagination; in the re-creation of the wild environment where the beautiful and sensuous essence of man, the world, and all the cosmos is yet to be discovered.

In fall, 1969, the beginning of the Year of Ecology, central solutions seem perilous to me and the Holocene Gazetteer's seem romantic. Past efforts to "define community interests and impose them on a global basis" have brought us the Crusades, fascism, communism, and Vietnam. Most interesting, therefore, to me are the people trying to avert the apocalypse by changing their own lives—despite all statistical evidence that it's futile. They believe that change must begin where you are.

There's Stephanie Mills, for example, the charming, keen-witted valedictorian of Mills College, Class of 1969, who announced she would have no children because the world was already overcrowded. With that personal, public commitment she evoked a response that the most brilliant speech on population could not have generated. She compelled those who heard her to relate to the abstract "population" in terms of their own babies, born or not. The press spread her message nationwide. She was flooded with mail praising her courage, accusing her of being against God, her country, and especially against motherhood.

Then there are the Humphreys, Clifford and Mary, co-founders of Ecology Action, who destroyed their family car, made it into a sculpture, and have ever since traveled by bicycle. They live what they preach with rigor, refusing to buy wastefully packaged goods, avoiding machines when their own energy suffices. They send out letters on used paper, enclosed in old envelopes they re-address and staple shut. They brook no separations between their present ways and future goals. Consequently, like Stephanie, they make some of us squirm because we notice that our own lives are not in keeping with our convictions. When people tell the Humphreys they're naïve idealists, they reply: "Pessimism has no survival value."

It's no accident that Stephanie Mills, the Humphreys and other leaders in this new movement live in the Bay area. This has long been a nesting place for various malcontents and rebels. Pacifists, anarchists, spiritual adventurers, and revolutionaries have found there was space and time here to try to build something of what they dreamed. The student rebellion started here in September, 1964, with the Free Speech Movement in Berkeley. The Black Panthers began in Oakland, the Beat poets did their early readings in San Francisco's North Beach coffee houses, the hippies had their flowering in the Haight-Ashbury.

The Bay area has also long been a conservationist stronghold. Nature unravaged is still accessible here and the spirit of the land is still strong. The city of San Francisco is perhaps the last livable city in the United States and many of its residents will fight hard when they believe it is threatened. So it is that the first freeway ever stopped in mid-construction looms on the waterfront, its ramp to nowhere a kind of monument. The Sierra Club has its headquarters here. And now, dozens of new groups, clustering under the banner word "ecology," are sprouting, setting patterns for groups elsewhere, breathing new life into elderly conservation establishments.

The septuagenarian Sierra Club, for instance, has until recently been known mostly for its handsome nature calendars and studio books, for its backpacking expeditions and campaigns to save remote wilderness sanctuaries. Now it is increasingly involved in much broader environmental battles, spurred on by the influence of newcomers like Ecology Action. Not long ago, the club urged the federal government to take steps to decrease population growth, to outlaw the internal combustion engine, and tax automobiles according to the amount of gas they consume. And it has hired some young rebels who are trying to push it even further into radical ecology, which is challenging the growth economy and the entire notion of progress.

In May, 1969, the club's longtime executive director David Brower resigned to form Friends of the Earth, announcing he would lobby internationally against what he called "the disease that now threatens the planet: cirrhosis of the environment."

Brower's group is considered militant by old-line conservationists but is seen as establishment-minded by radicals. Like the Sierra Club, FOE puts out handsomely illustrated publications, lobbies for environmental bills, and tries to forestall what it considers environmental disaster by litigation. It has thus helped to stall the Alaska oil pipeline, and has fought against the California water project, a colossal system for moving northern water to the deserts of the south. Many environmentalists view this project as the single greatest disaster underway in the state. It will bring more development to areas already suffocating in smog, hasten land exploitation in the Great Central Valley, deplete marine lifeways in the north, and hasten the extinction of some fish and wildlife.

FOE likes petitions with weighty signatures. But it's not above picketing. One of its most successful campaigns, headed by Brower's dynamic assistant Joan McIntyre, brought the wealthy beautiful people out into the streets with placards to save threatened species. The result: it's now unfashionable—indeed, bad taste—to wear sealskin, leopard, and other endangered animals' skins.

Each of the groups has a different constituency. In the FOE office, one is likely to find bright and well-educated women in hip elegant clothes—ladies comfortably enough situated to spend time on a smart worthy cause, able to pull off a benefit dance and concert and to call in donations of special skills and talents. Some young people who feel more detached from society are more likely to find kindred folk elsewhere—in Berkeley's Ecology Center, for instance.

Started in June, 1969, the Center was within months a model for groups in other cities. It's a storefront near the campus, designed to be an information and energy exchange. People who come in with an idea are steered to whoever else is interested, or invited to go ahead and try to carry it out. The structure is loose, the activities depend on what walks in the door. Volunteer staffers include professors, students, businessmen, housewives. Among the people I met there was Garrett DeBell, who not long ago was working on a doctorate at the university, writing a thesis titled: "Ecology and Bio-energetics: The Lycosid Spider at the Hastings Natural History Reservation."

"It was interesting, but a luxury," he told me. "It had nothing to do with people starving." He gave it up, together with a comfortable study grant, to cross the street into practical ecology. His first project was to try to devise a scheme for recycling aluminum, hoping it would become a first step toward legally mandatory recycling. (The idea would become an excellent merchandizing gimmick for aluminum companies within a year.) He seeks to expand the understanding of what's involved by asking: "If unemployed people burn cities—is that a cost of not recycling?"

That's the kind of question that, more and more, is demanding consideration. It brings together liberals, radicals, and psychedelic dropouts, all working in their own ways toward shared goals.

When a bill to protect San Francisco Bay from fillers and dumpers was being tugged through the state legislature, for instance, the Sierra Club and Friends of the Earth lobbied for it in the traditional ways while Ecology Action went down to the Bay shore with fifty money bags from a bank, filled them with mud and delivered them to the offices of corporations that had Bay fill plans. A local paper ran a photo of this "Bay unfilling" on the front page and a certain impact was undeniable.

United on a common objective, the various clans of environmentalists can be a formidable political force. There is, however, a noticeable absence of poor people among them. The poor are usually first victims in any environmental catastrophe. They live in the smoggiest places, eat the worst food, have the fewest choices. But their immediate interests sometimes conflict with those of ecology activists. They tend to support factories that pollute and real estate developments that ravage the landscape if these offer a promise of jobs. Environmental considerations become secondary when the rent is due and the phone has been disconnected. Ecology tends to look like a rich folk's preoccupation.

Some Navajos support the strip mining of the Black Mesa because while it's happening, they have work. When the coal is gone, their jobs will be gone too—and so, almost certainly, their ancient lifeways. Coal mining is destroying the fragile eco-systems within which the Indian people had found a place. But unfortunately, those who tried to keep the coal company out did not have alternative income sources to offer.

Some of the ecology movement's leaders live on low, even minimal, incomes, though they have the option of earning more. Cliff and Mary Humphrey, for instance, survive, with four children, on $250 a month, with foodstamps, tailends of educational loans, and a small income from a course taught by Cliff on "the ecological dynamics of social change" at the University of California's San Francisco Extension. They practice a frugality that Mary learned growing up as the youngest of the six children of an Irish immigrant in Medford, Massachusetts. Her father, she says, "when he worked his way up in the world, dug ditches for the city of Boston."

Their house in the Berkeley flats spills over with ecology action. Someone is always on the phone; someone else is answering letters, running the mimeograph machine, typing. Leaflets lie in piles on the kitchen table and the couch. Kids and visitors weave in and out.

The Humphreys give much of their time to a kind of street theater designed to get people to look at what's happening around them. One of their recent projects was a "fault tour" during which they draped buildings on the San Andreas fault with bright purple crepe paper. (On that very day a mild earthquake shook the city.)

"Ecology Action is a movement rather than an organization," Cliff explains. "Anyone can do his or her thing and we don't even have to know about it."

The Resistance members who hid in the Colorado wilderness near the site of an underground nuclear blast were engaged in a form of ecology action unbeknown to the Humphreys. They tried to prevent the explosion by playing hide-and-seek with helicopters and though they only succeeded in delaying it, the news coverage they provoked had an impact on people's awareness. That was Project Gasbuggy, planned to release natural gas supplies. What else was released by the explosion is still being discovered.

These Resisters were engaged in ecology action in its highest form: a total theater-protest-experience that must be lived as it is acted out. The performers must do more than take on personae for the duration. They must expose themselves to risks as whole persons. If their action is successful, it generates change by proffering epiphanies that lead to perceptual shifts.

Another instance of this sort of action was "Liferaft Earth," staged this same autumn by Stewart Brand, founder of the *Whole Earth Catalog*, and billed as "a flamboyant, pointed piece of media theater on crowding and hunger: a group of people spending a week together in a plastic bubble set up in a highly public place, partaking only of water."

The idea came to Brand in the course of a long train ride through the Midwest. He was reading Paul Ehrlich's *Population Bomb*, watching America roll by, and he had this vision of a country that was ocean-to-ocean people. So he decided to help others see what he saw.

A few years before, Brand helped launch the psychedelic era by putting together the first Trips Festival with Ken Kesey, Bill Graham, and others who remained anonymous. The public was invited to share a "simulated" LSD experience. Stoned freaks danced for three nights in San Francisco's Longshoremen's Hall and flower power was born. "Liferaft Earth" was Brand's bit for the dawning eco-era.

There was no shortage of prospective starvers. But finding a place for "Liferaft Earth" was something else. No big hotel wanted it, nor did any public institution Brand approached—except for the Office of Economic Opportunity, which offered an out-of-the way parking lot in Hayward, a remote East Bay suburb. The fire department banned the bubble so the hunger artists had to stay in the open air, within a polyethylene bubble fence. About a hundred people took part, mostly longhairs. The Hog Farm Commune was there, a lot of vegetarians and communards, and Stephanie Mills, slim and smart, somewhat intimidated by all that hipness. She came mainly to make another gesture for the media. But eating nothing for a week had to be more than a gesture.

The first day was rather exhilarating. On the second, she had a headache and hunger pains. On the third, diarrhea. On the fourth day it rained. Stephanie wasn't used to standing out in the rain, having grown up in Phoenix. When it rained again on the sixth night, a cold late-autumn rain, she stepped out of the hunger pale and ate a peanut butter cupcake. With that, as far as "Liferaft Earth" was concerned, she "died."

The show did get some coverage in the press. But its impact was strongest on the participants. Stephanie went away feeling she now at last understood what she had been talking about. At the time, she was working for the Alameda County Planned Parenthood Association, making speeches on campuses and at conferences, trying to encourage "less motherhood and more brotherhood." But now she wondered: did anybody learn anything from speeches? Shouldn't she, instead, be trying to get Hunger I and Hunger II included in school curricula?

My friend Lectric Lulu doesn't care much for the ecology activists. She finds them too self-righteous and devoid of humor. To change anything for the better, she believes, you have to focus on life rather than death. She herself is an artist, constantly busy with stitcheries that glow and glitter with velvets, silks, feathers, and bright beads. These she trades for other things she needs, having more or less dropped out of the whole money economy.

It is true; the apocalyptics aren't laughing or dancing. The burden of all that bad news has got them down and, in conversation, they never exhaust their litany of dire facts.

Shortly after the Hunger Show, Stephanie Mills quit her job with Planned Parenthood and became the editor of the short-lived ecology newspaper *Earth Times*. It was a rather dreary publication to read—full of well-documented outrages against the planet and its creatures, devoid of hope and joy.

Nor was there much to lift the spirit in early issues of the *Earth Read-Out*, a new venture by Keith Lampe, a poet-activist who dropped out of the Yippies after the Chicago Convention because he felt the situation had grown too serious for laughter. His little newspaper arrived closely printed on both sides of yellow mimeograph paper (saving trees), and packed with facts I'd rather not know, culled from *Science, Scientific American, Natural History, Environment,* and similar journals.

During the coming months, Lampe predicted, "psychedelic

(i.e., mind-expanding, mind-opening) experience . . . will result much less often from chemically induced pansensual delight, much more often from old-fashioned cerebral homework. Having learned that the mind in fact is merely one of several senses, we must now return to a sober husbandry of the sense-of-think."

So it's frugality and sobriety again. So dreary. As Thoreau (now much quoted) remarked: "Why should we not meet, not always as dyspeptics, to tell our bad dreams, but sometimes as *eu*peptics to congratulate each other on the ever-glorious morning?"

That vision of the ever-glorious morning is the life-force in this new movement. A few attempts have been made to set it into words.

In September, 1969, Ecology Action held a ceremony at the Berkeley City dump. The press was invited. Cliff Humphrey unrolled a document he had drawn up: The Declaration of Interdependence. One by one, eco-activists stepped up to sign. It read, in part:

> We hold these truths to be self-evident that all species have evolved with equal and unalienable rights, that among these are Life, Liberty and the pursuit of Happiness—That to insure these rights, nature has instituted certain principles for the sustenance of all species. . . . We therefore, among the mortal representatives of the eternal process of life and evolutionary principles, in mutual humbleness, explicitly stated, appealing to the ecological consciousness of the world for rectitude of our intentions, do solemnly publish and declare that all species are interdependent; that they are all free to realize these relationships to the full extent of their capabilities; that each species is subservient to the requirements of the natural processes that sustain all life. . . .

It was an attempt to state the basics of the emerging ecological mind-set.

A short while later, other radical ecologists went further with a manifesto called "Four Changes"; here excerpted:

I. Population

THE CONDITION

... Man is but a part of the fabric of life—dependent on the whole fabric for his very existence. As the most highly developed tool-using animal, he must recognize that the unknown evolutionary destinies of other life forms are to be respected, and act as gentle steward of the earth's community of being.

... there are now too many human beings, and the problem is growing rapidly worse. It is potentially disastrous not only for the human race but for most other life forms.

... The goal would be half of the present world population, or less.

ACTION

... Work ceaselessly to have all political questions be seen in the light of this prime problem.

... Explore other social structures and marriage forms, such as group marriage and polyandrous marriage, which provide family life but may produce less children. Share the pleasure of raising children widely, so that all need not directly reproduce to enter into this basic human experience. ... Adopt children. Let reverence for life and reverence for the feminine mean also a reverence for other species, and future human lives, most of which are threatened.

... Love, love-making, a man and woman together, seen as the vehicle of mutual realization, where the creation of new selves and a new world of being is as important as reproducing our kind.

II. Pollution

THE CONDITION

... The human race in the last century has allowed its production and scattering of wastes, by-products, and various chemicals to become excessive. ... We are fouling our air and water, and living in noise and filth that no "animal" would tolerate, while advertising and politicians try to tell us "we've never had it so good." The dependence of the modern governments on this kind of untruth leads to shameful mind-pollution: mass media and most school education.

Goal: Clean air, clean clear-running rivers, the presence of Pelican and Osprey and Gray Whale in our lives; salmon and trout in our streams; unmuddied language and good dreams.

ACTION

. . . Recycling should be the basic principle behind all waste-disposal thinking. . . . Share rides, legalize hitch-hiking, and build hitch-hiker waiting stations along the highways. . . . Also walk more; look for the best routes through beautiful countryside for long-distance walking trips. . . . Learn how to use your own manure as fertilizer if you're in the country—as the far East has done for centuries. There's a way, and it's safe. . . . Don't work in any way for or with an industry which pollutes, and don't be drafted into the military. Don't waste. (A monk and an old master were once walking in the mountains. They noticed a little hut upstream. The monk said, "A wise hermit must live there" —the master said, "That's no wise hermit, you see that lettuce leaf floating down the stream, he's a Waster." Just then an old man came running down the hill with his beard flying and caught the floating lettuce leaf.)

. . . *There is something in western culture that wants to totally wipe out creepy-crawlies, and feels repugnance for toadstools and snakes. This is fear of one's own deepest natural inner-self wilderness areas, and the answer is, relax.** Relax around bugs, snakes, and your own hairy dreams. . . . In the realm of thought, inner experience, consciousness, as in the outward realm of interconnection, there is a difference between balanced cycle, and the excess which cannot be handled. When the balance is right, the mind recycles from highest illuminations to the stillness of dreamless sleep; the alchemical "transmutation."

---

* Italics author's.

III. Consumption

THE CONDITION

To grossly use more than you need to destroy, is biologically unsound. Most of the production and consumption of modern societies is not necessary or conducive to spiritual and cultural growth, let alone survival and is behind much greed and envy, age-old causes of social and international discord. . . . *True affluence is not needing anything.*

ACTION

. . . It must be demonstrated ceaselessly that a continually "growing economy" is no longer healthy, but a Cancer. And that the criminal waste which is allowed in the name of competition—especially that ultimate in wasteful needless competition, hot wars and cold wars with "communism" (or "capitalism")—must be halted totally with ferocious energy and decision. Economics must be seen as a small sub-branch of Ecology, and production/distribution/consumption handled by companies or unions with the same elegance and spareness one sees in nature. . . . Protection for all predators and varmints, "Support your right to arm bears."

. . . The power of renunciation: If enough Americans refused to buy a new car for one given year it would permanently alter the American economy. Recycling clothes and equipment. Support handicrafts—gardening, home skills, midwifery, herbs—all the things that can make us independent, beautiful and whole. *Learn to break the habit of unnecessary possessions—a monkey on everybody's back—but avoid a self-abnegating anti-joyous self-righteousness. Simplicity is light, carefree, neat, and loving—not a self-punishing ascetic trip.* . . . Don't shoot a deer if you don't know how to use all the meat and preserve that which you can't eat, to tan the hide and use the leather—use it all, with gratitude, right down to the sinew and hooves. Simplicity and mindfulness in diet is a starting point for many people.

. . . To live lightly on the earth, to be aware and alive, to be free of egotism, to be in contact with plants and animals, starts with simple concrete acts. The inner principle is the insight that we are interdependent energy-fields of great potential wisdom and compassion—expressed in each person as a superb mind, a handsome and complex body, and the almost magical capacity of language. To these potentials and capacities, "owning things" can add nothing of authenticity. "Clad in the sky, with the earth for a pillow."

IV. Transformation

THE CONDITION

. . . We have it within our deepest powers not only to change our "selves" but to change our culture. If a man is to remain on earth he must transform the five-millennia-long urbanizing civilization tradition into a new ecologically-sensitive harmony-oriented wild-minded scientific/spiritual culture . . . . civilization, which has made us so successful a species, has overshot itself and now threatens us with its inertia. . . . nothing short of total transformation will do much good. What we envision is a planet on which the human population lives harmoniously and dynamically by employing a sophisticated and unobtrusive technology in a world environment which is "left natural." Specific points in this vision:

- A healthy and spare population of all races, much less in number than today.
- Cultural and individual pluralism, unified by a type of world tribal council. Division by natural and cultural boundaries rather than arbitrary political boundaries.
- A technology of communication, education, and quiet transportation, land-use being sensitive to the properties of each region. Allowing, thus, the Bison to return to much of the high plains. Careful but intensive agriculture in the great alluvial valleys; deserts left wild for those who would trot in them. Computer technicians who run the plant part of the year and walk along with the Elk in their migrations during the rest.
- A basic cultural outlook and social organization that inhibits power and property-seeking while encouraging exploration and challenge in things like music, meditation, mathematics, mountaineering, magic, and all other ways of authentic being-in-the-world. Women totally free and equal. A new kind of family—responsible, but more festive and relaxed—is implicit.

ACTION

Social/political: It seems evident that there are throughout the world certain social and religious forces which have worked through history toward an ecologically and culturally enlightened state of affairs. Let these be encouraged: Gnostics, hip Marxists, Teilhard de Chardin Catholics, Druids, Taoists, Biologists, Witches, Yogins, Bhikkus, Quakers, Sufis, Tibetans, Zens, Shamans, Bushmen, American Indians, Polynesians, Anarchists, Alchemists . . . the list is long. All primitive cultures, all communal and ashram movements. *Since it doesn't seem practical or even desirable to think that direct bloody force will achieve much, it would be best to consider this a continuing "revolution of consciousness" which will be won not by guns but by seizing the key images, myths, archetypes, eschatologies, and ecstasies so that life won't seem worth living unless one's on the transforming energy's side. By taking over "science and technology" and releasing its real possibilities and powers in the service of this planet—which, after all, produced us and it.*

Our community: New schools, new classes, walking in the woods and cleaning up the streets. Find psychological techniques for creating an awareness of "self" which includes the social and natural environment. "Consideration of what specific language forms—symbolic systems—and social institutions constitute obstacles to ecological awareness." Let no one be ignorant of the facts of biology and related disciplines; bring up our children as part of the wild-life. Some communities can establish themselves in backwater rural areas and flourish —others maintain themselves in urban centers, and the two types work together—a two-way flow of experience, people, money, and home-grown vegetables. Ultimately cities will exist only as joyous tribal gatherings and fairs, to dissolve after a few weeks. Investigating new life-styles is our work, as is the exploration of Ways to explore our inner realms—with the known dangers of crashing that go with such. We should work with political-minded people where it helps, hoping to enlarge their vision, and with people of all varieties of politics or thought at whatever point they become aware of environmental urgencies. *Master the archaic and the primitive as models of basic nature-*

related cultures—as well as the most imaginative extensions of science —and build a community where these two vectors cross.
Our own heads: is where it starts. . . . to look clearly into the eyes of the wild and see our self-hood, our family, there. . . . to go beyond the idea of "man's survival" or "the survival of the biosphere" and to draw our strength from the realization that at the heart of things is some kind of serene and ecstatic process which is actually beyond qualities and certainly beyond birth-and-death. "No need to survive!" "In the fires that destroy the universe at the end of the kalpa, what survives?"—"The iron tree blooms in the void!"
Knowing that nothing need be done, is where we begin to move from.

Gary Snyder, the poet, wrote the "Four Changes," drawing on the contributions of many others. He had recently returned from Japan, where he studied Zen for eight years and was ordained a Buddhist priest. Since his return, he had become a spiritual leader for the eco-activists, but sought as much anonymity as possible. At the Sierra Club's 1969 Wilderness Conference, for instance, he distributed his "Smokey the Bear Sutra," anonymously, with the notation: "May be reproduced free forever"— a gift. He brought Keith Lampe along to that conference and so turned him away from politics and toward eco-activism.

Snyder has explored the world from many perspectives. He's been a forest lookout, and a fireman aboard an oil tanker. He played guitar for Henry Wallace, planted sweet potatoes on a volcanic island in Japan, meditated on the volcano's edge. Lately he has been writing:

> . . . *the most*
> *Revolutionary consciousness is to be found*
> *Among the most ruthlessly exploited classes:*
> *Animals, trees, water, air, grasses.* . . .

That's in the book *Earth Household*, as is an essay titled "Buddhism and the Coming Revolution," in which he says: "The practice of meditation, for which one needs only 'the ground beneath one's feet' wipes out mountains of junk being pumped into the mind by the mass media and supermarket universities."

With things grim among scientists and activists, it seems wise to seek out priests and poets. So one breezy morning I drive to see Gary Snyder. The route takes me north on Highway 1 as it curves along the sheer edge of the continent, then sharply down a dirt road into a leafy canyon. Leaving behind the broad vistas of ocean and mesa, I wind down into the trees. From the heady edge into the inner core—is that the direction?

Snyder is staying in someone's vine-covered house. His wife Masa, pregnant with their second child, opens the door.

"He's down shooting arrows with Alan Watts," she says. "I'll call him."

Going into the living room, she reaches above a doorway and brings down a conch, then walks to the edge of the veranda, where the slope drops into a maze of vines and trees, blows twice, then listens. "He has answered," she says, though I didn't hear a thing.

Masa disappears into the house and I sit down on a bench by a redwood table. No hurry here and no doom gloom. Insects buzz in the vines. The sun makes leafy patterns on table and floor.

Snyder comes up from the green maze, his eighteen-month-old son Kai on his back, a bow in his right hand. He takes the child to Masa, then returns to sit opposite me and smiles across. I know right away that this will be a memorable encounter.

Snyder has the luminous look I saw in Suzuki Roshi, at the Tassajara Zen Mountain Center. There's a clarity, a complete absence of ambiguity, about him. When he walked in a moment ago, he was walking. He was a man who might walk across a room or across the world with equally light strides. Now he's here listening. Each moment is complete. I'm reminded of a Zen student whom Alan Watts, I think, quotes in one of his books, who says that before he began to study Zen, mountains were mountains. Then, after some study they were no longer mountains. But at last they are mountains again. Snyder has apparently reached the point where mountains are once more mountains. There is asceticism in his face but it does not exclude love of pleasure. It seems a distillation of joyful energy rather than the Puritan self-punishment that some American Zen Buddhists convey. His hair is pulled back and knotted at the back of his head. His arms rest at ease on the table.

What takes place between us is more than an interview in which I ask questions and write things down in a notebook. It is a full meeting in which, much of the time, we communicate by word, inflection, gesture, and pause within I-Thou regard.

Snyder talks about the American Indians who saw themselves as custodians of the land rather than its owners or users; about destructive logging practices in India and China and the way the damage began long ago, before Christianity and industrialization. The average peasant in India had a higher living standard 2000 years ago than he does now, he says. There were fewer people then and more fruit, game, and water for each.

"It's a beautiful paradox," he says. "Man has reached the point of his greatest knowledge and power and has come to a dialectical turning point, where, if he is to become greater, he must become smaller."

He hopes to further that process by continuing to write poetry and by moving to some land in the Sierras he has bought together with Allen Ginsberg, Richard Baker, head priest of the San Francisco Zen Center, and a few others. He will build a house, learn to live by hunting and gathering, try to make acorn flour as the Indians did. As we walk to my car, he talks about his belief that our society might fall apart within about fifteen years. His son might need to know how to live off the land then, he says.

Stephanie Mills had told me, "If it turns out we have to become a hunting and gathering society I think I'll blow my brains out. There are too many things I like."

I'm with her. Give me those rotten urban pleasures even if

they do mean breathing is the equivalent of smoking two packs of cigarettes a day. Acorn flour reminds me of fall-out shelters.

Still, in the months to come, I will find myself thinking back repeatedly on that meeting with Gary Snyder. Not so much on what he said. His words were as gloomy as Kenneth Watt's, Stephanie Mills's, and others. But his presence had conveyed the sense of wholeness I had sensed at Adam's. It seemed to speak, somehow, to the heart of things.

3

People's Park

❈

Orthodox Jews hold that you must always be able to walk to the temple. The ancient Greeks believed that a city should never be bigger than one man's voice, so that when all citizens were assembled, each could be heard. The Indians placed their tepees in a circle, each "a nest within a nest," and held open council where all could speak.

But our institutions are no longer scaled to a man's pace and voice, and so our power systems no longer reflect the will of the people. Some saw that vividly during the People's Park conflagration in Berkeley, in spring, 1968.

The story was covered by the press nationally, since it was good theater. (So much of what we consider news is really theater.) It was a morality play, with specific events and characters representing much broader forces at war in society.

At first the drama revolved around a little park that some young people built in a burst of spring fever on a vacant lot owned by the University of California in downtown Berkeley. The University provoked a riot by fencing it and locking it up. But the conflict expanded until the whole town was involved and pitted against the state. At stake, in the end, was democracy—and democracy lost. The state stomped on the clearly stated will of the city council, a united campus (students, faculty, administration), and the citizenry.

In the process, many came to understand that to be free, we have to gain control over the place where we live—first our minds/bodies, then our neighborhoods, cities, and institutions. The people who made the decision to destroy the park never shared in its life. They dealt with it as an abstraction.

I thought of the People's Park the other day at a neighborhood meeting about a mini-park that is to be built across the street from where we live in San Francisco. As a member of the "community" I had a chance to have a say on the design.

"Community" is the word used in such contexts by city bureaucrats and social agencies. But most of us urban dwellers don't live in communities, really; we reside in contiguities—at fixed addresses next to this or that. Our neighborhood is on the edge of Russian Hill. Within a few blocks we have expensive homes, middle-income flats, and houses where the passerby would never suspect that swarms of Chinese children crowd behind curtained windows.

The children have no decent play space. The old people stay indoors or sit on steps because there are no benches within easy walking distance. A park, even if tiny, could mean a lot. Therefore, I helped to plaster the neighborhood with announcements of the meeting, in English and Chinese. Eight people came. A community we are not.

Still, those eight of us were clear on one thing: we did not want the standard city park. No cement benches, cement horses, no chain link fence.

A lot of exciting ideas were proposed. A park can fire the imagination. But one by one, most of them were regretfully turned down. We couldn't have sand because dog shit would soon ruin it for children. Wooden benches were dangerous. There had been one on the block once and kids stacked dry Christmas trees on it and burned it. We certainly couldn't have flowers because no one would take care of them. In the cities of Today-USA, public parks must be near-indestructible or supervised. No flower will survive without a fence to protect it.

With some nostalgia, then, I remembered how I stopped one warm April evening in 1968 to look at the People's Park in Berkeley. I saw many flowers, carefully tended, wooden benches, mobile sculptures. On a wooden stage, a puppet show was underway. Stopping to watch, I stepped on the newly laid grass. Right away a girl beside me politely asked me to keep off. There was no fence.

"People are worse than pigs," a young mother said in disgust at my neighborhood mini-park meeting. "No individual responsibility."

But responsibility implies that someone wants your response and is ready to respond in turn. And who, of the people who govern our environment, wants our response? Nobody wanted it during the People's Park crisis. Politicians seek only our vote or, at best, our mandate. The real-estate interests who tear down and build on the streets where we live want profits—a goal fully sanctioned by society. At this neighborhood meeting, people scarcely believed that their wishes would be attended to in any way.

What stirred us all so about the People's Park was that it was a breakaway from all that urban anomie, a sudden blossoming of community. And then this creative thing that was trying to happen was extinguished by institutions that fear the unpredictability of freedom and to whom safety means control.

In covering the People's Park story for the *Washington Post*, I began as an "objective" observer. But by the time it was all over, I was emotionally involved, identifying with the longhaired, rumpled park leaders much more than with the wealthy and fatigued men who exert power over the university and the state. The park kids were the ones who were saner and more open to life. I trusted them more.

Briefly, what happened was this. Early in spring, 1968, some habitués of the cafés on Berkeley's Telegraph Avenue were sitting around talking about the dismal winter and the dismal state of the world. But it was spring, and after a while their talk turned toward things more connected with the season. Why not give everyone a lift, someone suggested, by building a park on that swamp the university had created a block off the avenue?

Nine months previously, the university had torn down some old Victorian houses, evicting considerable numbers of students and other young people from inexpensive quarters. The announced intent was to build student residences, but so far nothing had happened. During the winter rains, the lot was a swampy eyesore. Now it was an informal parking lot and a particularly blatant example of the university's callousness toward the community.

Basically there was nothing radical in the idea of turning a vacant lot into a park. That was happening in many cities, with the blessings of authorities and property owners. Lady Bird Johnson had gone around the country urging people to beautify America by planting flowers.

But the people planning this particular park happened to include a number of radicals: Stew Albert, a Yippie; Mike Delacour, owner of the Red Square Dress Shop; Wendy Schlesinger, a sharp-witted young woman in the process of dropping out; and Superjoel, famous for having inserted a flower into a soldier's gun barrel during the 1967 siege of the Pentagon. Their style tended toward the flamboyant.

Stew Albert drew up a proclamation that appeared in the *Berkeley Barb*, then the leading underground newspaper in the area. In part, it read:

PEOPLE'S PARK

Hear Ye, Hear Ye,
A park will be built this Sunday between Dwight and Haste. The land is owned by the University which tore down a lot of beautiful houses in order to build a swamp. . . . On Sunday we will stop this shit. Bring shovels, hoses, chains, grass, paints, flowers, trees, bulldozers, top soil, colorful smiles, laughter and lots of sweat. . . . We want the park to be a cultural, political freak out and rap center for the Western world. . . . Nobody supervises and the trip belongs to whoever dreams.

Signed,
Robin Hood's Park Commissioner.

More than a hundred people showed up on Sunday, April 20. Many of them were so-called street people—hairy and usually stoned denizens of the sidewalks of Telegraph Avenue, which had succeeded the Haight-Ashbury as dropout mecca. To see them sweating in constructive labor would have warmed the heart of many a daddy. They cleaned up trash, hauled away rocks, leveled part of the lot, put down rolls of sod, planted shrubs.

Afterward, Stew Albert wrote in the *Barb*: "For the first time in my life I enjoyed working. I think lots of people had that experience. Ever since I was eighteen I hated every job and either quit or was fired. But this was something different, with aching back and sweat on my brow, there was no boss. What we were creating was our own desires, so we worked like madmen and loved it."

Some Telegraph Avenue merchants contributed money for the park, hoping it would draw the unsightly street people away from the sidewalks and into the trees. All kinds of folks showed up the following Sunday. Passersby stopped to watch, went away, returned with food, drink, shovels, welded sculptures, benches. A sandlot and a set of swings appeared. Someone brought a rototiller and put in "the people's revolutionary corn garden."

Before long, the People's Park was a neighborhood center where folks who usually avoided each other discovered they could share common space. Students and faculty from the university's College of Environmental Design came to marvel at this case study of self-generated community improvement. Proper middle-class mothers brought youngsters to the sandboxes and swings, despite the presence of dope fiends. On the third Sunday, the Reverend Richard York, an Episcopalian clergyman ministering to street people through the Free Church, blessed the park. "Holy Land," read the headline on the report in the *Barb*.

But one blessing was sorely missing—the university's. And while many never thought of the omission, others were aware of it and were preparing for what they knew had to be a fight. In Berkeley, you never know how seriously to take a penciled sign staking out a "revolutionary corn garden." Berkeley radicals tend to take a cosmic view. What might have been a mere minipark in New York or Detroit was a revolutionary People's Park here.

On the whole, good humor prevailed easily over confrontation politics at Dwight and Haste. Stopping to read notices on the park's bulletin board one afternoon, I found information about plants, instruction about watering, announcements of assorted meetings in town. There were a few notices, though, hinting at confrontation. One was headed "Proclamation by Madmen" and threatened to destroy university property if the university tried to destroy the park.

Whom did this notice, unsigned, represent? In Berkeley, you can walk across campus most any day and pick up enough proclamations for a bonfire that will burn in the rain. Many speak only for the persons who wrote them.

The park itself, however, was real beyond rhetoric and, by its nature, a powerful symbol. It was not just a park, it was territory, like Hamburger Hill in Vietnam. It was land—and that very word, land, echoes with home, mother, blood. It was also real estate and property.

To the dropped-out intellectuals-turned-carpenters, the many artists and craftsmen of Berkeley, the park was a chance to create an environment. They worked together, infecting each other with enthusiasm, in anarchistic anonymity. The stage was there for any performer or speaker who wanted to use it, and almost daily someone or some group did. Through it all wafted, now and then, the aroma of the benevolent weed.

Meanwhile, the university was getting nervous. A meeting of the Board of Regents was coming up and questions would surely be asked. On April 30, the administration announced that it planned to use the land for a playing field but was "willing to discuss the design of the field, and possible uses of the area by the community." Nobody stepped forward to take up the offer in behalf of the park builders. There was nobody in charge.

On May 13, Chancellor Heyns announced that "It is now clear that no one can speak for the anonymous developers, and no one can control the growing safety, health and liability problems in the area.... We will have to put up a fence to reestablish the conveniently forgotten fact that the field is indeed the university's and to exclude unauthorized persons from the site."

At that, the three ministers of the Free Church hastened to publish an open letter to the chancellor warning that he was courting trouble: "Do you really want to declare war on this community?... It is in your hands to determine whether it will turn to tearing down or building up.... As followers of Jesus, we are committed to stand with ... the spirit of the poor and alienated trying to create a new world on the vacant lots of the old."

At the urging of Sim Van de Ryn, professor at the College of Environmental Design, the park builders finally did organize. About 200 gathered and elected a committee of eleven, including students and street people, to represent the Park before the university administration. But by now Heyns was out of town and other wheels were rolling.

At dawn on Thursday, May 15, afterward known as Bloody

Thursday, a work-crew arrived with police escort, surrounded the park with an eight-foot chain link fence and locked it. That noon, Dan Siegel, president-elect of the Associated Students, stepped up to a microphone atop the steps of Sproul Hall, the gray stone administration building. Sproul faces the glass-walled student union building across the main campus entrance at Telegraph Avenue. There's some kind of rally there most noons but no more than a few hundred usually pause to listen. Today, however, the crowd was huge and angry.

Siegel spoke of the morning's events and invited the students to "go down and take the park." Later, at his trial on the charge of inciting a riot, he said he had not finished speaking. But at those words, the crowd surged toward Telegraph.

From here on, the story has different versions. Police were to claim later that they were "overrun," that their lives were in danger, that Alameda County sheriff's deputies, who were called in to help, ran out of tear gas and were unable to scatter the crowd by firing into the air. They produced steel rods and rocks as evidence that they had been attacked.

Others produced photographs of officers aiming at people who were apparently watching on rooftops. One photograph showed an officer about to fire at the back of a fleeing man. They pointed out that though about fifty officers were treated in hospitals, none was injured seriously enough to require hospitalization.

One fact could not be disputed: late that afternoon, James Rector, twenty five, a wanderer visiting Berkeley, lay dying of buckshot wounds. Allan Blanchard, a carpenter and also a bystander, was blinded by birdshot. Thirty-four people had been hit by gunfire, scores of others treated for tear gas, cuts, bruises, and other injuries. For the first time in recent history, peace officers had used firearms on a crowd of predominantly white young people and students on North American city streets. All the bullets fired seemed to have come from police guns.

Governor Ronald Reagan declared a state of extreme emergency and called out the National Guard. By the following morning, soldiers had pitched camp among the revolutionary cornstalks, the swings, lawns, and sculptures. Looking in at them through the fence, I recalled how, toward the end of World War II, I had stared through a trolley car window in the Austrian city of Graz at the Russian soldiers who had moved in overnight. I'd been frightened then, for we had left Lithuania in flight from the Russians. But *these* soldiers were not scary. They were just out of place. This was no military occupation, it was some kind of playacting—wasn't it?

Saturday, May 17—Hundreds of young people moving through downtown, chanting "We want the park" and ululating à la *Battle of Algiers*, a movie everybody has seen. Eerie sound—u-lu-lu-lu-lu-lu—high pitched, suggesting something foreign and wild—a swarm of locusts, perhaps?—something gathering force, unstoppable. Frightening.

I run along with the crowd, notebook in hand, trying to keep close to those who look like leaders. But the aim is to keep the cops on the run, to distract and disrupt by darting here and there, scattering and again massing, confusing by constant direction change. This is guerrilla action.

A heavy-set, large-boned man on a corner of Shattuck Avenue looks like he knows what he's doing. He's directing the crowd, urging it on with his clapping and angry repetition of "We want the park." I watch him for a while—a cheerleader of sorts. Then I go up to ask a question and his name. He looks at me incredulously, smiles, turns away. I realize I've been naïvely trying to cover this as I've covered peace rallies.

In doorways, older people frown and shake heads. "Shameful . . . incredible . . . no respect."

Monday, May 19—The front page of the *San Francisco Chronicle* features a two-column shot of a helmeted Berkeley policeman, eyes hidden by visor, in the act of ripping out a sapling. An already uprooted plant is in his left hand. He stands there like the gorilla giant we've all seen in horror movies, the one with the tiny human in his paw, ready to snatch up another. But how preposterous a role for a peace officer!

The story explains that yesterday, a crowd armed with picks, shovels, and plants wandered through Berkeley streets illicitly planting. Another vacant lot had been claimed as People's Park Annex. It was above the newly laid tracks of the new subway. (The Bay Area Rapid Transit Authority, unlike the university, did not panic. The park would remain there peacefully for years.)

Meanwhile, I read in my paper, the Apollo X astronauts enjoyed a wholly round view of earth from outer space:

" 'You know,' said astronaut Eugene A. Cernan, 'you blink your eyes and look out there and you know it's three-dimensional but it's just sitting out there in the middle of nowhere.' "

The great ball they saw was blue brown green, set in "the blackest black you ever did see."

In Vietnam, paratroopers spent the seventh day in battle over a barren peak they had named Hamburger Hill because so many were killed and maimed there.

"Sure we want the hill," a soldier told a UPI reporter. "We want it because we can't get the hell out of here until we get it."

I wondered if Governor Reagan and Chancellor Heyns connected those stories in any way. They were all about ways of relating to the planet. Sometimes the newspaper could be read like the *I Ching*.

Tuesday, May 20—James Rector is dead. National Guardsmen stand a few feet apart all around city hall while the city council meets inside. It meets all day, deplores violence, hopes for peace, takes no action.

"It's not a piece of land that's in dispute," Councilman

Wilmot Sweeney says, speaking for nearly everybody. "It's the principles by which we live."

The noon memorial march for James Rector is stopped on the campus edge by police. Nothing more seems likely to happen, I conclude at 2 P.M. A line of Guardsmen backed by jeeps still blocks traffic between Telegraph Avenue and Sproul Plaza, but the crowd seems to be dispersing for the day.

Suddenly I'm startled by a voice through a bullhorn, speaking from the Student Union balcony:

"Clear the plaza. Chemical reagents will be dropped in the next five minutes."

Chemical reagents? The voice repeats. I write down the message and wait. What are chemical reagents? Some students duck into buildings. Others try to leave the plaza but find themselves corralled on all sides by Guardsmen. A National Guard helicopter clatters above us, swoops low, releases a white plume of gas.

Sneezing and coughing, I run into the Student Union cafeteria. The gas is CS, a tear gas commonly used in Vietnam, stronger than the common domestic variety. Effects include vomiting and stomach cramps.

The stinging fumes are everywhere. They drift into classrooms, abruptly ending instruction, and into the university hospital where a paralyzed patient is rushed into a sealed room. In Strawberry Canyon, faculty children begin to cry and mothers hurry away with them. It drifts into homes and nearby schools. On Telegraph Avenue, shopkeepers stand behind shut doors, damp handkerchiefs over their faces.

As the gas clears, a National Guardsman suddenly rips off his helmet and mask, drops his rifle and tries to tear off his flak jacket. I see the MPs lead him away.

In the days that follow, street action is sporadic. As in Paris student demonstrations, red and black flags signal directions to crowds. Black is the anarchists' banner; red represents revolution. But the park people add another color—green, the color of growing things.

On Thursday, May 23, the day after the Apollo X rockets into moon orbit, about 500 demonstrators are corralled in a Bank of America parking lot, arrested, and sent to Santa Rita Rehabilitation Center. There they are forced to lie on the cement of the courtyard for hours. Some are struck with clubs, threatened, and forced to kneel. Tim Finley, reporter for the *San Francisco Chronicle*, is one of a group forced to trot in formation and, in response to a guard's shout: "Whom do we love?" to reply: "The blue meanies!"

I file a piece Saturday morning, then drive to our country cabin for the rest of the weekend. On the way back, shortly after dawn Monday, the whole story begins to take shape. The highway winds along the Russian River, past vineyards and sloping meadows, then widens into a freeway. At that point, as usual, I switch on the radio, tuned to KCBS, the "all the news, all the time" station.

The Apollo crew is preparing for a splashdown in the Pacific. Reports of its progress rattle out in a rapid-fire mix of other news and commercials. So far, nothing much seems to be happening in Berkeley. I keep the radio on, hearing the same round of news over and over. The words hammer into my skull, make my nerves dance, create an illusion I'm plugged into what's happening (The Important News! Now!). They numb me and rev me up simultaneously.

After a while the voice of Mission Control begins to merge with my mind-movies of last week's events and to blend with messages in behalf of Compoz, Excedrin, etc. It all combines into one single story. Suddenly I'm sharply awake.

Here we've done this incredible thing, we've orbited the moon. It took sacrifice, though, more than we realize. We had to rally all our energies and powers into a single thrust, discarding everything that did not seem directly relevant. And now we're hooked to that rocket, disintegrating in reentry burn-out—as witnessed by our increasing reliance on Compoz-Excedrin-Etc., our rotting, burning cities and the preposterous People's Park fight.

How was it that a bunch of shaggy street rebels, doing something so innocuous as building a park, could drive the leaders of a great state and a great university to military force and violence? What threat was posed? Why couldn't the duly constituted authorities deal with the matter with grace?

I'm speeding along the freeway, in transit from a place where life is simple, quiet, and connected, to the discontinuities of a city where, a few hours later, I will dictate into a telephone a story that will appear, in print, six hours later, on streets at the other rim of the continent. Tracking the astronauts, Berkeley on my mind, traces of country-mellowness still with me, I know how it all comes together.

To get to the moon we crushed everything that seemed irrelevant or against progress. The mountain lion was shot because he sometimes ate a sheep. Indians were slaughtered because they took up space. Old people were put out of sight because they slowed us down and reminded us of that great American taboo—death. Chickens and cows were converted into food production machines. We moved fast and straight, beamed to our goal.

Soon we would walk on the moon. But our rockets were powered with hubris. The spirits of the put-away and done-away life forms waited on the edge of our consciousness. All the rejected gods and goblins (rejected aspects of ourselves) merely needed the right moment to surface and wreak havoc with the order we had imposed on nature.

Those prison guards must have welcomed an opportunity to get their hands on some longhaired kids. Their very existence was threatening as it had apparently been to the university authorities who tried to get rid of some weird folks by tearing down the houses that stood on the People's Park site. The park people are basically the same crowd, of course, that lived in those houses. They didn't disappear, no more than the poor, the blacks, and the old "cleared" by urban renewal ever disappear.

I reach Berkeley just as the Apollo crew lands. How incongruous is Today-USA.

In the largest turnout in its history, the students at the University of California, Berkeley, vote 85 percent in favor of continuing People's Park. Faculty votes overwhelmingly for removal of the fence. Support pours in from notables across the country. Jane Jacobs, critic of urban planning and author, tells the park builders they've "affirmed that parks are for people and the world is for people." Thomas Hoving, director of the Metropolitan Museum of Art in New York and former parks commissioner under Mayor John Lindsay, comes out against "the obscene stupidity of people in high places who will take something like this and crush it and react to it with shooting and gassings and instruments of war." Architectural critic Allan Temko says, "The People's Park is the most significant innovation in recreational design since the great public parks of the 19th and early 20th centuries, such as Central Park in New York, Fairmount Park in Philadelphia, Golden Gate Park in San Francisco." He says, "the kids really showed what life could be if senseless and needless bureaucratic impediments were removed."

To show beyond all question that the park is really the people's, a massive march is called for Memorial Day. The march sponsors announce a theatrical streategy. They will march from the People's Park Annex to People's Park. But if, getting there, they find a fence, they will surround it with an enormous park. "We'll fence in the fence," says Jim Holly of the Radical Student Union, "with trees and grass and sod, with music and people in the streets. . . . We'll continue to build the park outward instead of inward."

And then, adds Wendy Schlesinger, "we'll sleep with a stranger."

On the eve of the event Chancellor Heyns invites the city of Berkeley to request a lease of the park site. The council does so at a late-night special meeting. The park people are jubilant. They have won over all local authorities. The matter is now in the hands of the university's Board of Regents, who are appointed by the governor from many parts of the state. To persuade them, a gigantic crowd turns out for the big march. Everyone is jittery. Will the police shoot again?

Five determined but fragile-looking old ladies walk together. "Aren't you afraid?" I ask.

"That's why I'm here," one snaps. "They haven't yet started to attack grayhaired women." She's a great-grandmother.

"I'm here for the children," says her companion. "We had relatives killed in Germany."

The park is much more than a park to people now. That was clear last night, when opponents testified at the city council. They were nearly all graying, balding men in business suits, startlingly alike in appearance—to the point of wearing near-identical heavy-rimmed glasses. They identified themselves as "longtime Berkeley citizens," as taxpayers, or as property owners.

"The main issue is that young people are getting away with anarchy."

"The issue is lawlessness. . . . These so-called flower children are puppets, they are pawns. . . ."

"Appeasing this minority group is not the answer to our problems."

"Munich produced Hitler. Hitler said he had no further territorial ambitions. These demands are being made by people wallowing in an emotional trough of their own manufacture. Their so-called parks are a real mess."

Whether they're for or against the park, the people of Berkeley have come to view it as much more than a patch of green play-space. They have made it into a powerful symbol.

I fall into step with a couple who are walking with two small children.

"We felt we had to put our lives on the line," the woman tells me. "Bringing them was a way to do that."

A man with a little boy on his shoulders says: "Sure I worried about him. But I got my ass shot off in Vietnam for nothing." This is, yes, Memorial Day.

Young and old, straight and hip, have been united by the park issue. I spot an accountant I know, walking hand in hand with his wife. For the past year they have been on the verge of divorce. But this park has, at least for the moment, reunited them.

The crowd seems endless. Estimates range between 15,000 and 35,000. And it stays wholly peaceful. *Time* Magazine, which has planned a sizable story, decides to skip it when no violence erupts.

At Telegraph Avenue, rolls of barbed wire have been laid across the street and Guardsmen are stationed behind it. Only one passage is open for the marchers. They weave flowers into the barbed wire and surge to weave more into the People's Park fence. The Guardsmen look out stoically as someone posts a sign: "People's Zoo."

I stop on someone's front steps opposite the fence. A bearded young man in front of me slowly and deliberately takes off all his clothes, folds them, puts them next to his toes, stands straight and nude for a moment, then dresses again. Nobody pays much attention.

"Why did you do that?" I ask.

"I am the Lord God," he replies. "I am too, yes I am."

Signs drift by above the crowd—"Green Power," "Sod Brother," and a silk-screened one in the form of an official No Parking sign: "Park Here Anytime." A lot of people are carrying green balloons.

As the trucks with the trees and sod reach the fence, people jump off with picks. They hack holes through the asphalt in the middle of the street and stick in the trees. Others lay out sod and bring on hoses. Three pretty girls take off their blouses and start dancing atop a truck. This is street theater and everyone is in the act. It is also something more; it's some kind of ceremony.

At 5:30, policemen with flowers stuck onto their helmets politely ask the crowd to disperse and there is a surge toward the People's Park Annex for celebration. I'm happy to see that someone remembers to rescue the trees from the asphalt. That's evidence, to me, that these people are really serious.

Now nobody could deny that the park has massive community support. But the fence is still up.

On June 7, the grounds and buildings committee of the Regents meets around a long oval table just off campus, beneath a banner reading *Fiat Luce*. But little light is shed.

To the men around the table, the People's Park is a "user-developed, user-maintained park" on the "Haste-Bowditch-Dwight" property. And the language in which they designate the matter on hand is an accurate mirror of their differences with the park builders. Theirs is a cumbersome description, fit for legal and procedural identification but devoid of life and magic. Your mind will not soar upon hearing "user-developed and user-maintained" the way it does at the sound of the word "people." We the people. By the people, for the people. Last year, during the long strike at San Francisco State College, police would order crowds to disperse in the name of the people. The students would shout back in chorus: "We are the people!" and surge on. The exchange was always emotionally rousing.

People are persons, whole beings. And the park, in its builders' minds, is vaguely linked with wholeness. It was an intuitive non-rational statement against the anonymity, impersonality and diminution of man that expressions like "user-developed and user-maintained" convey. The park was, to them, not there to be merely used; it was to be known. It was not just to be developed and maintained; it was to be nurtured and lived with.

As you can hear the gulf between the two groups in their choice of words, so you can see it in their physical presence. The men around the table are all successful in society's definition of success. They are all, within their special fields, in command of other people and of money. But they are not growing old gracefully. Looking around at them I see pinched and dissatisfied faces, pampered faces. University President Charles Hitch has lines running down the inside edges of his cheeks toward a narrow mouth that is closed severely. Lieutenant Governor Ed Reinecke was probably popular with the sorority girls. His eyes look out boyishly from a middle-aged face to charm and record approval. I would not choose him for my jury.

In the tier of spectators sit Charles Palmer, president of the Associated Students, properly suited and shorthaired though with mustache; Mike Delacour, in wrinkled white shirt of Indian mirror cloth, his long black hair unkempt. Beside him is little Wendy Schlesinger, looking very comfortable in her tight jersey and tight jeans, the straight blond hair streaming down around her. Wendy has been on TV a lot, especially the day she wore nothing up top but a net bra with a People's Park button green on each nipple. Her loud street urchin's voice and college-trained articulateness has made her one of the park people's leading witches.

This is a meeting of two very different reality sets. To connect, they could perhaps begin by sitting in a circle or going to the park together. Or at least they could watch film clips of recent events before attempting to settle anything. At the very least, both sides should listen at length to each other.

At the park supporters' meetings I've attended, problems were discussed thoroughly but informally. The most preposterous ideas were entertained without resort to the safeguards of parliamentary procedure, yet somehow the decisions that emerged always made sense. The kids had some basic if unspoken shared understanding that made a free weighing of alternatives possible. No such understanding is sought between the two groups at this meeting.

Instead, the Regents talk about insurance. Berkeley's Mayor Wallace Johnson says the city cannot afford to take the insurance risk on the park. And though a People's Park Corporation has just been formed and is willing to sublease and manage the lot, it is, the mayor says, "for all practical purposes uninsurable."

Not so, argues Jon Reed, a landscape architect representing park people. The corporation they've just formed has a near-guarantee of insurance. Its thirty-one-member board includes a bishop, the president of the Berkeley school board, the chairman of the university's school of architecture, an insurance man, and Scott Newhall, editor of the *San Francisco Chronicle*.

The corporation's assets include "promises by the Jefferson Airplane and other rock groups to play anytime any place," says Reed. Besides, he reminds everyone, Thomas Hoving has said he had no insurance problems with mini-parks in even the worst of New York City neighborhoods.

The Regents remain unimpressed. They talk about law and order. What would happen, William French Smith, a Los Angeles lawyer, wants to know, "if one group appears with an avocado tree and clashes with a group with an orange tree? Who will have the authority to decide what's planted?"

"Well," replies Reed, "a large pool was started the other day. The announced intention was for a swimming pool. But one person came along and started filling the pool in again. So about a hundred people gathered round, talked for ninety minutes and agreed that a swimming pool wouldn't be a good idea but a smaller pool would be. It's difficult, but it can be worked out."

"What if another group wants to take over?"

"That's what gets us into real creative situations," says Reed.

"What sort of thing would be built?"

Reed says he doesn't know. "We're not trying to construct

the definitive park," he explains. "It's a process, ongoing and unstructured, much like sculpture with only so much clay that's used over and over."

"Would there be shanties?" someone asks.

"There could be Watts Towers three miles high. It would depend on the energy."

Now that's not the kind of thing a person familiar with the ways of bureaucracy would ever say if he wanted approval for some project. That sort of openness and fantasy flight will always frighten people who make decisions from memoranda that have been mimeographed and stapled and sent to them in advance in tidy folders, listing alternatives and their implications, letting them believe—no matter if falsely—that they know exactly what they are choosing.

At this point Reed is startled to hear:

"What position does the corporation take on the thirteen points?"

The morning's *Chronicle* reported that some Berkeley radicals had drawn up yet another manifesto, spelling out goals and directions for the future. Reed knows nothing about it. He tries to get the Regents to realize that they're talking only about a little park, not about any plot to overthrow the government.

"When we went out for the first park we had no idea of the dynamics that would be developed," he says. "We went out much the way you would put a Christmas tree in a vacant lot. . . . It was the way I went into business for myself. I didn't feel like I was Castro going to the hills. Once we saw what the situation was we organized a corporation. We're playing it on your terms. The governor's seal is on the corporation papers."

His voice is pleading, urgent. The Regents don't understand what the park now means to the community. It has become Camelot, destroyed in its first flowering, before any problems—self-policing, for instance—had fully emerged. Had it been permitted to go on longer, the inner tensions within the subculture might have caused it to self-destruct, as many a commune, started with high ideals, had self-destructed. But now, after Rector's death, after the huge march and the various other expressions of support from students, faculty, and the community, the lost park stands for democracy, harmony, and hope. It is remembered not for its urchins with STP but for the variety of people working together spontaneously in the spring sunshine.

Charles Palmer tries to say this to the Regents when his turn comes for a brief statement: "The park is an incredibly important thing and I just hope you people can respond to it. It sounds overdramatic but it's like the Berlin Wall. It's a symbol and more than a symbol."

Chancellor Heyns speaks for the park, having quite lost his earlier tentativeness on the matter. But instead of responding, the Regents talk of alternatives. They tangle in motions and numbers and amendments. They talk about ways to get student housing up right away.

As I listen, the reality of the park and the street recedes. This is a world of papers and rules that are somehow supposed to contain and order reality. But these people have no idea. They know so little about what is actually happening out there it's terrifying. I'm reminded of the congressmen who, two years ago, looked with disgust on the rabble from Resurrection City in their antiseptic halls, having no notion that these might be the last group of black people to come plead so humbly before them.

On June 19, the full Board of Regents, with Governor Ronald Reagan presiding, votes to build student housing on the "Haste-Bowditch-Dwight property" as quickly as possible and meanwhile, to put in a playing field for students and—can I be hearing correctly?—to pave part of the park for a parking lot. Heyns, without a word, walks out of the meeting.

A year later, Dan Siegel, acquitted of the riot charge and about to retire as president of the Associated Students, will tell me:

What we learned is that power in this country is wielded by people who are not responsive to the will of the majority and that when an issue comes up that's important to those people they drop all pretense of democracy and due process or regard for law and justice and simply maintain their position by naked force. We went through all the steps of working in the community, getting support from students and finally came up against the Regents and were told no. That made a lot of people reach the conclusion that the only possibility at all was revolution.

Charles Palmer, during commencement, tells it much the same way to the faculty, students, and friends assembled in the university's huge stadium. Then from up on the stage, where he stands in cap and gown representing all the students, a graduate every parent can't help but be proud of, Palmer leads a walkout toward the park. Several hundred, at least, follow him. He tosses a bucketful of water through the cyclone fence at some plants, then proceeds to a nearby hillside to an informal counter-commencement and thence to law school and the presidency of the National Student Association.

During the summer, the university spent $35,000 to bulldoze the People's Park and build the playing field–parking lot complex. But a full year after Bloody Thursday, both remained empty. No student group would use the playing field. The concession for the parking lot went begging. An Orange County firm finally took it up. But the few people who chose to leave their cars on that lot risked punctured tires. The fence remained brightly lit at night and was still protected by a uniformed guard.

By this time, the country had been rent even further. Four students had been gunned down by armed authorities at Kent State University, six at Jackson State College. Twelve sheriff's deputies were indicted in the People's Park shootings but all were acquitted.

But in the wake of the People's Park experience, many were more radical. Some lost faith in the sanctioned processes of social change and began to look toward revolution. Others turned away from politics and set out to create new communities that would be as independent as possible from the existing socio-economic system. They took up self-defense, printing, gardening, fishing, communal life. Wendy Schlesinger, who first met women's libbers at the Park, put away her sexy clothes, got some hiking boots and a motorcycle jacket, began karate lessons and a book to be called, tentatively, "Call Me Chickie and I'll Kick Your Balls In."

Sim Van de Ryn left Berkeley for West Marin County. He took sabbatical leave, then continued, on a Guggenheim Fellowship, to search for ways to involve people directly in shaping their environment. He worked with free schools and community planning groups. In 1971, he returned to teaching—but in a new way. He devised a course that required architecture students to live and build in a wilderness area.

Everyone moved on, and most moved out.

In the spring of 1971, a friend of mine gave a lift to a longhaired couple hitchhiking toward Berkeley. The young man was returning for the first time after the People's Park drama. He had been a student then and very much involved: had even heaved a brick on Bloody Thursday and been struck on the head with some object. But now he believed that nobody had won in that fight. So he was living with his girl up on the side of Mount Shasta, growing a garden and making candles and leather things in a place where the vibes were still good and the air still clean. They had realized, he said, that the People's Park had to include the whole planet and that it had to start with the way they lived their lives.

A new shift was beginning within the Movement, indicated in a letter from Keith Lampe to Frank Bardacke and Tom Hayden, which appeared during the summer of 1969 in the underground press. Bardacke and Hayden had written a scenario describing victory by SDS and Yippie-type revolutionaries. Lampe extended the scenario in light of some of the environmental information beginning to gain public attention:

The White House is surrounded and besieged. Meanwhile, through the years the rising concentrations of carbon monoxide in the atmosphere have caused mean planetary Fahrenheits to rise several degrees. The ice caps have melted and a wall of water 400 feet high advances toward both temperate zones from both poles. Concentrations of DDT in the seas have become so great that phyloplankton are extincted and the planet's oxygen supply greatly reduced. The siege of the White House progresses efficiently and soon the rebels are dashing up the steps front and rear and approaching those infamous portals. But wait! The rebels on the rear steps fall asphyxiated just as those on the front steps drown in the wall of water. . . .

> Power to the imagination
> Support your local wild animal
> The earth: love it or leave it
> Power to the people, the birds, the fishes,
>   the grasses, the serpents
> All power to the life-support system.
>   Keith Lampe

In the months that followed, the first wave of the ecology movement built to its crest. Assorted eco-catastrophes brought the facts home to increasing numbers of people.

In Santa Barbara, oil from an off-shore drilling rig oozed over the white beaches and launched Santa Barbarans into a crash course in the politics of ecology. The fight to get oil out of the channel pitted them against the most powerful industry in the world. They came to experience themselves, these comfortable well-to-do Santa Barbarans, as powerless versus the oil establishment as the People's Park folks had been versus the state and the university.

4

The Political Education of Santa Barbara

❦

At 6,000 feet above the Santa Barbara Channel the twin-engine plane went into a dive, nose aimed at the oil rig. Lois Sidenberg had jammed down her wheel and now sat calmly in the co-pilot's seat, looking down at the water. In front of her, unnoticed, the altimeter raced along a dial: 5,000 feet, 4,000 feet, 3,000 feet. All she cared about at this moment was that the target would be destroyed upon impact.

For months she had been rational and eminently sensible. Ever since the big blowout on Union Oil's Platform A dumped miles of ooze on her city's beautiful beaches, she had fought for the rights of her community in the proper democratic way. She had organized neighbors into a group called GOO! (Get Oil Out!) and had taken part in appeals to courts, legislators, the President.

Nothing had been of use. All GOO! had achieved since the disaster began—January 28, 1969, more than three months before—was publicity and sympathy. Nothing could really stop oil power. The ooze was still seeping, boats still got messy, surfers had gotten into the habit of bringing cleaning paste to beaches. But oil was being pumped again. And then—despite everything that had been disclosed about the dangers of drilling in such an unstable geological formation—this new rig was about to be brought in by Sun Oil.

She was very calm, just watching, as the plane continued downward. Beside the target that grew larger below her every split second, Mrs. Sidenberg saw little boats bobbing at anchor. GOO! had organized a "fish-in" when all other means of stopping Sun Oil from installing this rig had failed.

A couple of days ago she too had participated, circling the Sun Oil site in a helicopter and dangling, as symbolic fishing line, a garden hose with sprinkler head attached. She held out a banner that announced: "100,000 PEOPLE SAY NO." The wind had caught it and nearly pulled her out of the chopper.

Never before had Lois Sidenberg taken part in a direct action protest. But the case was so clear. Even the forces of nature seemed to be against oil's intrusion: as the rig was being tugged into place, it had suddenly toppled off the barge, right in front of the little boats and the TV cameras. All America saw it happen on the evening news. There it was, the steel tower clearly visible upside down just below. Very soon, when she touched . . .

"Hey, what are you doing?"

The alarmed pilot's voice cut through Lois Sidenberg's trance. On the panel before her, the red light was flashing. The dial read 1000 feet.

"What am I doing?" she echoed as the pilot yanked the plane upward again.

So she lived to tell of that kamikaze moment. It was only a moment. But what matters is that it happened. Lois Sidenberg is a grandmother, a Republican, a longtime leader in the League of Women Voters. She was brought up in fashionable Greenwich, Connecticut. For many years, she had been an avid fox hunter.

She had worked for many community causes but always in a deliberate, rational way. Never as a desperado.

She plays tennis, flies a plane, and wears smart pant suits—all of which may set her apart from most grandmothers and testify to her energy. But ordinarily, nobody would liken her to a campus crazy.

And yet in that moment of blind fury above the channel she did behave much like one of those irrational young people she would normally deplore.

Many other well-to-do and usually reserved Santa Barbarans who took part in the frustrating struggle to get oil out of their channel have known similar moments of helpless rage—the kind familiar to poor people, black people, and university students; very much the sort of impotent anger that prevailed in Berkeley during the fight about People's Park.

It made no difference that Mrs. Sidenberg had dined socially with former Secretary of Interior Stewart Udall; that Alvin C. Weingand, the former GOO! president, had been a state senator; that others called high government officials by first names.

Lois Sidenberg did not go on to become a terrorist oil bomber, of course. She continued as the vigorous president of GOO! in her usual sensible way. It would be an exaggeration to talk, as some people have, about the "radicalization of the rich" in Santa Barbara. There weren't any GOO! leaders in the mob that threw rocks at police and burned a branch of the Bank of America during the riots of February, 1970. But the oil spill forced on many solid citizens a crash course in practical politics and ecology. It rattled their comfortable faith in the basic rightness of the American political and economic system. It changed them.

All that most GOO! leaders wanted, really, was protection for their backyard, as it were: their boats, their harbor, their beaches, their ocean view. But this modest objective forced them to delve into the intricate and shadowy relationships between the petroleum industry and government and to examine the implications of the society's heavy dependence on oil.

They found that nearly all oil experts were somehow connected with the industry. Those at universities often had grants or contracts from oil companies. Those in government tended to rely on oil firms for technical data—the data on which they based their decisions affecting those same companies. The public was not allowed access to this same information.

All this, the people in Santa Barbara discovered, helped to explain why drilling was permitted despite the many signs that it could lead to a spill. Later, the U.S. Geological Survey was to admit that even while the ill-fated first Union Oil platform was being built, there was evidence of natural seepage.

"We found that oil is King," was one Goo! fighter's blunt conclusion.

If ever there was a community equipped to fight oil power, it was Santa Barbara. It not only has the local University of California campus and the Center for Study of Democratic Institutions as resources, it is rich in talented, prosperous and well-connected citizens who have the know-how and the time for a cause of this sort.

White and tranquil, its homes climbing the mountainside to look out over beach and ocean, Santa Barbara has, since the 1880s, been "a respite from the horrors of big cities—actually a respite for people who made big cities horrible," says William Botwright, an ex-newsman turned public relations man for the University of California and an anti-oil activist.

Santa Barbarans took pains to keep out unpleasant industry and made sure the waterfront stayed open and clean. They pioneered in environmental law with a local billboard ordinance, validated by a Superior court, and with legislation that protects the city's white-walled, red-tiled charm against the pressures of the real estate industry.

The community even has an ordinance banning sonic booms

—unenforceable but effective. "Can you picture a city marshal walking out on the tarmac there at the Air Force base and giving a ticket to some lieutenant colonel getting out of a jet?" Botwright chuckled. "But there are no sonic booms over Santa Barbara because we shamed them into not doing that any more." ("Well, there are some," corrects Lois Sidenberg, "but not many.")

More recently, litigation was set into motion that could have momentous significance throughout the country. The city and county, as well as some citizens supported by the American Civil Liberties Union, filed suit in 1969 against the oil companies and the Secretary of Interior, challenging the constitutionality of the Outer Continental Shelf Lands Act, which permits off-shore drilling. Their argument was that the people have the right to free use of their environment. The case had the potential of placing many environmental issues under civil rights regulation.

All this—plus a special flair for publicity—enabled GOO! to build its community cause into a national one. The Santa Barbara disaster became nationally famous while oil spillage elsewhere— off Texas, Louisiana, Nova Scotia, Florida—was barely mentioned in the news when it occurred. And it all gave Santa Barbarans a feeling of mission.

On a sunny day in January, 1970, with the beaches white again and no oil visible on surf or shore, William Gawzner, a ruddy yachtsman and prosperous hotel owner, sits down with me at the bar of the Yacht Club to reflect on the year since the spill. In this community, a lot of things are dated as before or after the spill.

Gawzner spends most of his time in the club and around the harbor. He makes sure there aren't any slicks in the path of boat races and generally keeps his eye on goings-on.

"You see that sea wall out there?" He points out the window. "Imagine that whole thing covered, absolutely black with oil. That was black fresh crude, much stickier than the stuff that comes out of the crankcase of your car. It was so thick in the harbor you could throw a broom on it and it wouldn't sink. Birds were walking on it. They didn't walk very far."

Thousands of birds died in the disaster, as did a lot of other sea and shore creatures.

"For a long time," Gawzner says, "I felt this was just a dead ocean. There was nothing out there. The water was black. And now there's less natural life than there used to be."

The oil gushed at a rate estimated as high as 21,000 gallons a day more than a week, covering more than 600 square miles of ocean. Even after the well was brought under control, it continued to flow and seep.

The oil companies' fumbling and ineffective efforts to stop the leak, compared to the sure-fire way they had gone about drilling, were proof to Gawzner of carelessness. And the response of Interior Department authorities to the spill—the misinformed statements, the admissions of ignorance—angered him and turned him political.

Before the drill, he had registered Republican, voted for Richard Nixon, Ronald Reagan, and other party candidates. But he didn't get involved beyond that. If a problem came up before a local governing body relating directly to his business, he could usually call on some official he knew socially.

Now, however, he has a file of letters to senators, representatives, and assemblymen, and a file of clippings on oil politics and economics. This very day one of his letters to editors, pertaining to an oil issue before the county board of supervisors, appears in the Santa Barbara *News-Press*.

"Reagan," he says bitterly. "Never once did he come down here to look at the damage. Nixon came." He laughs. "He landed right here on the beach about a block and a half away, after they cleaned up the beach so it was absolutely spotless.

"They kept all Santa Barbara residents about a hundred feet away. I was next to Al Weingand, who was then president of GOO! He had a petition with about a hundred thousand signatures on it but they wouldn't let him through the line. They wouldn't let any of us. There were banners; people were chanting 'Get Oil Out!' but he couldn't even hear us.

"They had three beach cleaners and they must have been from the Actors Guild. They arrived in new uniforms about two hours before he arrived. The beach had been cleaned already. They got up there with the rakes. When his chopper landed they started to rake. There was nothing to rake but they raked it up anyway. He walked down to them, talked to 'the common people,' turned around, walked to the chopper. They put the rakes back on their shoulders and walked off. . . . He didn't even acknowledge us."

The White House press corps contingent flew in with the President and off with him. Only the local reporters, Gawzner says, realized that other beaches were still oozing with oil. And that petition was still waiting to be presented a full year later, despite many appeals to the White House. GOO! had lugged the sheaves of signatures to Washington, to Sacramento. By January, they had more than 175,000 names on their request to end the drilling.

Finally, the angry Santa Barbarans resorted to a less orthodox approach in trying to get it to the President. One day when Nixon was at the so-called western White House, his house in San Clemente, three GOO! members piled the paper into a boat and picketed from the ocean. But if the President saw their little boat with its orange banner, he gave no sign.

Mrs. Sidenberg began to daydream of flying over San Clemente and dropping some oil on the President's roof. Others were ready to put the petition into a hearse and display it around town.

"Maybe we're not acting exactly like college students but the same frustration is there," Gawzner tells me. "We had all the tools that democracy makes available to a citizen but they didn't work. We feel that the oil industry really owns the government. . . . They keep oil out of the country, which means it costs you more. The government talks about inflation and they make inflation because they make the consumer spend more for gasoline."

A white paper on the oil disaster, prepared for GOO! by Charles E. McCarty with the help of the UC–Santa Barbara's Walter J. Mead, a petroleum economist, explains how a complex system of tax subsidies, depletion allowances, and import quotas keeps American oil prices consistently above free world market prices. "The leases in the channel could be purchased only because such operations were made profitable by the subsidy system," the paper states.

So Gawzner feels that he, as well as everyone who signed that petition and everyone who drives a car in America, was forced to subsidize those hated oil rigs.

"It's virtually a national scandal," another Republican, Harold Beveridge, says to me the same day, echoing Gawzner. "My guess is that the oil companies' tax advantage is several times the total profits of the military-industrial complex."

Beveridge is part of that complex—the General Research Corporation, which he founded, handles defense work. He also dealt in million-dollar contracts in Washington when he was in technical charge of the ABM system.

He joined GOO! ("despite the name," he says) because he was "utterly dismayed" to find oil two feet up the hull of his sail boat. Since then, he has been surprised to find himself labeled a protest leader and pleased to hear his twelve-year-old son say, "Dad, I'm proud of what you did." His sail bag still has a red mark on it where an oil worker threw a brush at it.

During the fish-in, Beveridge's yacht was anchored at the scene. He was also present at the final confrontation on November 25, when the platform, once again righted, was tugged into place. That was when he experienced what poor people, black people, and students often complain of: how federal officers can act as if they were agents of private interests.

That night was calm and bright at sea. On what was believed to be the site of the new platform, the chartered boat *Suzie* lay at anchor with three men aboard. They knew that, according to ocean rules of the road, a vessel underway has to stay clear of a vessel at anchor. They intended to stay at anchor.

The *Suzie*'s communications were out, so Beveridge and his boat stood by.

Shortly before 10 P.M., the three men on the *Suzie* later reported, a Coast Guard cutter approached them and pinned them with floodlights. Aboard was Donald W. Solanas, regional oil and gas administrator for the Interior Department. He told them that a barge and rig in a condition of "critical buoyancy" were being towed in and that the companies involved in the building of a platform had legal rights to do so.

"Mr. Solanas informed us that he had recorded our names and the name of the boat and was going to turn this information over to the Department of Justice," the *Suzie*'s crew reported.

The *Suzie* stayed put. But unfortunately, GOO! had slightly miscalculated the site of the new platform. The barge was towed in anyway.

That confrontation with Solanas, however, outraged Beveridge. "I think it was outright intimidation," he tells me. "He acted like he belonged to the oil companies." (Solanas, asked for comment, had none.)

Since the spill, Beveridge has developed some doubts about whether the representative process is as representative as he had assumed it to be.

On a trip to Sacramento regarding the oil issue, he says, "I was a little appalled to find there were five hundred lobbyists and a hundred and twenty-five lawmakers," he says. "Perhaps there ought to be an equal amount of money spent on the other side. Tax the lobbyists or something. Maybe there should be an ombudsman or something. We should have someone who represents the people and good land and good water."

A trace of the unease from which such ideas arose is audible in his words. Then Beveridge leans back in his desk chair and self-confidence returns to his voice as he waxes rhetorical.

"I think we're fighting the battle for the whole country here," he says. "We're as good a test case as we're going to get. If we fail, maybe there's no hope. Are we going to have dead seas, forests slashed to the ground, wildlife gone—is the country going to do itself in or are we going to have a soul-satisfying land in which to live?"

He could have said "planet" instead of "land." For oil pollution is a global problem. In May, 1969, Dr. Max Blumer of the Woods Hole Oceanography Institute reported that a research ship collecting sargasso weed in the Sargasso Sea towed a net for 630 miles and brought in three times more oil tar lumps than sargasso weed. "Oil pollution is not only on our shores, where it is very evident, but it is spreading worldwide," he told a meeting of fellow scientists.

Off-shore drilling and oil-bearing ocean traffic are expanding. And the danger of spills grows proportionally. The building of larger tankers further increases the hazard.

The long-term effects of oil spills are still largely unknown, but there is evidence that they are persistent. In March, 1957, the tanker *Tampico* ran aground in a cove of the Pacific Coast off Baja California, spilling its diesel oil and killing much sea life, lobsters, mussels, and abalone.

Seven years later, the shellfish population was considerably reduced, according to a study by Wheeler J. North, Michael Neushul, Jr., and Kenneth A. Clendenning. But vastly greater numbers of plants were found shutting out sun from underwater areas and being cast upon beaches, upsetting complex marine ecosystems.

Julian McCaull, a biologist at the University of Washington, sees the most serious threat to phytoplankton, the one-celled plants that float in the upper seawater and provide food for the tiny zooplankton that fish eat. Man, of course, is at the top of this food chain.

And so it followed that on the morning of January 28, 1970,

the first anniversary of the big spill, Harold Beveridge and a few others sailed to the spot where the oil first gushed and placed a buoy, with an attached canister containing the newly written "Santa Barbara Declaration of Environmental Rights:"

All men have the right to an environment capable of sustaining life and promoting happiness. If the accumulated actions of the past become destructive of this right, men now living have the further right to repudiate the past for the benefit of the future. . . .

We propose a revolution in conduct toward an environment which is rising in revolt against us. Granted that ideas and institutions long established are not easily changed; yet today is the first day of the rest of our life on this planet. We will begin anew.

The fight to get oil out of the Santa Barbara Channel continued, with Lois Sidenberg ever vigilant in the lead, knowing what Margot Patterson Doss, the Bay area conservationist, had discovered: that in conservation, you can't afford to lose sight of the next battle. You only need to lose one to lose the whole war.

On April 21, 1971, the Nixon Administration submitted to Congress a proposal to cancel thirty-five of the Channel's seventy-one oil leases, with leaseholders to be compensated. The intent was to create a federal oil-free sanctuary adjacent to one already created by the state. Santa Barbarans were pleased but the bill languished.

On September 2, oil seemed to have won. The Department of Interior sent a "final environmental impact statement" to the President's Council on Environmental Quality, recommending that permission be granted for two more drilling platforms requested by Union Oil and Sun Oil. The department took note of the fact that the channel's geology was unstable but concluded that two more platforms would reduce oil seepage and lessen undersea pressures that could set off another blowout.

GOO! fighters rushed to importune political and environmentalist friends for help. Both California senators, Alan Cranston and John Tunney, pleaded for the President's intervention. So did Representative Charles Teague.

Bowing to pressure, the administration did an about-face. On September 20, Secretary of Interior Rogers Morton took the unprecedented step of reversing his department's authorization. He denied permits to install the platforms "because of overriding environmental considerations." It was understood that the White House had stepped in.

That close victory helped to restore some Santa Barbarans' confidence in the responsiveness of their government and gave them new energy to attempt to keep oil power at bay.

But more important, perhaps, than the outcome of that fight was its effect on the people who waged it and on others who learned from it. By late 1971, the community had become more alert to threats and disturbances in the environment. Noise pollution had become a big issue as had population growth. On the local campus, serious consideration was being given to the banning of cars. Plans were dropped for a freeway that would have cut across part of one of the three remaining coastal wetland areas on the Pacific Flyway in California.

"The whole business of whether people should be moving around so much is being questioned," Botwright told me. He himself had just answered the question for himself in the negative by selling his car, moving closer to his job, and acquiring a bicycle.

In his view, the community was undergoing a profound transformation. "The centers of power—assemblymen, senators, city councilmen—are still conservative," he said, "but they're under strenuous challenge in elections and under daily siege from environmentalists. And everybody seems to be an environmentalist now."

But the universe is not simultaneous, as R. Buckminster Fuller likes to point out. On February 10, 1970, thirteen months after the Santa Barbara disaster, eight wells on a Chevron Oil Company platform blew out near the coast of Louisiana and the platform caught fire. For a full month, until the blaze was brought under control, oil gushed into the water—sometimes up to 42,000 gallons in a day, twice as much as in Santa Barbara. The last blowing well was not controlled until March 31 and even after that the spill continued. It was the largest spill ever known on this planet.

Walter J. Hickel, then secretary of interior, toured the Gulf of Mexico by helicopter a month after the blowout and, according to the *Los Angeles Times–Washington Post* news service, remarked: "Compared to Santa Barbara this is a disaster. There is more oil involved, more pollution, a wider area, and it will take much longer and be much harder to clean up."

The blowout occurred only eleven miles from the eastern edge of the coastal marshlands, an immensely rich watery world of bayous, ponds, saline troughs, brackish shallows, and salt water bays that nurtures a vast variety of animals and plants: snowgeese, deer, otters, shrimp, oysters, fish.

"Two-thirds of this nation's marine catch is estuary-dependent and the Gulf's largest and most fertile nursery is the Louisiana marshlands," according to Wesley Marx in the April, 1970, *Sierra Club Bulletin*. "As food demands rise and marine technology expands, Louisiana, more than any other coastal state, has at its doorstep an unmatched food factory which requires no fertilizers, pesticides or plows. At the same time, as leisure demands rise, Louisiana finds itself next door to a vast marine parkland that requires no bulkheading, dredging or fingering to accommodate thousands of pleasure-cruising craft."

It was mostly thanks to the winds, which blow southerly in the winter, that the oil was washed into the open rather than into this delta, where it would have been nearly impossible to clean out.

Chevron subsequently paid one million dollars in fines, pleading no contest to charges that it had violated federal drilling regulations. Drilling was temporarily suspended.

But Louisiana, unlike Santa Barbara, depends on oil for much of its income. Thousands of oil wells dot the coastal waters and the marshes. The priceless life of the delta has been mortgaged for income from oil.

No wave of outrage followed the disaster in Louisiana. The newly formed ecology center rallied a small band to a short demonstration in front of the Standard Oil Building, in New Orleans, but that was about all. Most people took the accident as a natural calamity, an act of God. The governor pressed for renewed drilling.

On TV one evening in New Orleans, while the fires still raged off-shore, I watched as the oil companies told what great things they were about to do for the Eskimo in Alaska in exploiting the North Slope. It would be a long while—perhaps too long for the living creatures of the Mississippi Delta—before the Santa Barbara perspective reached New Orleans.

5

Speed Fix

The news filters down and settles in our minds like ashes. By winter-spring, 1970, nearly everyone is vaguely scared.

Item: A "maximum security" subdivision of $200,000 homes is planned eight miles from Washington, D.C. It will be almost as inacessible as the White House. All residents will carry ID cards. All visitors will be cleared by guards. A fence with electronic sensors will keep off intruders.

Item: National Park Service officials report a major reproductive failure among sooty terns: only 2 percent of 40,000 terns in the area of Fort Jefferson, southern Florida, reproduced successfully. DDT and sonic booms are suspected causes of the trouble.

I wouldn't know a sooty tern from a seagull and will probably never have occasion to visit that luxurious self-prison in Potomac, Maryland. But such bulletins gather in the mind, feeding a growing unease. The death of birds is often the first sign of impending catastrophe. When the canary stops singing, the coal miner drops everything and runs.

When you're scared, you tense. Your extremities grow cold. You lock your door, avoid strangers' eyes. You prepare to fight or to run. Your breath constricts; an ashen haze suffuses the vision. And a paralysis of imagination sets in.

The bulletins keep pouring in, something to touch everyone.

"Pollution along the spectacular Monterey seacoast has become so serious that immunization against typhoid fever and hepatitis is now being recommended by Dr. Richard S. Fraser, county health director."—*San Francisco Chronicle*, January 20, 1970.

"*Stockholm, UPI*—The newspaper *Social-Democraten* reported that concrete boxes with 7000 tons of arsenic dumped into the Baltic Sea by a mining company thirty-eight years ago were crumbling. The arsenic is enough to kill three times the world's population." —*Earth Read-Out*, culled from *The New York Times*.

I spent my early childhood summers on the Baltic Coast in Lithuania, so this one's for me. In school I learned that the Baltic Sea is shaped like a maiden kneeling in prayer. Her arms and hands form the gulf between Finland and Estonia. Leningrad is at her fingertips; Sweden is at her back; Lithuania hugs her thighs. Before I could read I knew that the Baltic Sea is the domain of the goddess Jurate who fell in love with the mortal fisherman Kastytis and took him down into her amber palace. The chief god Perkunas (Thunder) was angry, sent a lightning bolt to shatter the palace and kill Kastytis. That's why you now find pieces of amber on the Baltic's shore and why sometimes, on stormy nights, you can hear Jurate weeping. I used to try to stay awake and listen.

In the July-August, 1970, issue of *Environment* I come upon an article called "The Stagnant Sea," by Stig R. Fonselius, oceanographer at the University of Göteborg in Sweden. It informs me that my Baltic is dying. Algae and phosphates from detergents and fertilizers are straining the oxygen supply near the surface. Cellulose

SPEED FIX

fibers from industrial wastes suffocate bottom life. Fishing gear is often fouled by ammunition and poison gas containers. Nobody knows how to remove the arsenic or the 20,000 tons of mustard gas in steel containers that could begin to leak anytime. The article does not mention the fate of the goddess Jurate. Perhaps, if we had listened more deeply to her, none of this would have happened.

But tell me no more. Information overload sets in. I begin to blank out.

The poet Michael McClure, who teaches English classes at the California College of Arts and Crafts, found that when he first started to include eco-facts in his lectures, many of his students stopped hearing him.

"Perhaps fear and fatigue in the land are so great that from now on not even our information can be confrontational," comments Keith Lampe in the *Earth Read-Out*. "Perhaps we have to learn how to present the information gently to the periphery of consciousness instead of trying to drive it straight through the forebrain and on down the throat. McClure suggests that the information, when spoken, be delivered slowly and selected carefully to avoid combinations of implications which overwhelm."

Alvin Toffler, in his book *Future Shock*, has tagged an apt label to the condition afflicting so many of us. The rate of change in our society is so great, he says, that the future careens into our present. We become confused, frightened. We go into shock.

I saw an extreme case of it in a middle-aged housewife who talked with me at length, in her comfortable home on the edge of Oakland, about what she and her neighbors were doing to fight crime. She told me how she and others kept an eye out for suspicious strangers, jotted down license numbers of cars and physical descriptions of drivers. When they thought something was odd, they called police. They watched for robbers, child molesters, drug-crazed addicts, and juvenile arsonists.

Several of her neighbors owned guns. She herself always slept with a knife at her side and a loaded pistol within easy reach. When she went out, she left on at least one light and one or two radios.

This woman had never been robbed in the sixteen years she had lived in this neighborhood. She had never been criminally accosted. No child molesters or other maniacs were known to have been around. There had been a recent increase in burglaries in the neighborhood, but not one had been violent.

At the heart of this lady's fright was that thing Toffler talks about—future shock. She came close to saying it toward the end of our conversation:

"We're living at such a fast pace that time is getting away from us. If you have children there's a subconscious fear always with you that they're growing up in this fast time."

Could it be, I wondered, that all that defense against malefactors was really a desperate effort to hold off the whole fast-timed world?

Fast time—compared to what? Isn't time a man-made concept? But yes. Once it paced and ordered our lives. It flowed in an inevitable progression from past toward future. You found your place in it and built your home in it. But now time is erratic and disordered. There are no more beginnings, middles, and ends to events.

The destruction of Jurate and all the other spirits of place has cast our own spirits adrift. The disorder of time has made us refugees in our own homes.

I first became aware of the disorder in our time experience during the events that followed the assassination of John F. Kennedy. I was in Washington at the time, reporting for *The Washington Post*. The day Jack Ruby shot Lee Harvey Oswald in front of the TV cameras, I was covering the arrival of various world leaders for the late President's funeral. Chiefs of state came in endless procession into Dulles Airport. Secretary of State Dean Rusk and some other man I've since forgotten went to meet each of them at the plane, escorted them into the terminal and toward the cameras. They would stand there a moment, their faces composed to appropriate solemnity, then proceed to their limousines.

In between arrivals, we watched TV. On the screen, the shooting of Oswald was repeated over and over. His grimace at the sight of Ruby's pistol engraved itself in my mind over the image of Dean Rusk's face before the cameras.

Like most people, I never turned off the TV or radio in those days, except when I was out covering further events in the story. Over and over I saw the Kennedys wave to the crowds in Dallas, the limousine's rush to the hospital, Oswald's face. And so the experience of those events did not end. It repeated itself, numbing me more each time.

During the funeral mass, I was outside in the street, walking along the route the procession was to take to Arlington Cemetery. The sidewalks were already packed with people, many of them listening on transistors to the Mass in St. Mark's Cathedral. As I walked past the radios, the sounds from the cathedral went with me. The whole city was listening—the whole nation. The cathedral had expanded to include the whole mourning country. We were all, for that brief hour, one body and one mind through the magic of radio.

But this magic soon turned against us. The body of the dead President was in the earth, but the murders and the funeral continued. We stayed hooked to our electronic antennae and the sound of the muffled drums and the sight of that procession pounded our senses until, in insomniac daze, we ceased experiencing. The media stole from us the catharsis that a funeral is designed to bring. Gradually, other images took over the screens and our attention. But because we never buried Kennedy, the nightmare stayed with us as a vague anxiety. The experience was never closed. Time could not heal the wound.

Some coffee shops along the major highways advertise: "We never close."

"Have you thought about how terrible that is," a psychiatrist in La Jolla asked me, "never to close? Never to rest?" Sartre's *No Exit*.

He told me some of his patients drive for hours along freeways with no destination in mind, spend whole days wandering through shopping centers and at those starkly fluorescent places. They themselves are afraid to close, he says, afraid to let go lest the lump in their throats escape in a scream. The momentum, they feel, is so great that to stop would mean instant disintegration.

But the speed fix will work only so long, then the body rebels. Like all other organisms, we must have cycles and rhythms. Our technology has allowed us to detach ourselves from the natural ones—for a while. But giving them up, we need substitutes. When the natural enemies of the garden pests are destroyed, we need pesticides. When people cannot live naturally, they resort to other things—fast cars, constant motion, drugs.

So it is that Librium has become the top-selling drug on the legal market. Some schools are giving tranquilizing drugs to children considered "hyperactive." More and more, the society is relying on psychoactive drugs—legal and illegal—for stimulation and relief, speeding up and slowing down. The drug problem, then, is inseparable from the sense of time disorder which, like many other social problems that are now so acute, arise out of a disorder in natural balances and rhythms.

A few months after the Kennedy funeral, some of the buildings that the caissons passed are gone. Ten years from now, will I be able to show my child the street corner where I stood watching? We've all shuddered, hearing about the way totalitarian governments try to erase history by destroying books. But we are erasing our past even more directly. And perhaps we've already erased our future. How can we help, then, but be scared?

Dr. David Hamburg, chief of psychiatry at Stanford University, says we must learn to replace our obsolete patterns of behavior not with new patterns but with the acceptance of constant change.

Dr. Frederick Perls, founder of Gestalt therapy, used to talk about allowing the river to flow. Kids of the counter-culture talk about "digging where you're at." Buddhism teaches that all learning and growth begins by accepting what is. The "Four Changes" has it this way: "Knowing that nothing need be done, is where we begin to move from."

In early 1970, I'm very much tuned in to the natural process and much aware, gladly, of the present. I'm pregnant with my first child. I want to give it the best chance it can have by eating right, sleeping right, avoiding artificial stimulants. According to some MDs I saw, I'm unwise to be pregnant. Cancer of the cervix (*carcinoma in situ*) has been diagnosed and though the biopsy probably removed it, the doctors can't be sure. "The treatment is a hysterectomy," I was told. The word should have been "sentence," not "treatment." But there were alternatives. Another doctor said I could try having a baby first.

Somewhere I read that cancer involves a failure of communication among cells. Normal human tissue cells signal each other by ionic current when they touch and so keep their growth in harmony with the needs of the organism they are part of. But cancer cells just go on, consuming the body—much the way homo sapiens is now consuming the planet body Earth. We must, then, restore lost connections among beings and cells. We must put ourselves in the power of life forces.

Gradually, as my belly grows larger, I am buoyed out of paranoia into a steady soft joyfulness. A woman at the clinic tells me she had four children because she liked the high of those nine months so much. I know what she means. Nothing can squelch that sense of spring everywhere. And yet, still, there is the threat everywhere. Loud noise, I read, harms the ear drums. A whole generation may be growing up partly deaf. Even the unborn are affected. And in Colorado, schools have been built on uranium mine tailings and must be aired out each morning to decrease radioactivity in classrooms. "Life is carcinogenic, not to mention fatal," sighs my friend Lil Lectric Lulu.

As the time of the birth approaches, the life forces become stronger. I'm in the country, lumbering and clumsy. Outside the cabin's door Spanish moss drips off heavy oak branches. Birds sing in them. Everywhere, swamps of fecundity are overcoming the dying. We have invaded Cambodia; students have been shot in Kent and Jackson State Colleges. The tragedy is, says Lil Lectric Lulu, that we are destroying what we need so badly. And yet I roll in those swamps of fecundity, letting the ooze come up between my spread fingers, oozing myself from every orifice, wallowing in the rich smells of birth out of dying.

The ranch is full of young animals. John has a baby great horned owl, Mary and Bruce a new baby and a puppy, some chickens, and a half-grown dog. Bob has a very woolly wiggly wolf-huskie. We have a black kitten. All kinds of children come visiting. We're planting an orchard. Some quiet people from country communes come to help. "They smile like Jesus but never like Lenny Bruce," someone says, cynically. But I'd rather learn to laugh like those monks in the Zen brush paintings.

The closer the birth date, the more time expands and the more I feel connected with all life and all beings. In my dreams, I dance one night with my grandmother, whom I love very much and who died a decade ago. She was wonderfully present again, happy with me. Another night I cry at the sight of a black kitten that comes up to me with its left eye hanging out bloody. I know it must be killed but can't do it. Three boys take it away. One puts its head in a plastic bag and holds it by the neck, a knife pointed at its throat. I sob. He laughs, looks at me, and laughs more. I stop sobbing and accept that there is no other way, that the kitten must die. Then a triangular tablet appears, with three friezes. The top and bottom ones show animals and men changing into one another. The middle one is full of prophets pointing. In between are enormously heavy letters.

SPEED FIX

In early spring, we spend a weekend with friends at Lake Tahoe. The alpine water is clear all the way down to the little white plastic knife beside the beer can tab. Everywhere signs of hurried development: shacks thrown up on half-acre lots, destroying the wilderness. Yet it's *because* of this wilderness people want these shacks. Cancer.

In the evening by the huge fireplace, I find the issue of the *New Yorker* with Thomas Whiteside's painfully detailed account of defoliation in Vietnam. It tells how Americans have dropped powerful poisons that may cause birth deformities and cancer over villages and waterways; how villagers have seen their crops shrivel and recorded an unusual number of miscarriages and abnormal births. Whiteside is thorough and avoids emotion. The facts, simply presented, scream loudly enough.

On the way back to the city, we stop by a waterfall. Tara, my eight-year-old stepdaughter, splashes barefoot. Mel and I lie down on a rock to wait for the baby's kick in my belly. But there is this sense of existing in some past time. This peace around us has already been slashed by the grieving Vietnamese mothers. Our children don't know it yet but at this moment they are already scarred by the napalm that burned the Vietnamese children.

Erwin Schroedinger, physicist: "No Self stands alone. Behind it stretches an immense chain of . . . events, to which it belongs as a reacting member and which it carries on."

A child born, he wrote, is "not really a new seed but the predetermined unfolding of a bud in the ancient, sacred tree of life." Birth—awakening from a deep sleep.

The Hopi Indian baby is kept in the dark for nineteen days, so its soul can make the transition from the protection of the Sun Father and the Corn Mother into that of the human parents. Our baby came suddenly into the bright fluorescent lights of the University of California Medical Center's delivery room. It was 5:11 A.M., July 2, 1970 (Sign of Cancer the Crab), dawn. So we called her Usha, which in the ancient Sanskrit language is Dawn. She slithered out of me and was placed on my belly where Mel cut the umbilical cord. Then a nurse held her up and she looked at me with wide open eyes and gave a huge wail. All of us in the delivery room were feeling very exalted. And she began her first day, as every American baby now does, with unknown quantities of DDT, DDE, dieldrin, and other toxins in her body tissues, inhaling unknown quantities of other poisons with her first breaths. She began to drink my milk, which is tainted, like the milk of all American mothers, with DDT. And as she sucked on my breast and then fell back, drunkenly sated and asleep, it was all so very very fine that I never once wondered, as I did later—is that what original sin is—being born tainted by our society's crimes against nature? She was born with an unknown quotient of freedom, a child whom I hope to teach what I know, most basically that, in the words of that wise man, Schroedinger, "The present is the only thing that has no end."

6

*Pollution of
Ecology*

❧

Just how much of a sham Earth Day, 1970, was did not become fully clear until a year later, when one of its organizers told the story in an article in the Washington *Post*.

"The idea that students had discovered a new supercause was largely a myth," wrote Stephen Cotton, a law student at Harvard, who had been press director for the event. "It was conjured up by the press and encouraged by a variety of well-intentioned and not-so-well-intentioned political figures. It was made possible by an energetic band of young people in the Washington office of Environmental Action, the national coordinating council."

Senator Gaylord Nelson first suggested the idea of Earth Day. He invited Representative Paul McCloskey of California as cosponsor and obtained funds from foundations and labor unions to hire Cotton and two other Harvard students.

"We accepted not because of any new-found interest in conservation, but out of a desire to rescue the country's environment in a broader sense," Cotton wrote. "Our concern was with poverty, war, racism and slums. We hoped that middle-class people who became indignant over dirty air and water could be persuaded that no one concerned about ecology could in conscience support continued destruction in Vietnam.

"Both students and reporters naturally tended to be suspicious that we were out to co-opt the anti-war movement. We weren't; actually, we were trying to co-opt the administration's Silent Majority."

Publishers and politicians were happy to see the ecology issue detracting—or so it seemed at the time—from student rebellion in the universities, and from street protests by blacks, welfare mothers, anti-war groups. Reporters flocked to the office of Environmental Action. To meet their expectations of hustle and bustle, wrote Cotton, "we must have wiped out a middle-sized forest churning out fact sheets and brochures."

But contrary to what the impression was through the media, very little was actually happening around the country on April 22, 1970. Cotton managed to list only fourteen events as suitable for coverage during the nine and a half hours of network time allotted to Earth Day. And eleven of those fourteen either didn't happen, he wrote, or were "dull beyond belief."

In an outraged response, the national coordinator of Environmental Action, Denis Hayes, labeled Cotton's article "a crazy, unstructured blend of truths, half-truths, exaggerations and outright—let's be charitable—mistakes."

Cotton's bitterness, however, was aimed less at Earth Day than at the failure of the ecology movement thus far to see the extent of society's predicament. As some of the more astute observers had long ago pointed out, much of what passed as ecology activism was in fact only verbiage, if not truth pollution.

This, in part, from an early spring issue of the *Spokane Natural*:

White House spokesmen recently announced that the President encouraged students and young people to demonstrate vigorously for fresh air and clean water. This is the same man who watched a football game while 500,000 peace demonstrators marched down Pennsylvania Avenue. . . . Crystal clear air amounts to nothing if it merely means a cop can get a better shot at a fleeing suspect, or vice versa. Limpid water in our lakes and rivers will not help the worker who doesn't have a job. . . . Noise abatement will matter little to the soldier who is losing his hearing, if not his life, on a foreign battlefield. . . . A government that fakes concern over pollution while using the issue to manipulate the people is worse than a government that does nothing at all. The appearance of action may lull the country into the fatal error of thinking the environment is being saved.

On the other hand, if the government cleans up on our industrial wasteland with funds from present and future social programs, the country won't be worth cleaning up.

In his May 4 newsletter, I. F. Stone pointed out that President Nixon had called air and water pollution a "now or never" task but, in his budget, allocated fifty-two cents of every general revenue dollar to the military and space—and only .4 of one cent of every such dollar to air and water pollution.

The incredible flow of platitudes on Earth Day did the eco-fad in. And in the subculture, what helped kill it was another media ploy—Earth People's Park. Like Earth Day, it was born of a mix of high hopes, misunderstanding, delusion, and self-serving.

On the winter solstice, 1969, some of the subculture's elders gathered in San Francisco. Among those present: Stuart Brand of the *Whole Earth Catalog*, Ken Kesey of the Merry Pranksters and *One Flew Over the Cuckoo's Nest*, the Diggers' Peter Coyote and Peter Berg, Paul Krassner, publisher of *The Realist*, Keith Lampe, and Wavy Gravy (Hugh Romney) of the Hog Farm Commune, which had raised Pigasus, pig candidate for president in 1968, and did much to keep things high and happy at the Woodstock rock festival.

The Earth People's Park idea was proposed by some hip-talking longhaired entrepreneurs, including Milan Melvin, a pop record producer and disc jockey, husband of Joan Baez's sister Mimi.

The idea was to buy about 50,000 acres of land somewhere in the Southwest as a home for what Abbie Hoffman had dubbed "The Woodstock Nation." Everyone who had been in Woodstock in body or spirit was asked to send one dollar, with the goal of raising a million dollars—and so, among other things, showing the size of the subculture.

The land would be open to anyone. All fences would be torn down. No private property, no cars, no money would be allowed. Ecologists and Indians would be called in to advise on the park's development but rules would be avoided. The acquisition of the land would be celebrated with a giant earth-warming festival.

The elders approved the idea, on the whole, though some objected and some were wary. Lampe argued that the project was a creature of "urban media junkies." It was too flamboyant and ecologically unsound, he said. And how was it, others asked, that the sponsors of the Earth People's Park idea did not themselves plan to live in it?

But the *Tribe* glowed that Earth People's Park was "an attempt to make a beachhead for a new order of civilization." There was coverage in many leading newspapers and on TV.

Handsome leaflets flowed out of the office of the Earth People's Park Corporation (non-profit) setup in the basement of a Union Street church. Handsome piles of letters, each containing a dollar, flowed in. A check from Tim Leary bounced but was proudly tacked to a wall.

The leaflets quoted Indians and emoted: "Can you remember the way we danced? Can you remember the way we sang? At Woodstock . . . in People's Park? . . . And what if all the people who can still remember how to dance and sing came together in wholly communion? . . . in the creation of a new nation—a non-nation—not of geographical boundaries but of free spirits howling at the moon." They talked of "a life style which cherishes the earth and man with equal reverence" and of "freeing a piece of Mother Earth."

But Woodstock was over. Squabbling and financial hassling had forced the cancellation of the Wild West rock festival in the Bay area. The last big rock gathering, at Altamont, had ended with beatings and a murder.

In February, a statement signed "Earth/Life Defense" appeared in the *Tribe,* summing up the criticism of the giant land idea mounting within the subculture. The Earth People's Park would be nothing but a "hippie ghetto in the desert," it predicted.

> They all talk about "ecology" but what's ecological about a zillion thirsty people, with no knowledge of survival in the desert, where every drop of water is already accounted for? What's ecological about a zillion electric rock show fanatics trampling the ground to dust, leaving their plastic wrapper, beer can, toilet paper reality behind them? . . . will the indian-chicano people see them as anything but another gringo invasion/ another (40,000 acre) territorial rip-off/ more urban middle-class hippies washing their clothes in the drinking water/ will they create anything for the southern Colorado and northern New Mexico communes except a million dollars worth of longhair hatred/ from people who've been fighting the gringos a hundred years for every inch of ground capable of supporting life? . . .
>
> what Earth People's Park is creating is the falsified (media) version of everything that's part of our real life: our everyday communal existence, and our visions of revolution and a new culture/ they sell us to the media (along with the movie rights, record rights, book rights). . . .
>
> the people who are really concerned about hip life/ the future of the communes/ our survival & the survival of our life-style/ are people who work quietly to build the real living units, the new institutions of a hip society/ they bake the bread, fix the cars, grow the gardens in city & country, deliver the babies, & start the schools for young children/ they create new forms for people getting together, new forms

of free exchange between individuals, between communes, & between city & country/ they hunt their own meat, fish their own fish, arm themselves for survival & eventual struggle, practice herbal & organic medicine to heal each other, yoga to put their mind back in their body, & karate to defend what they build.

By March, money was still coming in, Wavy Gravy and his Hog Farm were still busing around the country collecting money for Earth People's Park, but the idea of a massive land purchase had been discarded. Inquiries about how the park was coming along were met with vague answers about smaller pieces of land that were about to be acquired.

The park had to begin closer to home, wrote Edward Baer, a KSAN disc jockey who had made a name for himself as an eco-freak in the Bay area. In a letter to "Dear Sisters and Brothers" that the Earth People's Park office sent out, he ventured that the Park had to begin "in mind, in body, at home."

"In order to give something to it all," he said wisely, "one must have something to give." So, people who share the vision might begin by sharing their homes, lives, and loves "so that a couch is earth people's park to a wanderer, their car is earth people's bus to a hitch-hiker, and their table is earth people's earth to a soul with hunger."

He trimmed the million-dollar, 50,000-acre dream to "a handsome well-made sticker roughly four inches square," with the symbol of Earth People's Park on it in Day-Glo, to be displayed by people with Earth People's Park vision.

Neither Earth Day nor Earth People's Park drew much attention from the most imaginative radical eco-thinkers. Cliff and Mary Humphrey were busy, during the winter-spring of 1970, with a 500-mile Survival Walk from Sacramento to Los Angeles. They had decided it was time to move from guerrilla theater action in city streets into contact with people in rural places. If a cultural transformation was to happen, it had to happen in places like Elyria, Ohio; Peoria, Illinois; Fenton, Michigan; Modesto, California. When it happened there, it would make things change in the state legislatures and in Washington.

So they made painstaking arrangements for a forty-eight-day trek through the Great Central Valley where pesticides and chemical fertilizers have meant prosperity—and where DDT no longer works because bugs are immune, nitrates are threatening water supplies, and air pollution affects food crops.

Many of those who took part in the journey had already made personal commitments toward what they saw as an ecologically sound way of life.

James Tremaine, a San Francisco architect, and his wife, Lynda, for instance, had sold their car and found they could get along without one. They had turned their home into a community center—a "life house" in Ecology Action language—where neighbors could come for information and conversation about environmental problems.

Before the march began on March 15, many participants attended weekly "rap sessions" at the Ecology Action headquarters in Berkeley and read books about major problems in the valley. Others took part in a course given by Ecology Action on the University of California campus and tried their hand at organic gardening.

The idea was to learn from the people of the valley as well as to bring them information. The walkers stopped to talk with crop dusters, farmers, field workers. They visited schools with leaflets and bibliographies, set up exhibits in town squares and shopping centers. Where they saw Shell No-Pest strips in food stores or restaurants, they left leaflets warning that dichlorvonos vapona, a powerful organo-phosphorous insecticide, was the active ingredient, and that the Department of Agriculture had ordered that the strips be packaged with labels cautioning: "Do not use in kitchens, restaurants, or areas where food is prepared or served." Shell was challenging the order through the courts, so the warning was not yet on the package, the leaflets explained.

As had happened in Stuart Brand's Hunger Show, the most intense encounters were among the participants. But glimpses into Valley lives also had their impact.

In the tiny town of Winton, Cliff stopped for iced tea in a coffee shop. He sat down at a counter with a few of the local folks. Cliff can look inconspicuous in most crowds. At first glance, he looks like a European professor. His brown hair is longish but worn unfashionably straight back from the forehead. His glasses are horn-rimmed, his expression studious. But when he smiles it's not the sardonic, worldly smile you'd expect but a grin that is completely guileless. He wears simple sporty shirts, trousers that tend to be baggy, old-man black shoes. From his belt hangs a brown leather pouch with notebook and pencil. You can't easily pigeonhole him into any category of person. And when you talk with him, he's disarming.

So nobody in the coffee shop paid much attention when he ordered his tea. He noticed however, that it was strangely quiet in the place. The only conversation came from a table by the window where a dapper black Air Force sergeant sat with a blond woman. Only when the couple left did the others come to life.

"Well, she didn't *look* like a pig," observed a truck driver.

"You can't go by looks anymore," replied the cook.

"These remarks were made automatically and without malice," Cliff wrote afterward in his column in the monthly *Freedom News*, a small community newspaper published in Richmond, California. "Immediately it became clear to me that this was a lesson for the politics of ecology. The lack of anger from those utterances indicates that the racist culture is no longer relevant to those that know it. They are only hollow utterances that beg for new information. . . . The old culture is only maintained because there is nothing yet to abandon it for."

Shortly after the walk ended, Cliff and Mary acted on this insight by leaving Berkeley for Modesto. In that Central Valley town, Cliff said he would try to "create an example of environmental sanity that would be a ray of hope for the rest of the country."

Modesto's 1970 population was 60,000, tripled in twenty years. The main industry: food processing. Food processing wastes dumped as landfill though they would compost into an excellent replacement for chemical fertilizers. Much of the employment seasonal. A hunger crisis every Christmas.

Near the railway station, an arch spans what used to be a proud avenue and the city's gateway. On it, a legend forged in bold letters: "Water Wealth Contentment Health," forlorn reminder of the hope and promise to settlers who came out a half-century ago to conquer nature and make the valley into a breadbasket for the nation. It used to stand proudly above a tree-lined street. Now it looms empty above the anonymous urban jumble on the city's fringe. Nature as enemy has proved invincible.

So, to Modesto Cliff and Mary brought their new dream, as spelled out in their Declaration of Interdependence their vision of the good life in harmony with nature.

But change is slow in the valley. People who came from the Dust Bowl thirty years ago are still called Okies. News from Berkeley often sounds like news from abroad. The Humphreys would need much patience.

They rented an economy-style office suite behind the Quik-Stop Market at Tully Road and Roseburg Avenue, a crossroads that could be anywhere, USA.: three gas stations, a coffee shop that serves coffee in paper containers, a grocery store, and a few nondescript shops in a nondescript building. Little houses marching off into tree-lined streets, each behind its little square of lawn.

When I drove down to visit them three months later, in January, 1971, it seemed at first as though they had been absorbed and made invisible by the drab anonymity of their surroundings. In their office window, the poster of Earth in a gas mask was no more dramatic than the paraphernalia of the beauty parlor next door. I recalled how, during the Survival Walk, I had seen the same thing happen in Stockton, where they had set up their catastrophe warning exhibits in the gleaming walkway of a new shopping arcade. The merchandise in the surrounding shops, fluorescent lights, and canned music somehow drained all the life out of their message. Consumerland has a way of consuming its would-be transformers.

But after I'd spent some time with the Humphreys I realized that they were competent to tackle Consumerland. They had the self-effacing perseverance and the contact with what politicians like to call "grass roots."

Cliff greeted me with a clipping, an editorial from the *Modesto Bee*. "Here," he said. "Our certificate of arrival. Now people refer to me as Cliff Humphrey of Modesto."

The editorial praised an agreement that the Ecology Action Educational Institute (consisting of the Humphreys and a young Modesto couple, Lester and Beverly Corn, who had taken part in the Survival Walk) had just reached with the Gallo Glass Company, the biggest wine bottler in the country, located right in town. Gallo would buy, at twenty dollars a ton, not just its own wine bottles but all clean jars and bottles Ecology Action could deliver.

A ton of glass would be about 1600 bottles, but that didn't seem like much to Cliff. Everyone he had contacted was eager to cooperate—the VFW, the Four-H Club, gas station operators, Boy Scouts. Everyone cared. Nobody really liked throwing away things that could be saved.

It's through such small but cumulatively important changes that the transformation can begin, Cliff believes. The sight of a neighbor separating jars and bottles means much more than the most eloquent article on waste. It develops a new consciousness that eventually will have to be recognized by the people who run governments and businesses. "We're changing what is politically feasible" Cliff likes to say of his work.

As we strolled across the street into the coffee shop, he told me how he saw ecology action in terms of the planet. Right now, he said, "We're still backing up catching a fly ball. We're going in reverse but there's no other way to catch it. It will be maybe fifty years before you'll begin to see a difference. It'll take that long for the education and the reclamation. The last thing to change will be the stinky rivers and the smog. The first will be people's minds.

"You have to know where to look for success and failure. We look whether increasing numbers of people are doing new things for new reasons. It's been only a year [since ecology became a household word] and I bet we have a million people throughout the country trying to manage their solid wastes, either by reducing their purchases or by recycling."

What's needed, he believes, is a cultural transformation greater than the industrial revolution's. The idea of progress must change "from dollar progress to progress toward serenity, tranquility." Everything has to slow down a bit and man must rediscover his connections with the earth and its other inhabitants.

When people change the way they live and think, the socioeconomic system will be compelled to respond. That is why Cliff and Mary so rigorously live the revolution in their everyday lives. Cliff told me he now only accepts rides if someone is going his way or if it's absolutely essential he do so. Otherwise, biking proves a benefit, providing a bit of physical exercise and a few moments of quiet even on busiest days.

Mary had become even more proficient in applying the economics of hard-working large-family poverty to the management of the earth household. She had cut down on her garbage by buying no more frozen or canned foods, taking her own shopping bags to market and declining to have merchandise placed in paper bags. Her vegetable parings, of course, went into the compost and her glass would now go to Gallo.

But the waste distressing her most at the moment was that of the human energy represented by the thick folder full of job applications in the office file. Most were from conscientious objectors seeking alternate service. They were willing to work for the barest subsistence and had useful skills to offer. One was a biologist, another a filmmaker, another a forestry graduate. Yet there was no way the Humphreys could take them on. They could barely pay the rent and the phone bill. Sometimes there was not enough left over for food stamps for their family.

Cliff had some income from his lectures, but not much. He would not ask a fee, believing that the information he offered should be free. Sometimes—at the 1970 Aspen Design Conference, for instance—he'd accept a speaking engagement and find, upon getting there, he did not even have enough money to eat. To most people, there's work and there's charity. You demand money for work and you pile up goodness credit for charity. Cliff's notion of work does not fit in. It is, actually, an Eastern notion. The Eastern guru is supported by students who come to him and ask to be taught.

But Cliff would not dwell on money matters. What mattered, he said, was that much had already been accomplished in Modesto. There had been a meeting with city department heads at the city manager's invitation. Public workshops, lectures, and classes had begun. Proposals had been made to the city about more sensible methods of garbage disposal. There was some possibility that food processing wastes from the packing plants might be salvaged and returned to the soil.

"The biggest reason for optimism," said Cliff, "is that there is no tolerable alternative."

While Earth Day and Earth People's Park marked the dying of the first phase of the ecology movement, the Humphreys' Survival Walk and their move to Modesto marked the beginning of the second phase, which was to be characterized by a narrowing of focus, a growing emphasis on regionalism, and a return to the land in search of lost connections. The Humphreys found their niche in the heart of mainstream America. Keith Lampe, meanwhile, sought to create it in the back country.

On Earth Day, Lampe and others associated with his *Earth*

Read-Out had left Berkeley in search of some remote hunk of land where they might try farming and prepare to shelter others during the great total systems collapse.

I was particularly interested in this new move by Lampe because several times in the past he had proved to be a bellwether for a dominant trend in the subculture. He had been through the beat scene with the poets in the 1950s, the civil rights movement in Mississippi in the 1960s, the anti-war movement, the Yippies, and in the ecology movement—always on the leading edge, always as an articulate spokesman. In his latest newsletter, he had run down his view of where things stood with the ecology movement:

It now seems that the old-timers—liberals, moderates, right-wingers, left-wingers—are sufficiently aroused to make possible in a few years the phasing out of the internal combustion engine plus short-term patchwork clean-up of certain rivers and lakes plus bans on the more persistent insecticides and on the SST.

All of which provides ERO with an opportunity to take new paths, to begin to define a more specifically radical ("root") approach to the emergency.

For openers, let's look at a few "root" mistakes the old-timers are about to make in the context of their new eco-concern. I use "old-timer" not as a pejorative but to indicate anybody—regardless of age—whose frames of reference are products of the *old time*, i.e., the industrial-revolution phase of history:

1—They are about to initiate massive programs within the old frames of centralized authority, of nation. Nations are such an artificial construct from an ecological point of view that any further energies poured into them are almost certain to do more long-term harm than good. Nations . . . must be phased out as quickly as possible and replaced with tribal or regional autonomous economies rational in root terms of planet topo/climate/water shed/ etc. Boycott the words "nation" and "international."

2—They are about to initiate massive programs within the old frames of a competitive society even though this will prove decisively contradictory in terms of our root insight into interdependence-of-species. Since interdependence can be sustained only in a context of cooperation, competition (capitalism) must be phased out and replaced with cooperative models.

3—They are about to initiate massive programs within the old frames of profit (and recognition, e.g., yr idealistic, militant photo on the cover of *Time*) even though our natural resources already have dwindled to the point where further manipulation of profit as a work incentive is intolerable. The phase-out of profit, then money, must follow the phase-out of competition. Survival itself once again is the incentive.

4—They are about to initiate massive programs within the old frames of growth and progress even though the planet's dwindled resources and exploded populations make continued use of those concepts imminently disastrous. Capitalism, phased out, cannot be replaced with socialism or communism because those forms too are growth-and-progress oriented. We have very little recent politico-economic inheritance to work from.

5—They are about to initiate massive programs within the old frames of faith-in-infinite-technology even though crucial limitations of planetary energy—energy as root solar E—mean the technology, no matter how brilliantly transformed, cannot prevent huge homo-sapiens die-backs and extinctions of thousands of other species. This sort of realism is difficult—yet overwhelmingly important—to reach: when we dropped out of the religions (e.g., Christianity, Judaism) we were originally trained to accept, we unconsciously transferred our sense-of-an-infinite into science and technology. Even some of the activists who recently have shifted into crime as a life-style trustingly assume that the techno-system will continue to produce goods worth stealing. We shall have to use a transformed technology to salvage what we can—but technology even at its best cannot save the whole scene.

6—They are about to initiate massive programs within the old frames of anthropocentricity even though interdependence-of-species means you have to care equally about all earth creatures. Humanism, despite its sweet surfaces, has been enormously unfortunate. Even worse than contemporary graduate-school humanism is the recent (1890) cook book which says: "Three days before the turkey is slaughtered it should have an English walnut forced down its throat three times a day and a glass of sherry once a day. The meat will be deliciously tender, and have a fine nutty flavor." Practical considerations of survival force us past humanism as fast as we can make it.

Just before Lampe left, I'd called him for an interview. After some hesitation, he invited me to lunch at his house, which turned out to be a spacious adobe in the prosperous Berkeley hills. Lampe was not exactly a down-and-out radical. Like a number of other activists who came from the white educated classes, he was being supported, at the time, by inherited money—in his case, his wife's.

We settled down in his basement study, among packing boxes, and he filled me in on changes within the past year. There was the latest arrest—his eighth. The previous seven had been in connection with anti-war demonstrations. This one was for lying down in front of a logging truck loaded with redwoods.

That was April, 1969, just before he started the *Earth Read-Out* as an effort to focus attention on ecological data that did not make it into the general circulation press. Did I remember the item about the two scientists who challenged present radiation safety standards? He believed he was the first to print that one. John Gofman, associate director of the Lawrence Radiation Laboratory, and his colleague Arthur Tamplin had estimated that if all Americans received the radiation dose currently allowed by the federal government, there would be 17,000 additional cases of cancer each year. They had made their statement at a scientific symposium but the general press missed it. Since he had put it into the October, 1969, *Read-Out*, though, it had been picked up.

The media were now pretty good about such stories, Lampe said, so he had tried to stay ahead in the perceptual shift by getting "crankier." He had lately suggested, for instance, that humans start eating "further down the food chain" and so save land. One acre is quite sufficient to support a human subsisting on grain and vegetables, but not near enough for a man who eats beef.

His latest thought, though, was that perhaps he should leave "typewriter ecology" lest he become another "urban media junkie." He was having serious doubts about the value of a newsletter that went out to a mailing list around the country. The move had to be from centralism to regionalism, he said. And away from words to their meaning. So he and Judy were selling the house and would use the money to buy land somewhere in the Southwest, together with two or three other couples. He wouldn't say where—being worried about a population influx.

Had he always been so nervous? His face was kind, thoughtful, and somehow aristocratic. Since I'd last seen him, his hair had grown longer but his paranoia did not seem to have decreased. I began to feel annoyed because I was disappointed—preferring, reportorial objectivity notwithstanding, to see my radicals as nobler than me.

"The Black Panthers are getting shot; there's the Chicago Seven Trial; there's the war," I said. "How do you relate all that to raising gardens?"

"I can't talk about it all right here," he replied, glancing at the phone. "The room might be bugged. The phone can be used as a transmitting device. But I'm not running away. At least I don't think so. For one thing, if we're scattered, it will be harder and more expensive to keep us under surveillance."

Way back in the first issue of the *Read-Out,* he had suggested: "What if the Pentagon had to deal with thousands of small tribes scattered across the American landscape? Tribes interiorly gentle but exteriorly capable of good offense and good defense. Knowing Indian survival techniques and capable of Indian-mobility. The suburban whites thus themselves surrounded—in fact opposed simultaneously front and rear. The strategic situation changes so much that possibly few shots will have to be fired."

I read that as romanticism then and that's how I still heard Keith now. The notion of this so thoroughly urban person, who moved his body in the rather stiff hulking manner of a man used to sedentary pursuits, the idea of him talking about living as an Indian!

We went upstairs to lunch on some health-food noodle soup with Steve Beckwitt, a biophysics graduate student at the University of California, Sam Abrams, a poet from New York who used to be chairman of the classical languages department at Drew University, Sam's wife Barbara, Keith's wife Judy. All were members of the *Read-Out* group ready to join the emigration. All seemed to me thoroughly urban intellectual types who probably didn't know any more about farming than I did. You could tell with just a look they hadn't been doing any heavy physical labor.

In a recent *Read-Out*, Beckwitt had written: "The crux is population size: it must decrease. How much is a question for the new science.... The patterns of our lives determine our offspring's success. Selection operates against: up-tight lives, urban dwellers, automobile users, meat eaters. The only people who will survive the environmental crisis are those who respect the earth." Now he was about to move to maximize his offspring's survival prospects.

"Rasa thinks we may be copping out," Keith said.

"When I'm up in the country," I said, "it's so lovely all around, there is such pleasure in just being part of the scenery, that Panthers getting shot in Oakland is very unreal. I don't want any newspapers. We planted an orchard and that was so . . ."

"You planted an orchard?" cut in Sam. "Did you have any stumps to take out?"

"No."

"Well, if you could have found some stumps to take out you would have gone to town and bought dynamite. You can't just walk into J. C. Penney's here in the city and ask for dynamite. Some people find ways to relate to Panthers while planting orchards."

"I guess that's not my way of relating," I said.

Sam shrugged. Diane di Prima, he said, explains how it is that man is so destructive: we have been invaded by creatures from outer space. Twelve hundred years ago, when we stopped hunting and gathering and began to plow the land. At that point we became the carrier—the louse, the mosquito—of the disease sent from outer space to turn the earth into desert. Now we can see that the microbes are getting ready to move out—see it by the international space race—because the earth is nearly finished. Sam was angry. So were Diane di Prima's poems. A lot of anger in this house.

Keith and I got into a conversation about newspapering. He had worked for INS in Paris for a while, just before it folded into UPI. He told me some of the lessons he learned, which killed his illusions about the idealism of the press and turned him elsewhere. He sensed that I must have had some of those same bitter lessons recently.

He was right. When *The New York Times* failed to stand wholly behind Earl Caldwell in his fight to keep notes and tapes of interviews with Black Panthers confidential, some of my remaining illusions took a tumble. We talked about that for a while. If superb newsmen like Earl Caldwell should be intimidated by subpoenas, the radical subculture would be even more dangerously isolated and misunderstood.

"Yes," says Keith. "They must put up with attacks and be careful not to blow their cover."

Blow their cover? I didn't see that kind of advanced guerrilla war.

"Just the way I have to put up with what you asked before," Keith said. " 'Aren't you shirking your responsibility?' "

A few days after this lunch, another issue of the *Read-Out* arrived in the mail, dated "Spring Equinox, 1970." Printed on both sides of half a sheet of orange-yellow mimeograph paper was a letter explaining that from now on the newsletter "will occur as events suggest—or perhaps we'll evolve a rhythm tuned to the moon."

"ERO also is beginning a desubscription drive. We've become victims of the eco-fad and as such have become just one more growth industry. We began in mid-May of 1969 with a mailing list of seventy; we now mail to six hundred thirty places. . . . If you don't need ERO, please let us know and we'll remove you from the list. Remember 'Four Changes': 'True affluence is not *needing* anything.'"

ERO would continue in "regional perspective." People should also start their own regional eco-newsletters. To "help establish a regionalist perspective from which a radical regionalist politics can be constructed," a "special issue" of the *Read-Out* was enclosed.

This turned out to be a glossy four-color topographical map of the United States, dividing the country into ten regions. On the back I read:

> Centrally defined borders imprison all life. The ecological crisis is the earth/organism shaking itself free of its human/imperialist chains.... No more nations. Nations are fantasies. Our own ways lead to realities. Topo realities. Watershed and airshed realities. Regions. A region is terrain within which ecological cycles can be closed without expenditures of non-renewable energy reserves. As regions close within themselves, nations lose ability to wage war: no more Colorado water for desert Imperial Valley lettuce which feeds L.A. munitions worker who kills Vietnamese.... Our ways go forth from civilization now; they lead to autonomous regional cultures once again.

Also enclosed was a beautifully printed copy of "The Holocene Gazette & Country Traveller," a poster-sized bulletin dated "Wolf Moon, 1970," in "Vermont Free Territory" and dedicated "for nature against art." It contained some of the basic radical ecology gospels, and some poems including "Revolutionary Letter #38" by Diane di Prima: "NOT PEOPLE'S PARK/PEOPLE'S PLANET. ..."

I looked over the packet and again felt annoyed, for some reason. It seemed to me that Keith Lampe had lost touch with reality. Here was this man who so many times had manifested a passion for social justice, turning out some paranoid mystic thing. Of what relevance could it possibly be?

Decentralization and regionalism, however, are words I now continue to hear from many directions. Vine Deloria, Jr., a Standing Rock Sioux, author of *Custer Died for Your Sins* and former executive director of the National Council of American Indians, echoes Keith Lampe. In the March 8, 1970, *New York Times Sunday Magazine*, he writes that many younger Indian leaders have turned back toward the tribe.

> By the fall of 1967, it was apparent that the national Indian scene was collapsing in favor of strong regional organizations. . . .
>
> Indian people are speaking more and more of sovereignty, of the great political technique of the open council, and of the need for gaining the community's consensus on all programs before putting them into effect.

We are discovering that when systems get too big, or move too fast, they overwhelm the human and extinguish the natural. The whole eco-problem can be examined in terms of scale and speed.

On the late night show in New Orleans, a white plumber watches a black community leader in Newark and becomes angry at what he hears. He cannot understand because the words come to him out of context. He cannot relate to that black ghetto man's experience. No more than I, having flown from San Francisco to New Orleans, can relate to the mountains and deserts I've passed. The airports are much the same in San Francisco and New Orleans. I don't even know the *extent* of what I can't relate to.

So it is with the eco-news of the past months. It's familiar, but we can't relate to most of it. Has anyone failed to hear that the world's population is doubling every thirty-seven years? That the United States consumes seventy-five percent of the world's non-renewable resources? That the Peruvian tuna we feed to our cats and chickens could be enough for all the Latin-American children who now suffer brain damage from protein deficiency?

We've all been told these things *ad nauseam* and we get angry at having to keep thinking about them without finding a way to act. The words build a vague fear and we try to screen them out of our minds. Then the consumerland wizards come along and kill their meaning by recycling them into sales pitches: "Help save the Bay. Make washday Ecology Day. Purex."

The terrible war news continues. "War isn't even the word for it anymore. It must have a new name," says my friend Elizabeth. We cease to hear.

Not long ago, the poet Robert Mezey selected excerpts from Max Picard's *The World of Silence* for an issue of *Earth Read-Out*, including this:

> Everything is carried along in the noise, and any and everything can develop out of it. Nothing arises any longer through a specific act, through a decision and through the creative. Everything turns up automatically: through a kind of mimicry the noise produces what is required by the circumstances of the moment. . . . Man is so much a part of the verbal noise going on all around him that he does not notice what is being conveyed to him. . . . If war reports were not blaring out from the radio every minute of the day the cannon fire and the wails of the dying would be heard everywhere. In the silence the wails of the dying would be heard and they would weigh down even the sound of the guns. In the silence the war would be heard so loud that it would become intolerable. But the constant noise of the war reports levels down the sound of guns and the cries of the dying to the general and universal noise.

The Humphreys and Keith Lampe's *Read-Out* family are trying to get through that noise by turning away from rhetoric and toward something that cannot be perverted. They're trying to change their own lives, so generating change in their society. They talk of slowing down and narrowing their focus, of moving from centralism to regionalism, of connecting with the earth by getting their hands into it.

Other activists, meanwhile, have chosen an opposite path, one charted by R. Buckminster Fuller. Their aim is to expand their focus to the limits of the universe and to speed up until universal patterns become clear.

7

Omni-Directional Bucky Fuller and His World Game

R. Buckminster Fuller is a man with good news in dark times. He believes it's now possible—right now, today—to provide for all humanity's basic material needs. Thanks to modern technology, he says, we now have the capability of achieving utopia. All that's lacking is a perceptual shift.

So, for several years now, he's been circumjetting the globe, talking, talking, trying to open minds to implications of the world's roundness.

Fuller is best known as the designer of the geodesic dome. He's also a mathematician, cartographer, architect, poet, philosopher, world man, evolutionary strategist, comprehensive and anticipatory design scientist. Marshall McLuhan has called him a modern Leonardo da Vinci. Heads of state, other great scientists, powerful people in government and industry, students the world over admire him. But it's as teacher that he may be most influential.

OMNI-DIRECTIONAL BUCKY FULLER

On a wall in his office at Southern Illinois University, Carbondale, Illinois, I saw a photograph of the boot of Italy taken from a plane, seeming to show the earth's curvature. His friend Norman Cousins, former editor of the *Saturday Review* (later to launch a new review, *World*), sent it, inscribed: ". . . of all the human beings I know, you have liberated yourself most from earth constrictions—not just specific gravity but general modes of fixed thought." Now Fuller's set himself the task of liberating others by showing them his vision of man and technology evolving together in the context of natural harmonies.

The morning I arrived in Carbondale, very little seemed fixed there. People and ideas were in rapid transit. Someone was just leaving for Israel; someone else had just arrived from New York; someone else prepared to depart for the West Coast. Fuller was on his way to the airport, having already spent four days—long, for him—at the home office.

I landed among some highly verbal, fast-talking young apprentices, all with world-sized projects in the works, all willing to pause for conversation, at length, about their Bucky. They showed a devotion to Fuller that rivaled that of the Chinese to Mao.

So enthusiastic and laden with data were these young men that very soon my head was spinning with dicta on tetrahedrons, domes, ephemeralization, the World Game. They spelled out connections between micro and macro with near-fanatical diligence. In one breath they moved from pollen to cosmic dust, social relations to astrophysics. And before long, they had drummed me into their frame of reference.

I began to be aware
That I sat on a chair
That was inside a building
Inside a town that was
Riding a sphere

*Spinning through space
Drifting omni-directionally
(Inward toward the DNA
Outward toward the farthest star).*

*Boggled by Bucky.
A whole new scale.*

Some months prior, someone in San Francisco told me of a similar perceptual whammy he felt after reading Fuller's *Nine Chains to the Moon*. Impressed by the argument that man's continued existence depends on his learning to perceive his everyday world in light of science, this fellow climbed a hill one evening to try a Fuller exercise: to sense a sunset as an earthturn.

He sat down on a rock, looked at the "sinking" sun and thought of what was actually happening. Before long he felt himself falling backward, at incredible speed, on a huge ball. Boggled by Bucky.

At the time he told me this story, it didn't mean much. He was even a little shy: "Maybe it was self-hypnosis." But talking with the Fuller folks in Carbondale I sensed something similar.

Of course, the apprentices said. Naturally. That's Bucky, always generating epiphanies and so nudging evolution a microstep forward each time. That's why they had come to this rather provincial campus. They had all been boggled by Bucky. Each could tell his tale if there were time for looking back. But with future careening into present so fast.... The point was, you have to keep moving. Bucky moves nearly all the time. He's almost constantly orbiting the planet, as fast as jet convenience will allow (alas, not yet the speed of light or even the speed of sound), clocking an average thousand miles a day, having gone three million miles during the first seventy-six years of his life, showing no sign of slowing. He's the man of the future, free of impediments, unattached to either place or time. He tries to see everything in whole-earth perspective.

Fuller's travel gear includes four watches: one set to the time at the place where he's just been, one to where he is, one to where he's going, the fourth to Carbondale time so he'll phone at appropriate hours. Businessmen, who must cross time zones frequently, suffer from jet lag and take time off to recover after each trip. Not Bucky. His biological clock runs on Fuller time.

But isn't such perpetual motion rather a waste of time, I wondered—all that waiting in airports, holding in pattern, inching through traffic? Couldn't he sometimes just write or phone or do a videotape?

No, said the Fuller people. He needs to move around to keep in touch with what's happening. And humanity needs to see and hear him. Its role on this planet will soon end unless it understands what he's been saying about synergy and our being passengers on a spaceship that is "a marvelous piece of design—every bit of it in view of the rest."

Fuller likes to compare his role in evolution to that of a jet plane's trimtab, a tiny rudder which changes the course of a skyship cutting through the air at 600 miles an hour. Just so, he is trying to turn humanity's course away from death and destruction and toward joy, abundance, and peace.

Fuller's Spaceship Earth metaphor has become a cliché already, yet few people know he is its author. Fewer still understand the metaphor's meaning. So Bucky keeps moving, talking, talking, racing toward speed of mind.

Even as I sat there he was en route. He'd pause in St. Louis for a TV interview on his recent proposal for redesign of the notorious slum city of East St. Louis. Then he'd move on to Colorado, Wisconsin, and California to speaking engagements. I had an appointment with Fuller in Los Angeles next week. My visit to Carbondale was mainly for the purpose of learning more about his World Game, which one of his young admirers had described to me as "Bucky's way to make the world work." Fuller's own definition is more complex:

> The World Game is a scientific means for exploring expeditious ways of employing the World's resources so efficiently and omni-considerately as to be able to provide a higher standard of living for all of humanity—higher than has heretofore been experienced by any humans—and on a continually sustainable basis for all generations to come, while enabling all of humanity to enjoy the whole planet Earth without any individual profiting at the expense of another and without interference with one another, while also rediverting the valuable chemistries known as pollution to effective uses elsewhere, conserving the wild resources and antiquities.

"I find humanity's general strategies in every known economy and ideology to be quite inadequate," Fuller told a subcommittee of the Senate Government Operations Committee, March 4, 1969. "This is why we are developing our World Game as the swiftest way in which to get humanity to understand both its dilemma and its potential egress from it."

As I understood it, this World Game was basically a process of world logistics and future simulation that Fuller was offering as his alternative to the war games now used in determination of national strategy.

War game strategy—as developed by the late Professor John Von Neumann and Oskar Morgenstern in the book *Theory of Games and Economic Behavior*—is based on the assumption that people or groups or nations seeking particular goals will pursue strategies that can be mathematically represented. They can then be anticipated and counter-acted. You make a mathematical calculation about what some country might do and then, on the basis of this calculation, devise your own strategy.

A basic assumption in war games is that nations must compete—one nation's gain is another's loss. Fuller's World Game, on the other hand, rests on the assumption that competition is obsolete and self-destructive, and that the goals all nations seek can only be achieved if we all learn to view ourselves as inextricably interdependent—no less so than the crew of a spaceship. The success of one is inseparable from the success of all.

Failure to perceive this fact, and to understand certain principles basic to the operation of Spaceship Earth, keep us from achieving all mankind's—and our own separate—well-being.

One of those basic principles is synergy, defined by Fuller as "behavior of whole systems unpredicted by behavior of any of the systems' parts." A simple case in point exists in metal alloys.

If you test the tensile strength of cobalt, nickel, and iron separately and then add them, you get 250,000 pounds per square inch. But the merged strength is greater: an alloy of the three metals will withstand 350,000 pounds of pressure.

Other examples abound because synergy is one of the basic principles governing the universe. (Universe, by the way, is "the aggregate of all humanity's consciously apprehended and communicated experience with the nonsimultaneous, nonidentical, and only partially overlapping, always complementary, weighable and unweighable, ever omni-transforming event sequences," according to Fuller's *Operating Manual for Spaceship Earth*.)

It is impossible to understand how the universe works without understanding synergy, says Fuller. And it's largely because so few people do understand it that we're headed for planetary catastrophe now.

One reason so few grasp the concept is that we tend to collect, examine, and analyse fragments rather than looking for wholes. That's the Western tradition. But the universe is in constant motion, its fragments (or rather, energy waves) combining into ever-new and unpredictable synergetic wholes that we cannot predict by projecting from segments of information. We must expect the unexpected, says Fuller, and look for it in whole systems.

The Earth is one obvious whole system. But we seldom view it as a whole. We confine our vision to nations, states, races, and other man-made categories. We have not, for instance, taken in the implications of the whole-earth fact that "in this century we have gone from less than one per cent of humanity being able to survive in any important kind of health and comfort to 44 per cent of humanity surviving at a standard of living unexperienced or undreamed of before—this without anyone's conscious effort, evolving out of the total thrust of humanity's activity."

That's good news, made possible in part by the trend toward ephemeralization—or "doing ever more with ever less," per given resource units of pounds, time, and energy. The bulky radio has yielded to the tiny transistor; the gramophone to the portable phonograph and the tape cassette. Intelsat IV, the three-quarter-ton communications satellite, can simultaneously relay fifteen times the messages that 175,000 tons of transatlantic cable used to carry. In each case, less material is being used to do more.

Now, says Fuller, technology has advanced to a point where "one hundred per cent success for humanity" is possible. That is, everyone could enjoy the food, shelter, education, medical care, and other physical aspects of survival that help to free people for the discovery of the good life. But because all planning, design, and accounting are confined to political and economic boundaries, nobody perceives the possibilities for all humanity.

Our choice, he says, is not whether or not we are to have technology but what kind of technology we are to have. A bird's nest is technology, extending the bird's power to rear and shelter its young. It is technology in harmony with nature. Our technology now too often violates nature. But the trend toward doing more with less could lead us to a wholly harmonious technology that would become less and less visible. Eventually, Fuller envisions an invisible technology.

To explain the possibilities of synergetic whole-earth technology, Fuller likes to talk of electricity. Presently, he points out, vast amounts of electric power are wasted because electricity cannot be stored and the demand for it varies according to time of day, day of week, and season. But if all the world's power grids were connected, the world's total generating capacity would triple without the addition of a single dam or power plant.

With the spread of electricity, more food would become available through improved storage and transport. Right now, for instance, much of the food in India rots or is eaten by mice.

Population growth would decelerate. Fuller has found a correlation between the birthrate and kilowatt hours of energy consumption. More power (Fuller speaks of it in terms of "energy slaves") makes possible more individual freedom and a diversification of life styles.

So, with a single synergetic move, the connection of electrical power grids, great benefits would accrue to humanity. The chances for peace would rise. People tend to fight wars, Fuller says, when they believe their survival is at stake.

Electricity is but one example. Others exist all around, mostly unseen. There is no adequate inventory of the world's resources, no global accounting system, and nobody is empowered to do whole-world designing. So we fail to become conscious of the extent of waste and destruction inherent in competition and of the way it is endangering all of us. We don't see the possible.

The World Game is Fuller's attempt to coax along evolution of the whole-world perspective we need to design whole-world solutions that could bring utopia closer.

Of course Fuller's thinking does not go undisputed. Some of his critics view him as naïve in expecting, as did the Technocrats who talked about hooking up electrical energy grids back in the 1930s, that technological change will bring about change in man.

To some eco-activists, he is a *bête noire*. They see him as an optimist who fails to appreciate the seriousness of the planetary crisis, dismisses the population problem and mistakenly assumes man can continue to play fast and loose with ecosystems.

Much of the criticism rises from misunderstandings of a very complex man. Fuller's stress on good news we've missed, for instance, does not mean he fails to see the bad. He simply sees no use in wasting energy on laments when he can, instead, coax positive trends along. He does not dismiss the population crisis. But he believes the birthrate will stabilize with world-around industrialization, which will make new opportunities in life available to more of humanity. As for his view on man's responsibility toward his environment, it is, in some ways, close to the Buddhist's: "You don't say to a new child—go back in there, you're not very responsible," he told me. (Stewart Brand's version: "You can't blame the baby for the afterbirth.")

Some of the confusion grows out of the fact that Fuller is both a scientist and a poet. He uses language in two different ways: to describe reality as precisely as possible and to evoke it. These ways sometimes conflict.

His fondness for technological metaphor arouses the suspicions of people who mistrust our modern technology. So they sometimes catch a few words of what Stuart Brand has called "the continuing raga" of R. Buckminster Fuller and come away thinking they've heard a long-winded engineer—while all the while he's been saying the very same thing they heard from nature poets and yogis.

I certainly did not think of Fuller as a mystic or poet before coming to Carbondale. Quite the contrary. I found his books indigestible and had heard that as a lecturer, he tended to ramble for hours. Aside from that, I knew only that he had designed the geodesic dome, had inspired Brand's *Whole Earth Catalog,* and had originated this thing called the World Game. In my mind I pictured him vaguely as an engineering genius who was somewhat mad.

The World Game seemed relevant to the ecology movement, so I felt duty-bound to learn something about it. It sounded like the exact opposite of my friend Adam's response to the planet alarm. I first heard of it from two young people I happened to meet in New Orleans during the time of the great Chevron oil blowout in the spring of 1970. They had come from Carbondale to deliver a slide lecture at Tulane University, in the course of a festival of life the local longhairs had organized. The morning I first saw them was generally glum. Oil was threatening oysterbeds; the festival had turned out to be a minor affair; not many people had come to the World Game lecture. But Mark Hansen and Elizabeth Woods were brimming with enthusiasm.

Mark, a kid from the Midwest with the blond, vitamin-fed, all-American look, was so charged with energy he could barely sit still. His words tumbled over one another. He told me World Game groups were being formed around the country to learn to play Fuller's peace game and contribute toward the inventory of world resources being set up, with giant computers, in Carbondale. (The giant computers, it was to develop, were but a fond hope, and the groups were not really playing the World Game. But of that later.)

A few weeks later, Mark and Elizabeth came to San Francisco and stayed with us. I learned they were out spreading World Game gospel as part of self-styled, post-college educational tours.

Mark was attending various meetings and conferences and looking up people whose ideas had impressed him. He asked a lot of questions and expected verbal answers. Sometimes, in the midst of a conversation, he would whip out a notebook and jot something down.

Elizabeth was more fluid, a listener and watcher, less speedy, more intuitive. She had left the University of Wisconsin a few months before with a list of fifty great men whom she wanted to visit. So far she had not gotten past Fuller.

My husband arranged for them to present their lecture at the California College of Arts and Crafts, where he teaches. I went to listen.

Mark did the talking while Elizabeth ran the slides. He laid on it, Fuller proposed that "a great world logistics game" (the World Game) "be played by introducing into the computers all the known inventory and whereabouts of the various metaphysical and physical resources of the earth . . . the inventory of human trends, known needs and fundamental behavior characteristics." Players would be invited to develop theories on "how to make the total world work successfully for all of humanity" and test them with the computerized system. "To win the World Game everybody must be made physically successful. Everybody must win," Fuller wrote.

He predicted that "as the world game is played progressively, it will disclose a myriad of politically untried, unprecedented yet amazingly effective ways of solving hitherto unsurmountable world-around problems." And as humanity gets itself into increasingly deeper trouble on its spaceship, he thought, popular pressure would force the adoption of these sensible solutions.

But the proposal for the exhibit was rejected. The dome was built, a translucent three-quarter sphere that dominated the fairscape and changed color with changes of light, perhaps the most beautiful of all Fuller's domes. (Privately, he has referred to it as his Taj Mahal.) But inside it, the USIA installed not a miniature earth but a funky pop art show. After the fair ended, the Canadian government began to use the dome as an aviary.

Fuller tried to find other sponsors for his idea. How about a computerized World Game Central, circling the globe once a year on a ship, he suggested to Southern Illinois University. The crew would be students of a world university. They would communicate with regional World Game centers around the planet, making the world resource data available to anyone.

How about using NASA's remote sensing and orbiting Skylab programs to compile accurate earth resource data, he suggested to federal officials; this data to be fed into a computerized world resources inventory, available freely to all?

SIU and NASA were both interested. Bills were introduced

in Congress to make the computerized free data bank possible. The Illinois legislature appropriated four million dollars in matching funds. In July, 1972, Skylab was launched, equipped and programmed to gather the data. But Bucky Fuller had come close before without seeing a vision realized. He remained, in his person, the only World Game Central extant.

Perhaps Fuller's logistical strategy system is a tool ahead of its time, as were the Dymaxion house, the Dymaxion car, and other Fuller inventions. The house, dating back to 1928, embodies ecologically sound principles that even now are avant garde. It was designed more like a tree or a ship than a conventional house and was to be mass-produced like a car.

Fuller had been studying the contrast between shipbuilding and the construction industry and making some interesting comparisons. He observed, for instance, that a hotel where he stayed in New York had the same number of occupants and the same amount of space as the Cunard Line steamship *Mauritania*. But the *Mauritania* moved through oceans, withstood storms, generated its own power, carried food and fuel for thirty days, and, with all that, weighed eighteen times less than the hotel. So Fuller designed a house to be more like the *Mauritania* than the hotel, using the structural principle of tension rather than compression and the basic structural unit of a triangle rather than a square. A central mast supported hexagonal floors and contained oil-generated power and plumbing systems. Fuel and septic tanks were at the base of the mast.

The outer walls were continuous translucent casein, a sheeting made of vegetable refuse. The floors were pneumatic so a child falling would bounce without hurting himself. Light was diffused by mirrors, prisms, and lenses. The house was air-conditioned, almost completely self-cleaning by means of a vacuumizing system, and contained a built-in washing machine.

The bathroom was a single unit stamped like a car body in two pieces. The toilet emptied into a waterless device that mechanically packaged and stored wastes for eventual pickup by a processing plant. You could shower with a "fog gun" squirting compressed air and one pint of recycled water. Fuller designed the shower after noting that, on a ship, fog and wind wash engine-room grease off human skin.

Growing up around Boston Bay and in Maine, he had known fishermen, yachtsmen, merchant seamen since childhood and been intrigued with their crafts. During World War I he served in the Navy. Many of his ideas and inventions have been inspired by ships, sailors and the sea.

But Dymaxion house also derived from his observations of mass production, acquired partly thanks to Harvard's expelling him twice. After the first expulsion he worked as apprentice to some cotton mill machinists in Canada. After the second, he got a job with Armour and Company, a giant packing house.

His house was to be produced on an assembly line, at a cost easily accessible to the average wage earner. It was light enough to be delivered by blimp, simple enough to be assembled on site in a day, intended to save time and provide maximum autonomy. There was no need to hook up with municipal water, sewer, and power systems, so it could be set up anywhere.

Fuller foresaw a time when people would move frequently and replace their houses as they replaced cars. Entire cities would be air-floatable as giant spherical cloud structures. Thousands of people would live anchored to mountaintops while others would populate the ocean in floating cities and submarine islands. Skyscrapers would be built with the technology of ship design and would be air-deliverable. Automation would free people from the need to be automatons. Instead of grubbing for a living, they would be able to give free rein to their imaginations.

Fuller's house, first named 4-D house, was to be a step toward that kind of future. Marshall Field was excited about it. He exhibited it in Chicago, renaming it Dymaxion house (from dynamic and maximum). Later Fuller began to use the word as sort of a trademark, redefining it to mean "maximum gain of advantage from minimal energy input."

But nobody mass-produced the house. To have done so would have upset some powerful industries—building, real estate, utilities. When Fuller offered the patent rights to the American Institute of Architects, his gift was turned down with the admonition that the AIA was "inherently opposed to any peas-in-the-pod-like reproducible designs." The traditional architect, of course, was unnecessary for such a house.

His Dymaxion car fared no better, appearing like an anachronism from the supersonic age in the midst of the squareback era. Its streamlined body was of aluminum, the chassis of chrome-molybdenum aircraft steel. It had a turning radius of a few feet, a rear engine, was air-conditioned, and could run on alcohol, expelling CO_2. Fuller turned out three prototypes between 1933 and 1935 but the auto industry would not even admit it to its annual show.

Such rejections did not stop Fuller from continuing to dream —about floating tetrahedral cities, about glass domes over existing cities. Many people considered him somewhat mad. Others borrowed his ideas without giving credit and adapted them to their own ends. Only the geodesic dome was mass-produced and credited to Fuller.

In his later years, he shifted his attention away from specifics and toward the larger frameworks that contain them. That was how the idea of the World Game evolved.

"Perhaps," mused Brendan O'Regan over dinner in a Carbondale steak house, "there's a built-in self-destruct—so you can't really play World Game until you lose the desire for power."

Fuller had been distressed and annoyed upon hearing that some of the World Game seminars had dissolved into emotional self-exploration events not unlike encounter groups. But perhaps that was inevitable, Brendan reflected. Contact with Fuller's global vision tends to lead people to examine their lives and minds.

"They discover that they *have* a world view," Brendan said. "It is the root core of that central phenomenon that gets touched. They've already decided that certain things are obsolete, that they don't need to know them. Then, when they discover this world view, they find they aren't educated. They discover they don't know how to find out, how to deal with information. Sometimes they don't even know the language it's in. The irrelevant suddenly becomes relevant. This creates an insecurity. It's part of a process initiated by a body of ideas."

Fuller's philosophy reinforces some of the values of the counter-culture and conflicts with some traditional American ones. Thinking about synergy leads to communes. Understanding Fuller's statement that "everything moves in angular wave patterning" conflicts with society's demand that we move full speed ahead in straight lines.

The seminars became way stations for personal change toward a synergetic world view. After a World Game seminar in Boston, ten participants moved into a house together as a commune. Several left school or jobs. And after the San Francisco one, Brendan O'Regan landed in Carbondale.

At the end of the seminar, he was invited to meet Fuller. He flew to Los Angeles and made his way to the home of Fuller's daughter Allegra Snyder, where he found Bucky sitting beside the swimming pool drinking tea.

"What's been happening in your life?" Fuller asked. The way he looked at him—seeing not Brendan, exactly, but something important about him—made Brendan realize he really wanted to hear. So Brendan told him.

He told him about his disappointment in the San Francisco seminar and about the car accident that had cut him loose from his past and sent him in quest of new connections.

He had survived a head-on collision in a Volkswagen, something near-miraculous. It happened on a highway, while he was moving about seventy miles per hour in the left-hand lane, with traffic on both sides and behind him. The other car had jumped the divider and come straight toward him and he knew there was nothing he could do to get out of the way. So he had let go. He took his hands off the wheel and relaxed. In the eternal split-second before the crash, his mind moved at the speed of light. His life sped across like a movie, he said yes to all of it and let it go. Just before the collision, he was excited and ready.

The story, as Brendan sketched it briefly over tea, must have struck a chord in Bucky Fuller because a confrontation with death had been pivotal in his own life. That was in 1927, the darkest year of his life. His daughter Allegra had just been born. His first, Alexandra, had died after contracting first polio, then spinal meningitis. He had begun to drink heavily and sink into ever deeper despair until, one night, he found himself standing on the edge of Lake Michigan contemplating suicide.

Later, he would date the beginning of what he calls his "second life" from that night. He turned away from the lake, deciding he did not have the right to kill himself because all humans belonged to each other, and he set himself a life task: to search for the principles governing the universe and help advance the evolution of humanity in accordance with them.

But first he underwent a kind of purge. He moved with his wife, Anne, and his new daughter to a Chicago slum and stopped talking almost completely for about a year, determined not to use words until he understood their meaning. His later passion for verbal accuracy, which explains his bulky sentences, endless speeches, neologisms, may date from that period. And his most creative work began then.

Perhaps Fuller thought back to 1927 when he inquired about O'Regan's interests. Brendan told him he had an honors degree (equivalent of Ph.D. candidacy) in chemistry from the National University of Ireland and had come to Indiana University for more studies in biochemistry, molecular biology, and psychology. He was particularly interested in finding ways to apply chemistry and mathematics to the study of memory. Lately, he had been doing brain research but had been disappointed in the way it was being conducted. Most of it, he said, failed to take account of synergy. Instead of trying to find organizing principles, brain researchers tried to piece together concepts from fragments of fact.

Paul Weiss of Rockefeller University, in an article titled "One Plus One Does Not Equal Two" in *Neurosciences: A Study Program* (1967), complains of a tendency "to endow differentials in an experiment with existence of their own, dissected from the context from which they were abstracted." He writes:

> Before we realize it, we have personified them as "actors." Genes for the difference between a white and a pink pea become simply genes for white and pink, respectively, throwing the peaness into discard; the differences between integrated brain functions before and after local lesions become transliterated to domiciles for specialist subfunctionaries, as if the rest of the brain were uninvolved; and so on.
>
> In trying to restore the loss of information suffered by thus lifting isolated fragments out of context, we have assigned the job of reintegration to a corps of anthropomorphic gremlins. As a result, we are now plagued—or blessed, depending on one's party view—with countless demigods, like those in antiquity, doing the jobs we do not understand: the organizers, operators, inductors, repressors, promoters, regulators, etc.—all prosthetic devices to make up for the amputations which we have allowed to be perpetrated on the organic wholeness, or, to put it more innocuously, the "systems" character of nature and of our thinking about nature.

Similar complaint has been lodged about research in molecular biology by Barry Commoner, who criticizes what he sees as a seeking of "the secret of life" within the DNA code. "The message which controls heredity is not carried by a single molecule but by the whole living cell," he wrote in *Science and Survival*. "The DNA and other factors in a cell interact in extremely complex ways.... The dominance of the molecular approach in biological research fosters inattention to the natural complexity of biological systems."

That's the sort of thing Fuller has in mind in pleading for attention to synergy. So he and Brendan talked about synergy over tea that afternoon. They also touched on Fuller's geometry, in which both were particularly interested.

And as they talked, "it flashed through my mind," recalled O'Regan, "that this would be a significant conversation I'd remember." He was unprepared for what followed. When it was time for Fuller to get ready for a dinner engagement, an aide of his, who had been listening, asked: "What do you want Brendan to do?" And O'Regan discovered he was now working for Fuller.

In Carbondale his special task was to help Fuller put together his work on synergetic and energetic geometry, another tool for the advancement of the whole-world perspective. With it, Fuller has sought to express mathematically the principles underlying all nature.

Plane geometry is flat-earth geometry, Fuller says. It is no longer of use in trying to understand the universe. In Archimedes' time, when the earth was still believed to be flat, it made sense to say that the shortest distance between two points is a straight line. It made sense to think of a square as a figure enclosed by two sets of parallel lines. But on a round earth, the shortest distance between two points is a curve, and a square is composed of four curves.

What's more, if you draw a square on a sphere, you divide that sphere into the space within and the space without. You create both in creating the one. And that is basic ecology, as well as Fuller geometry. "We are inherently responsible for the complementary transformation of universe, inwardly, outwardly and all around every system which we alter," Fuller wrote in "Planetary Planning," the Jawaharlal Nehru Memorial Lecture, 1969.

Plane geometry is useful as a tool for the carpenter. But as cosmic framework it is obsolete because "science has found no solids, no continuous surfaces, no infinity, no straight lines, no 180 degree angular continuums," wrote Fuller. "To the best of our experimentally informed knowledge, all such formerly accepted axiomatic [self-evident] concepts are false."

The modern scientist's universe has no ups and downs—only ins and outs: in toward various masses and out from them. But these are not mirror images of each other. One is discrete, the other general. "The rubber glove stripped inside-outingly from off the left hand now fits only the right hand. . . . When physics finds experimentally that a unique energy patterning—erroneously referred to in archaic terms as a particle—is annihilated, the annihilation is only of the rubber glove kind," Fuller continued in the published version of that lecture in New Delhi.

Therefore his geometry, like nature, is composed of minimum energy, multi-loop feedback systems with an inside and an outside. His models are all resilient and can be phased down to tetrahedrons.

The tetrahedron, a shape found in many crystals, encloses the least volume with the most surface, can be turned inside out, is most resistant to external pressure, and is synergetic: if you stack three equilateral triangles, as in a three-sided tent, you get a fourth at the base. One plus two equals four. Synergy. Take away one and only two are left.

The sphere encloses maximum volume with minimum surface and is most resistant to internal pressure. In the geodesic dome, a spherical network of tetrahedrons, the virtues of both forms combine. The dome encloses maximum volume with maximum resistance to internal and external pressure. In it, tension and compression work together synergetically. The larger the dome, the stronger it is. Therefore it is not only a useful structure but also an excellent example of synergy, ephemeralization, and design harmonious with nature.

To Fuller admirers, the building of a dome is more than

erection of cheap shelter. It often is a philosophical commitment. Unfortunately, many of these domes, constructed with plywood, plastic, or sheets of metal from cannibalized cars, are not pleasing to the eyes. In one poem, Gary Snyder saw them "stuck like warts in the woods." They fall far short of the potential Fuller envisions, which came closest to expression in the translucent, glowing Montreal dome.

In recent years, as precision instruments have allowed Western scientists to penetrate deeper into reality beyond reach of the senses, Fuller's geometry has been found congruent with discoveries in other fields. The DNA molecule can be modeled tetrahedrally. Membranes of certain viruses have geodetic structures. Nature uses minimum energy systems with sixty-degree coordination, like Fuller. All this surprises some scientists and mathematicians, but not Bucky Fuller—for he got his ideas from nature in the first place.

There is also a startling similarity between Fuller's geometric models and Tantric art. But this also should not be surprising: the universe of Albert Einstein, Max Planck, and Buckminster Fuller is more like the Eastern mystic's than the Western dualist's. It is a universe of balance, movement, and regeneration rather than of beginnings and ends, locations, results. In it, cause and effect have no meaning. It is process emerging from impenetrable mystery. Erwin Schroedinger, the Austrian who won the Nobel Prize for his work in theoretical physics, and who was a student of Vedanta, has pointed out that in the West philosophy relies on logical deduction, proof, and definition while in the East one looks at a crystal, its many facets showing many pictures of the same object.

But the vast gap continues between what scientists and mystics know and what the general public understands and lives by. It continues in part, according to Fuller, because children are still taught flat-earth geometry.

Children know intuitively that survival requires an understanding of nature. They ask comprehensive, fundamental questions until they're told to mind their ABCs. And if the world is to continue to include human children, they must learn fundamental answers—and fast. So, Fuller would have them build Dymaxion toys that show them how nature is omni-directional and how nobody lives on a plane.

He would also clean the language of flat-earth expressions. It's important, he says, to stop saying "up" and "down" when we mean in and out. When the Gemini astronauts whirled above China, he recalls, Mission Control asked from Texas: "Well, how are things up there today, boys?" ignoring the fact that the "boys" were under Mission Control's feet just then.

All right, but isn't that just semantic quibbling? people ask. Surely every child knows that the people in China are not upside down. No, insists Fuller. Words like "sunrise" and expressions like "four corners of the earth," "wide world," and "ends of the earth" reflect flat-earth consciousness. And flat-earth thinking continues to get us into trouble. We may have learned in school but we forget in our everyday life that we live on an incredibly wondrous spaceship, that the universe is non-simultaneous. Those light dots in the night sky are light from stars that may have burned out long ago. Looking at them we see something that is no longer there. These are facts that bear on our present and our future.

In Carbondale, Illinois, Fuller's highly verbal apprentices laced their talk with references to speed of light, electromagnetic fields, energy mass, and space/time continuums. They explained how going out into space is down to earth: how to conquer hunger, war, and pollution we must explore the frontiers of life-supporting existence with our minds and our bodies.

Survival in space requires knowledge of chemistry, physics, ecology. The "extraterrestial astrogator," says Fuller, cannot fudge. He has almost no margin for error. He must be quick, reliable, exact. His behavior must have integrity: wholeness, cohesion, reliability. His spaceship is a whole system, providing life support and using energy with maximum economy. Waste, sloppiness, or contention can mean death.

"We have discovered that the higher the speed and the more angularly contradictory to gravity humanity's communicating facilities have become, the higher the integrity of total thinking, as well as behavior, and the higher the performance realized per each unit of resource invested," Fuller has said.

The technological and behavioral lessons of the space program can supply answers for survival problems on the mother spaceship Earth. The "little black box" designed for supporting life on a spaceship can be adapted to supply food and save resources on earth. The realization that we are space travelers, who must perish together if we don't work together, can mean defense— de-fence, the removing of fences.

Yes, but *how* do we realize that? We have been given the photograph of the whole earth as seen from space. The data has been conveyed and became cliché before it was comprehended. We are here. How do we get there?

"As a happy but popularly unrealized consequence [of the space program], a new and large section of our economic system has been elevated to an entirely new level of incorruptible reliability," Fuller declared optimistically in "Vertical Is to Live— Horizontal Is to Die," in *American Scholar*, Winter, 1969–70.

You can't fudge on building a space vehicle, true. But how explain the appearance of one of the astronauts in a commercial for Standard Oil's alleged anti-pollutant, F-310, which the Federal Trade Commission has called deceptive? The view from space has not transformed astronavigators into bodhisattvas.

After talking with most of the Fuller folks in the office, watching a movie, reading a pile of Fuller writings, I took the little two-propeller plane from Carbondale to St. Louis. We flew fairly low and I looked down at the curves of rivers, the checkerboards of earth, woods, meadows, and here and there the scars of strip mines.

Fuller takes the long view, looks at big patterns—like these, from the plane. He attributes this tendency to an abnormal farsightedness that was not discovered until he was four and forced him to depend on big pattern clues.

Now I think about how that relates to the big pictures. To know what a strip mine does to land, for instance, you can't just look at the scar from up above. That's easily covered with bulldozers and some tough grasses. But if you get down close to the soil and examine the grasses, you see how incredibly complex plant communities are and how impossible it is to rearrange the scenery without leaving a wasteland.

Indians have lived for centuries on land that barely will support human existence by living very closely attuned to nature. I think of Smohalla, as quoted in an untitled, beautiful Indian magazine put out by the Mohawk poet Peter Blue Cloud and others in 1971:

You ask me to plow the ground. Shall I take a knife and tear my mother's breast? Then when I die she will not take me to her bosom to rest.

You ask me to dig for stone. Shall I dig under her skin for bones? Then when I die I cannot enter her body to be born again.

You ask me to cut grass and make hay and sell it, and be rich like white men. But how dare I cut off my mother's hair?

The Indians' sacred Black Mesa is now being ripped apart by the giant machinery of the strip miners. Meanwhile, journalists, most of whom write from big patterns—taking in the scene *en passant*, between hotels and airports—report that coal companies are making great strides in "reclaiming" strip-mined land. Most of these journalists live in cities and know little of the complexities of life-support systems that depend upon coyotes, cactuses, and a delicate water supply.

Over St. Louis, I noticed a factory spewing something orange from its stacks. The whole plant, adjoining streets, and a lagoon were completely orange. I asked the stewardess if she knew what kind of plant that was.

"I don't know. Sorry," she said. "But you're missing the view." She pointed to the opposite window, through which I saw the elegant arch by Eero Saarinen rise beside the river.

Fuller would see both views, surely. He would explain how the orange stuff that to me is pollution is in fact a mixture of some of the ninety-two elements and part of the world's wealth. He would see how these elements could be channeled into the regeneration of life. He would make the connection between that smokestack and the strip mine on the Black Mesa and imagine some alternatives to both. So why should I be uneasy because he talks about operating a spaceship while the Hopis talk about honoring the corn mother and the sun father?

The pilot of a ship—spaceship or any other kind of ship—knows that survival depends on accurate perception of currents, pressures, flows. Control is out of the question. The ship moves by riding prevailing forces.

Strip mines, the California water project, and related brutalities are the work of landlubbers. Fuller has learned about nature from the sea and the men who live off it. That should reassure me. But those seamen still keep cleaning oil out of their bilges into the ocean, where it kills birds and fish.

Fuller is distressing mainly because he seems to assume that the earth is *man's* spaceship. He never mentions in his *Operation Manual* whether other living creatures are fellow passengers or part of the equipment. Are whales resources or living beings? Where is Mother Earth in relation to Spaceship Earth?

With questions along these lines I fly to Los Angeles to interview Fuller himself at the home of his daughter. It's Sunday afternoon. I find him at a dinette table, in kimono and moccasins, with a teapot beside him and the Sunday *Los Angeles Times* in front of him, scribbling something on a long yellow pad.

When he stands up, I'm surprised to see how short he is—shorter than my five feet five; very straight, a little gnarled, a nononsense New Englander who could be both stern and kindly. He looks at me sharply through his spectacles, makes a few polite remarks about the view out the window—boats on the bay beyond terraced roofs and gardens—and escorts me to a chair and table arrangement. He sits down facing the bay-view window and I set up my tape recorder.

I've come with some written questions, partly because I half-expected him to be some sort of non-stop lecture machine, I guess. I thought if he just talked on and on I'd put the questions in front of him. But I can see right away that was foolish for he's clearly very much in contact with the moment.

He wears a hearing aid but still strains to hear, cupping his left ear and leaning slightly forward when I say something. So I talk slowly, loudly, and try to pronounce very clearly, which makes the interview just a little strained.

When he talks he looks off toward the bay most of the time. The light reflects in his glasses and he's distant. But when he listens, he looks at me and is completely attentive. In both instances, he is fully involved and demands the same of me.

"He generates integrity," one of his staff-men in Carbondale had said, trying to describe the effect of Fuller's presence.

And O'Regan had advised: "You don't go to Bucky and ask him a specific question. He gives you a huge view so you can then go back and find the answer. You have to get into a different state of consciousness, really, to hear him. He answers very much according to the way he intuits you. He'd be different with a molecular biologist, a crystallographer, a mathematician.

During the two and a half hours to follow, however, I ask quite a few specific questions. The intuitive apparatus jams and sends off discordant sparks. Only in retrospect, as I listen to the tape, will a lot of it turn out to be enlightening.

"I'm perfectly confident that the way we are going to get around pollution and so forth is by developing much better tools for handling energy," he says. "You make [a tool] and you have it available. If it does work it makes things obsolete that have been inadequate. . . . Desperate people say, 'I'm not going to pollute.' But oil is coming out of the refinery down there and people are using the automobile. People can't design their own automobiles. They can't design refineries as a body politic. Somebody has to take the trouble to discover how you refine and how you don't pollute. This can be done."

The needed tools will become available, he says, when people come to see the need for them—when they perceive their situation on the planet correctly. So a first step is a shift in perspective from flat-earth to whole-earth thinking. That's why, he says, he wants to computerize World Game and "develop large mechanical devices, great miniature earths where society could see things happening. I find that unless people see things move they don't pay much attention to them. . . .

"Not only do we have a very limited color spectrum—of red, orange, green, blue, violet, which are less than a millionth of all frequencies operative in physical universe, but we have a very limited motion spectrum. You don't even see the hands of the clock move. We do have after-image enough to remember that the hands were over there.

"You don't see the tree grow and you don't see the child grow. So I've learned that when you do see things move you change. And it is possible to take a moving picture and accelerate the picture. In one of the pictures Bob Snyder (his son-in-law who makes films of Bucky and his work) has, you see—the Kaiser dome in Hawaii I believe it was—you see it all put together in one minute or a half-minute. So it is possible to accelerate in such a way that people will understand what they're seeing.

"Or you decelerate. Like those atoms that are moving at such speed that you don't see them in motion at all so it looks like a solid. It is possible to slow that whole thing down so that you can comprehend it. In my population movie, every second is a hundred years. You see it growing around the world like a bonfire. . . . Being a sailor, mechanic, a scientist, I can visualize my boat in motion. I find lots of people don't do that. I can think of the different angles of keel. I can look at trends, I can look at figures. There's a case of that this morning." He gets up, goes to the table, and returns with a clipping from the front page of the *Los Angeles Times*, a story about air pollution getting worse in Los Angeles, and with a yellow legal-sized tablet on which he has been making calculations.

"Read it, then I'll show you what kind of things I get out of it."

I read about increased quantities of various chemicals in the air. But Fuller extracts the fact that sulphur oxide is descending and says that's good news. Sulphur and large particles spread in the mist and make it heavier, blanketing the city and trapping automobile fumes that otherwise would disperse in the atmosphere and drift away over the mountains. So sulphur going down means that other things would not be pocketed.

"I've been fighting—many of us have—to stop having sulphur going into the sky," he says. "The Edison electric generating stations all around the country are bad culprits about this. As you fly over the different cities you see smog and you look where it comes from and a dozen chimneys provide the whole darn thing, primarily Edison chimneys. I was the speaker three weeks ago in Hartford at the National Edison Institute of America, all the executives. . . . The host was one of the large engineering manufacturers of boiler equipment. And while talking with engineers and research men I found that the equipment exists and is highly perfected to take all of the sulphur out. The cost it would add to the production of electricity would be only thirty percent and you'd have no fumes in the sky."

"Thirty percent?"

"Yes, practically nothing."

"Isn't that kind of high?" I ask.

Fuller has been looking out toward the bay. But at this he snaps around, claps his hands together sharply, and glares at me. "High? High for what?" he shouts. There's fury in his face.

"High for what, dah'lin', high for what?" he repeats, straining to speak more calmly.

"The company would think it high," I stumble.

"High for death or high for life?"

"I understand you, Dr. Fuller, but . . ."

"To take the fumes out of the sky would cost thirty percent more," he interrupts. "The Edison men think it's so high that the industrial companies that could generate their own electricity but buy it from them would start generating their own. So they don't want to put the price up."

"I was thinking *they* would think it high." All I meant was that under current conditions a thirty percent price rise was unrealistic.

But later, when I reflect upon that incident, I decide he was the realist, not I. I recall that Cliff Humphrey, head of Ecology Action, had said he was engaged in "changing what was politically feasible." That's what Fuller was doing too. And the obstacle for both of them was the sort of timidity of expectation I had just manifested.

Fuller spoke radically, that is, from the root of the thing. He assumed that people had the right to expect industry to stop poisoning them. And that right would be recognized only when enough consumers and citizens stopped believing industry's propaganda about what was politically and economically feasible.

But now I want to move to another subject. While Fuller

has been talking of expanding the range of perception by computers, cameras, and other technological devices, I remembered an incident in Carlos Castaneda's A *Separate Place: Further Conversations with Don Juan*. The Yaqui Indian shaman, Don Juan, has taken Castaneda into the mountains, has given him a mixture of herbs to smoke, and has told him to sit and watch for holes. Castaneda does not understand but sits quietly, looking at a mountain range before him, listening to the sounds around him. He begins to hear the wind brushing through grass and swaying the trees, the sound of insects and birds separately, with distinct rhythms, and then in rhythm with the wind. The sounds assume an ever-richer pattern for him. He begins to notice spaces between sound sequences and to listen to these "holes." Then he notices that there seems to be a gap in the mountain range before him. Sound and visual holes flow into each other. As they merge, Castaneda perceives the spirit he has come to seek.

So now I ask Fuller if he does not think that we can also expand our range of perception with tools developed by shamans and mystics as well as with tools of Western technology. His reply is long and confirms my suspicion that he has not explored such mind discipline.

"In 1927 I said, 'I'm deeply concerned with thought—the fact that man has the capability to think and remember, a capability it is very clear animals don't have.' [That's not all so clear to me. How does he know?] I was very aware of yoga, very aware of Indian cults. Thinkers. People who spend all their time in meditation, thinking. . . . But to be able to sit and think you also ought to have some fuel coming in, otherwise you can think for only about thirty days and then you fall over.

"So somebody had to be producing something. So people who were sitting around thinking usually belonged to some religious sect and they had some peasants out there. They'd say: 'We'll do the thinking for you and you raise the vegetables.' That's what happened to most of the churches, most of the cults. I'm very interested in how you grow the food that people who are going to do the thinking eat, and I began to say—these people talked with great pride of their mystical capabilities, getting through to greater presence and great ecstasies—I said: 'What moves me is that we were given the ability to think. What also moves me very much is that we were given limited capabilities. We don't have any manifestation of being able to get on without the rest of the universe. So that I cannot get on without food or air, I cannot get on without the balance going on between vegetation and mammals—it is perfectly clear to me I could not. I could not get on without anything in universe that is in universe. It's a very complex and beautiful piece of design there, and the fact that I wake up and go to sleep, that people are born and die, that we get our information in packages and we articulate in packages—no continuum at all about it—so, the fact that I'm given the capability to think is very extraordinary. And to remember. And to be able to formulate. To take advantage of earlier experience. . . . To have a mind and be able to think of alternate ways of carrying on which other species don't have.' [How about the dolphins who have a language, and the humpbacked whale who sings? But interruption is out of the question now. Fuller is looking out the window.]

"So I said, 'I think what I am going to do is to accept the wisdom and the brilliance of the design of universe itself which is *a priori* to me, in which design it is apparently clearly designed that I would have limitation. . . . And all these people who sit, then, trying to use the thinking thing to break through limits of thinking that are not permitted—and waste their thinking capability trying to think about ways not allowed them—it's a complete waste and a lack of appreciation of the great design.' I said, I'm going to ramify the thinkable . . . not disconnecting from understanding in trying to break through to some new universe."

"But it's not a new universe," I put in. "There are simply other dimensions."

"I'm simply telling you that I'd rather not have any traffic with disconnects," he cuts in impatiently. I wanted to ask how he knew what was "permitted" to man, as he and Adam, for instance, would both have different views on the matter. But Fuller is laying it out, he's not open to my questioning now.

"I'm very aware of Hindu thinking," he continues. "I'm also very aware that the fact that many things I have been able to discover in my own thought, Hindu thinkers have come to me and said: 'You apparently are having the same thoughts. How did you get them?' And I said, 'I thought it myself.'"

More and more, I'm hearing in him a quixotic blend of arrogance and humility, of the scientist's passion for accuracy and the poet's license.

"All science starts with absolute mystery," he says. ". . . I'm not discontent with the fact there's *a priori* mystery. . . . I'm only interested in how useful I am to the other guy. If I'm not useful to the other man I'd like to do away with myself quickly."

To me, that's an attitude close to the classical martyr-mother's: "I live only for my children. If they don't need me I might as well do myself in."

"I'm only interested in the rest of man; I'm only interested in love. I'm not interested in self," Fuller says. But when I question his Spaceship Earth metaphor he becomes annoyed and distressed. "It is a spaceship. That's not an analogy. It's a fact," he says.

"But a spaceship is built by man, all the factors have been designed for a particular known purpose. The earth is an organic thing on which we live," I argue.

"The planet is designed—superbly designed—by a greater intellect than that of man," he says. "And it's moving through space."

"But are we passengers or an organic part of it?"

"We've got three billion and a half passengers on board."

"What about the plants, whales, horses—are they also passengers?"

"A passenger is someone taking passage aboard a vehicle," he says with a sharp edge of impatience. "You are aboard a vehicle moving at sixty thousand miles an hour through the heavens and you're aboard as a passenger. I'm sorry but your objection is invalid."

So decreed Justice Fuller. I try a different angle having, apparently, failed to make myself understood: "There's an organization that was just formed in San Francisco called Living Creatures Associates. It's a press agency claiming to represent other species—whales, garter snakes, foxes—represent them publicly on their own terms, with a right to exist on this spaceship, then, in the same way as I do. With some rights that conflict, perhaps, with those of men."

"Did the foxes invite them? Did the daisies elect them? . . . I have no objection to other people's doing what they do but nothing could be more remote from me," says Fuller. "I call this a do-gooder organization, idealistic and so forth. And their effectiveness approximately zero. . . . I think it is a very nice manifest of consciousness of man. He's beginning to think about things."

"The idea is that . . . we must accept the rights of other beings."

"What happened to those dragons?" he replies. "What happened to the flying creatures of a few million years ago? What happened about their rights? What about the rights of the volcanoes when the whole earth was volcanic? Who took their rights away?"

"But it's a fact that certain birds and animals are dying because of man's actions. Don't we have to take responsibility for that?"

"We have to take the responsibility of being responsible. So far we have not been very responsible. You don't say to a new child, 'You better go back in there, you're not very responsible. . . .' They're just using words—foxes and daisies. . . . I say: What might I do that made it logical for man not to do these things? That's what I'm caring about. That's what design science is. . . .

"I looked on a tree as beautiful when I was a little child. Now I can see why that tree is designed the way it is. I really feel the design of the tree. As comprehensive anticipatory design scientist I understand why that tree is there, what its relation to me is. I really feel it too. It's not something superficial to draw a picture of. I really feel how it's handling the wind and the rain and what it's doing. It's a beautiful mechanism. Fantastic technology. You try to pick up a bucket of water, hold it out at arm's length. Suppose it's fifty pounds. You can't hold fifty pounds horizontally. And this tree is holding out a branch that weighs five tons—horizontally. And it's able to handle a hurricane and not get into trouble, and with all those leaves. Quite a piece of design! And I know exactly how it's done now. I began to design like that."

He has taken me through another loop along the spiral; we seem to have traveled into a deeper understanding. I turn off my tape recorder. He gets up abruptly and leaves the room. I go to the phone to call a taxi to take me back to the airport.

But when he returns he sits down again. He says he has been feeling guilty about having been "short" with me and had asked himself why he had been. He concluded that he was reacting to a feeling that I was "an intuitive, sensitive person" who was not, however, sensitive to him. He was shocked that I found fault with his Spaceship Earth analogy.

"I invented this phrase, Spaceship Earth, a number of years ago when I was trying to get man to—trying to help him, personally, particularly young people, to shake themselves loose of preoccupation with the powerfully conditioned reflex that there is something called earth and something called space, this heaven and earth idea. I used to have students say to me, 'I wonder what it would be like to be on a spaceship?' And I'd say: 'What does it feel like?'

"The relative size of things. . . . When you get to the size of our earth in space, eight thousand miles' diameter—the sun's corona, when you look at it with filters through a telescope we can actually see it—in the larger magnification, one of the flames would be about an inch. One inch of flame is often an altitude over a hundred times the diameter of our earth. The size of our planet would be undetectable on one of those flames.

"The distance to the next-nearest star to our sun takes light, coming seven hundred million miles an hour, four and two-thirds years to get here. So somewhere between that kind of distance we have a tiny invisible spot of eight thousand miles' diameter, our planet, going around the sun at sixty thousand miles an hour. And the sun itself, and the galactic system . . . sum totally we're making something like a million miles an hour right now."

Now usually, when someone mentions a multi-digit number to me, I blank out. But Fuller has led me out into those interstellar spaces. That's Fuller the poet, conveying reality, not describing, with words.

"So we couldn't be more of a spaceship and we couldn't be tinier and we couldn't be more beautifully designed. . . . If I were to say that man was God, if that's what you're objecting to, that this design is so much better, then OK. But nevertheless, I call it a design. . . . The space is *a priori* mystery that the space vehicle goes in. And you don't think it's a mysterious thing that he had the capability to get there? It's all part of the same mystery." He sounds hurt.

"Perhaps the trouble is that people who listen to you . . ." I'm responding to that hurt tone now.

"People who listen to me say, 'Here's a man who's selling screwdrivers,'" he says, and I wonder whether he doesn't mean some of his apprentices, the ones who convey him so much as the master-packager-engineer, as well as others. "They don't realize how mysterious screwing is. . . . I've been identified only with the physical so far. I went through twenty-five, thirty years of people saying: this is the bathroom man, or the automobile man—that's all they thought about me. It's only in the last couple of years that they discover I'm a thinker. And I started as a thinker.

I didn't start with bathrooms. I started off with God and my charge was to work on the physical. That's where I had the capability; that's why we're here. I accepted this. And to find myself identified, then, with just being a fishing-pole salesman! I find this thing echoed when you say that about my analogy, 'cause I use a very good tool there. I have helped to shock man into realizing he's on board a space vehicle. He's a passenger on it and he's intimately related to it. . . .

"At any rate, first I felt very apologetic about being rigorous with you but wondering why I was. Intuitively I'd say you're very sensitive. Yet if your sensitivity isn't tuning into my sensitivity, when I feel gears aren't meshing I tend to be a little abrupt."

Jetting back to San Francisco, completing in late afternoon the round trip of nearly a thousand miles (Fuller's daily average) that began late morning, I think I at last understand the true reason for Fuller's perpetual motion. It's his form of yoga. Eastern holy men have learned, with centuries of arduous trying, to move from the inside out—detaching themselves from fixed bearings by means of the mind. Their bodies follow and they hardly move them at all. Really high Tibetans, I've heard, could read books by the light of their bodies. Saddhus in samadhi subsist with almost no food, manage to be simultaneously present in several places at once. But in the West we tend to do things from the outside in, wastefully and expensively. The rocket builders are our holy men.

I recall that Stewart Brand told me he conceived the idea of the Hunger Show while riding a train across the country. He decided to start the *Whole Earth Catalog* in a plane over Nebraska, returning to California from his father's funeral in Illinois. Other writers and artists tell of beginning new works while driving on freeways or moving rapidly in some other fashion. I myself often practice a form of meditation on the trip between our city apartment and country cabin. But can we afford automotive, not to mention supersonic, yoga? I don't think so.

Back home, I dig into Fuller's texts. The encounter has helped cut through the words. The writing has been getting lighter lately, I notice. He calls some of it, set in verse form, "ventilated prose." Others call it poetry.

The contrast between his perspective and Castaneda's Don Juan stays in mind. Fuller speaks of "environment," "design," "resources," "the 92 elements." Don Juan taught his apprentice to address lizards with respect and remember that if he picked more of some herb or plant than he needed he was courting trouble. Fuller wonders at the way a tree works. Don Juan sought to meet the tree's spirit. Both may be talking about the same thing. But the way Fuller formulates it all encourages an I-it attitude toward nature while Don Juan invites an I-Thou relation. That I-it attitude made progress possible. It both built and undermined Western civilization.

Fuller's perspective derives in large part from his experiences in navigation, mass production, the building industry, Western science, study of the technology of nature, and from jetting around the globe wearing four watches. Don Juan's comes from his native mountains and deserts, the study of shamanistic arts, and from mind-body travel via psychedelic substances and spiritual discipline.

We need them both, surely.

Gradually, the presumptions and inconsistencies in Fuller the man of reason peel away to reveal the much brighter core of Fuller the poet who speaks the language of technicians. Perhaps he can turn them to wholly round thinking by showing that machines, to work perfectly, must be tuned to the universe.

Perhaps what I failed to understand—and why he was so bothered by my questioning his Spaceship Earth metaphor—was that he has taken on the task of transforming machines for destruction into machines for life through subversion. To disarm the technicians' minds so they could hear him, he has to put up with being called a fishing-pole salesman.

Reading Fuller leads me to read Einstein and to become aware how the borders of knowledge as seen by physicists coincide with those seen with the mystical vision of C. G. Jung—with pleroma, primeval ooze, nothingness. Scientists, mystics, and poets arrive at the same meeting ground. Fuller, Teilhard de Chardin, Schroedinger, Einstein—one leads to the other.

"You will hardly find one among the profounder sort of scientific minds without a religious feeling," wrote Einstein.

His religious feeling takes the form of a rapturous amazement at the harmony of natural law, which reveals an intelligence of such superiority that, compared with it, all the systematic thinking and acting of human beings is an utterly insignificant reflection. This feeling is the guiding spirit of his life and work, in so far as he succeeds in keeping himself from the shackles of selfish desire. It is beyond question closely akin to that which has possessed the religious geniuses of all ages.

In July, 1971, Fuller met with the Maharishi Mahesh Yogi at Amherst College. The Maharishi has an advanced degree in physics, but his teaching takes quite a different form from that of Fuller. They talked together for three days and seemed to understand each other perfectly, Brendan O'Regan reported.

Couldn't we, then, learn to fly around, omni-surviving in our own mechanical living capsules? We cannot all return to nature the way my friend Adam did on his mountain. Not enough of us have the independence of Adam and we're fast running out of available mountains. Why shouldn't we then, with the help of Don Juan and Bucky Fuller, evolve a technology that would be as gentle, strong, and unobtrusive as a spider's web?

In late 1971, Fuller sped most of his apprentices away from Carbondale and sent out word that the World Game concept was, for the moment, dormant. Apparently not enough people were yet ready to play it, not having achieved the necessary perceptual shift. He continued to play the game more or less alone.

But the vision spread. The cost of running Spaceship Earth on batteries was becoming inescapably apparent.

8

Dinosaurs out of the Ocean

❧

The oil plague hit the Bay on the day Mr. and Mrs. Lee were murdered, so for a long time it was, to me, merely the background to that personal sorrow. The Lees were our landlords and friends. They ran a little grocery store on the corner across the street. On January 18, 1971, shortly before 10 P.M. closing, somebody shot them both dead.

Their youngest son found the bodies. Mr. Lee had fallen behind the counter and died while trying to crawl toward where Mrs. Lee lay at the back of the store, by the door of the tiny back room where they rested and drank tea. The cash register was open; there was money still inside. They knew better than to resist a robbery. Yet somebody had come in and killed them.

RUSSIAN HILL GROCERS MURDERED. A typical story. Happens somewhere most weeks. A classic of Today-USA. They had worked long hours, side by side, for twenty-two years. By keeping the store open daily from 9 A.M. to 10 P.M. and practicing untold economies, they had made enough to raise six children, send them to school and college, and even to acquire a couple of other buildings on the block. Now the children were raising grandchildren and Cheuck and Tuey How Lee, finding it hard to climb stairs, had been preparing to retire.

The crowd at the door. The shocked neighbors. "They were such nice people." "Everyone liked them." The boarded windows, the detective who keeps a lookout for several days, the search for some memory traces of suspicious persons. The people who won't help the cops because they're afraid.

In Today-USA there is no public weeping, no catharsis of shared grief. It's everyone for himself behind locked doors and drawn shades. You lower your eyes when passing one of the family. Edvard Munch's portrait of the woman on the bridge, her eyes great whirling circles, her mouth wide. Francis Bacon's Pope Innocent, gaping, blind. A side of slaughtered beef.

Mel and I lay in bed all night listening. The children and grandchildren were gathered downstairs. Their lights stayed on through the night. But we heard no voices. Was there the faint sound of Chinese mourning music? Not clear. Could be imagined. Outside, cats mewling like sick babies. Foghorns. Emptiness. *Terrain vague* means empty lot in French. The walls were suddenly rice-paper thin and we were exposed in the midst of the war zone. Toward dawn, a sharp sob—downstairs or in my dream? We made love.

Meanwhile, out on the Bay, birds were dying by the hundreds. Grebes, ducks, and herons struggled in vain against the greenish-brown stickiness that coated the water. Two Standard Oil tankers had collided in the early morning fog in the Golden Gateway. About 845,000 gallons of bunker C fuel oil poured into watery habitats—four times more than had spilled in the Santa Barbara disaster.

In the *San Francisco Chronicle*, the story of the Lees' murder was on the bottom of page one, below a four-column cut of seals stranded on a buoy.

I had to get away from the house so I drove down to Aquatic Park to look at the oil damage. Straw had been spread on the water to catch the mess as it came in on the tide. Dozens of people were scooping up oily straw with pitchforks while others tossed out more clean straw. The smell was foul. A third-grade teacher had brought down a flock of children to witness a lesson in ecology. Richard Brautigan stood in the midst of the action, dour, jotting notes. Gary Near, an environmental lawyer, said he expected there would be lawsuits against Standard Oil because the fog was too thick for safe sailing, especially when the tankers lacked proper ship-to-shore communications equipment.

The oil harvesters were running out of straw, so I volunteered to go and call KSAN, the rock music station that had taken on the role of information relay center.

The nearest public phone was in Ghirardelli Square, the quaintly picturesque warren of smart little shops and restaurants just above the park. There I found the canned music tinkling as usual, the tourists window-shopping as on any other day. Hey, I wanted to tell a man with camera aimed at the mermaids of the fountain, hey, there's a more interesting scene down below.

At the public phone, a pouf-haired, powdered southern woman in a pastel green coat and tan pumps was saying: "I found the cutest place. Let's meet at 1:30. I'll save a table." KSAN said more straw was already on the way.

I drove down to the Marina to check the action at the Saint Francis Yacht Basin where, according to KSAN, a bird-cleaning station had been set up. Inside a trailer, two young men bent over a table covered with white cloth, holding an oil-coated egret. His beak was open and he struggled to breathe. His eyes were full of fear. Mrs. Lee, looking into the gun barrel, at her husband, at the gun. The men gave up their efforts to open the nostrils with Q-Tips and mineral oil. They wrapped a cloth around the trembling little body and held the bird up at the trailer door. "Can somebody take this to the ASPCA? It's an emergency."

Hands reached up. There was no shortage of workers. Entire schools had come down, bringing rags, mineral oil, food. The egret stood no chance and even the boy running with it toward a car must have known that. But at least these people had found something they could do. Nothing more could be done for the Lees.

I heard the police siren while talking with a friend on the phone from Los Angeles. "Your baby has strong lungs," he had said. He really thought it was Usha crying. At that moment, Mr. Lee, his lungs thrice punctured, lay behind the counter of his grocery store. "It's a fire engine, I think," I told my friend. But moments later a neighbor brought the news.

Who would do it
They had no enemies
I don't believe it

On the way home from St. Francis Yacht Basin I passed the store. The youngest son was locking up.

The next morning there were even more people at the Yacht Basin beach. Some had been hired by Standard Oil; more were volunteers. They were actually competing for pitchforks. Those who didn't have one did without. Boys and girls stood in the winter-cold water, black gunk all over their arms and legs and sometimes faces, scooping up straw and wading back with it. They brought in straw that wasn't even oily.

It was silly, in a way—all these people on this single little beach, tumbling all over one another when the oil was washing in everywhere along miles and miles of shoreline. Just a few hundred feet away I saw it come in to coat rocks and not a human harvester was in sight. But the enthusiasm here was nevertheless extraordinary and exhilarating. Strangers were united into community—as had happened during the Great Blackout in New York a few years back. Suddenly it was all right to talk with anyone. A wild-haired friend of mine conversed with a truckdriver who looked like the red-faced epitome of beer-guzzling hardhat. They were completely unself-conscious with each other.

I spotted an elderly couple standing atop the retaining wall behind the beach. They looked like brother and sister but that could have been a result of long living together. Mr. and Mrs. Lee didn't look alike but they were so incredibly complementary, they worked together so perfectly, that I wondered sometimes whether they even needed to talk.

"Some people are suing Standard Oil," I said to the elderly couple, as opener.

"Yes," he said.

"What do you think of that?"

"Well, it was an accident. Couldn't be helped."

"This man who's suing, Dr. Eugene Schoenfeld, says that they don't even have to ship oil by tanker. They just do it because it costs more money by rail, he says."

"Well, I don't know." The old man looked uncomfortable. He was probably thinking I was some radical agitator. "The extra expense would be passed on to the consumer," he said.

"Instead," put in a kid who'd stopped to listen, "they pass on to us this." He gestured sweepingly toward the Bay.

Near the bird-cleaning station, two young girls were rubbing their arms with rags, getting ready for coffee and sandwiches.

"I'm so mad," one of them said.

"At whom?" I asked.

"Just mad." She was about sixteen; maybe her teacher would help her channel that anger into understanding. I wished I were a high school teacher right then. These kids were really ripe for lessons about politics, economics, biology, ecology.

The other girl said she thought Standard Oil should pay for the mess but that she herself didn't care about pay. She had come out because she felt it her duty as a citizen to do so.

Leaving the beach, I drove to the Presidio where, in a huge

hall made available by the Army, a larger bird-cleaning station had just been opened. Long tables were covered with cloth, as for a banquet. Where the salt and pepper shakers would have been stood bottles of mineral oil.

A middle-aged woman with apple-pink cheeks said no birds had been brought in yet. She had blisters on her hands from tossing straw into the waves the previous night. Not since she harvested potatoes as a member of the Women's Land Army of World War II had she had such blisters.

"I'd like to take the captains of both those ships and tie a rope around their necks and tie them to a block and take them out to sea," she said slowly, as if savoring each part of the process.

For eliciting such righteous anger, there could be no easier villain, really, than Standard Oil, no more lovable victim than the snowy egret or blue heron. The oil company had clearly tried hard to assuage such ire. It had hired clean-up crews and deployed them along the highly visible beaches. It had set out catered food for volunteers, filled gas tanks for free. Assemblywoman March K. Fong, of Oakland, even said that Standard Oil had promised to replace the seabirds killed. She said the company promised to "buy and import them into the Bay area." (This to the bitter amusement of conservationists who knew of no way such a thing could be done.) But people mad enough to march to the beach with pitchforks are not easily mollified.

"How nice," my friend Lil Lectric Lulu commented, "that you can keep hating the old villains. It takes so much energy to get to know new ones."

Last night, at a North Beach movie theater where Lulu goes often because you get to see a double feature for only a dollar, someone set off a firecracker. As it arched in slow motion from the rear of the dark house into the crowd, she did not know whether it was a firecracker or a bomb. The new villains strike out of the dark like bombs that shatter the bones of Indochinese children, like the killer of Mr. and Mrs. Lee. To them, land is real estate;

whales are raw material. Seabirds, to them, are replaceable. They're bigger than just Standard Oil.

Back home, I sit down at my desk, lean my elbows on the typewriter, and look out through the venetian blinds. Someone stands across the street, looking toward the store. I close my eyes. A wave of blue rolls past my eyelids and into a landscape of dusty clay. A lump of clay that lay dry and forgotten under something for years has been lifted into daylight. I try to hold it a moment, to look at it, and let it fall.

"We're all at the mercy of everything; there is no protection for anyone," said my friend Lee Hastings, putting her baby into the car seat, on the way to pick up her little girl from school.

Accept.

I started to go to the wake but went to a Chinese restaurant instead. The idea of sitting in a funeral parlor and staring at the husks of two people, done up no doubt, into life-mocking masks, had nothing to do, for me, with honoring the dead. My sorrow was for the living Lees, for their children with their stoic smiles, and for myself.

I'd known them two and a half years, since the Sunday afternoon when, new to San Francisco, I came down Leavenworth Street in search of an apartment. I'd been looking for weeks with no luck and had long given up on want ads and real estate agents. Now I just walked streets in neighborhoods I liked, searching for places that appeared vacant.

In the lobby of an old Victorian building on the edge of Russian Hill, I spotted some mailboxes with no names. I rang a bell to inquire and was directed across the street to the grocery store.

It was the sort of store you go to between trips to the supermarket. It stocked the standard necessities, some wine and liquor, a few Chinese specialties. On a shelf near the ceiling, some bottles of grenadine syrup gathered dust, remnants from the days when more Italians lived in the neighborhood. Lately, Chinese had been moving in. Outside the door, fruit and vegetable bins and the newsstand. On the counter, a couple of well-tended houseplants.

Mrs. Lee was a comfortably plump woman with a roundish, kind face, graying hair combed smoothly back and done in small braids that were pinned at the nape of her neck.

"One?" she asked, holding up her right index finger. Her English was minimal.

"One," I said.

She nodded, searched in a box of keys, brought out a bunch on a ring, called toward the back of the store. Mr. Lee, thin, gray, and slightly stooped, came forward to take over behind the counter while she crossed the street with me and climbed three flights to open a door into a freshly painted tiny place. It was only one large room, bathroom, and tiny kitchen. But it had lots of light and felt good. I moved in the next day. The Lees asked for no references or guarantees, for which fact I immediately liked them.

The building was a warren of young people with long and short hair, dull jobs, and mysterious occupations. It had dogs, cats, and plants and pleasing aromas often drifted into the halls. From the roof, you could see the Bay and Golden Gate Bridge. I often went up to watch the sunsets. When my friend Lil Lectric Lulu came from New York, she moved into a place downstairs.

Only two things were a bother—the cold and the roaches. No matter what the weather, the radiators never started sizzling before 6 P.M. And no matter how often you spoke to Mr. Lee about the bugs, they stayed. He would come around and spray, but the roaches merely took cover.

Eventually someone called the health department. An inspector arrived and, in his wake, a man from the Rose Exterminator Company. The Rose man came every month and the roaches vanished. But from that time on, the heat started a half hour later. Mr. Lee knew his landlord economics.

When Mel and I started to live together, the place became

too small. I asked Mr. Lee if he had another one but he said: "When you married." There was no way I could persuade him that we were as good as. We stayed in that tiny place another year.

After we did have a wedding, I walked into the store with a gold ring. The following morning, to my amazement, Mr. Lee knocked on the door to offer me a choice of a bigger apartment in the same building or a flat next door.

That flat was the most marvelous wedding present. There was room enough for me to write, room enough for Mel's daughter Tara to play when she was with us, room enough for a baby.

When I told Mrs. Lee we were going to have a baby she laughed a wonderful laugh which came from all over her, that laugh which reminded me of the grandmother I had loved very much.

A shiny new grocery opened across the street, just half a block away. It was much more interestingly stocked, but we continued to shop at the Lees out of loyalty. During Chinese New Year we brought them an azalea. They responded with leechee nuts, tea, and tangerines.

We did not know much about their lives beyond what we saw right there in the store, but they were friends. Mrs. Lee would usually greet me with "Nice day, uh?" or "Cold!" and I would respond with something equally commonplace. Mr. Lee would come out from the back to say hello. When Usha was born, Mrs. Lee for the first time came to the house, bringing gifts: a little white coat and two tiny red envelopes printed with gold design, each with a dollar inside for good luck. I put them under Usha's mattress.

At the door of the funeral chapel, near-identical little envelopes were distributed to mourners, each with a few cents and some candy inside. Except for that, though, what happened at the final ceremony, maybe the only time a big fuss was made about Cheuck and Tuey How Lee since their wedding, was alien to all the little I knew about them.

It was the typical Today-USA funeral. The officiating minister spoke like an automaton, mispronouncing names. The people—at least a couple of hundred crowded the chapel—were almost all Chinese, and a Chinese minister had also been scheduled to speak. But he was remembered only when the coffins were being carried down the aisles and the doors to the street were open. Everyone sat down again and the coffins were once more set down, but the noise of the street traffic drowned most of the rest.

The cortege of automobiles slid quietly through the city, past the little store and onto the freeway. The old couple, whom I had seen daily for two and a half years on our block and never anywhere else, were sped to burial in a graveyard at the city's edge.

In Ghana they dance and young people court during funerals, so doing homage to the continuation of life. At an Irish wake, feasting and drunkenness are proper and stories about the dear departed are exchanged. In Lithuania, when a funeral passed, people stopped, bowed their heads, crossed themselves, and said a prayer. In Mexico I once rode with a cabdriver who had a plastic skull on his dashboard. When I asked why, he said: "Death is good. She will always be your friend."

But in Today-USA death is impersonal. It is also embarrassing. People titter about it the way their grandparents tittered about sex. Dying is "terminal illness." Pre-death establishments for old people are "convalescent homes." Corpses are not allowed to rot in the ground and fertilize grass and flowers, they are preserved chemically in waterproof containers. At many funerals, you never see the coffin lowered into the earth. It's left above the grave, which is hidden by a carpet of fake grass. You go away with the job unfinished and the grief unspent. Denying death, Today-USA is haunted by the fear of it. Only through full acceptance does healing begin.

The Lees' children had taken pains to do everything properly, according to standard. But as I drove home, alone, I still felt that need to wail out loud together with everyone who knew them.

Several months later, Suzuki Roshi, who did so much to help Zen Buddhism take root in this country, taught a lesson about dying. He did it as he himself died. When my friend Elizabeth came back from his funeral she was exhilarated because she understood how death can be the final exhalation, the ultimate letting go. Because of the way the Roshi had lived, died, and been mourned, the Zen community he built was left stronger.

"When something dies," said Dr. John Doss, a shaman-poet-doctor, "energy is released." It was so strong during the oil spill, he said, that he could feel the surge of it as he approached the water. It was as if liquid dinosaurs were rising from the waves.

In his journal of the Bay Oil Plague, the poet Lewis MacAdams reported:

The sun was burning a pale light through the fog. . . . The sea was grey and flat and sickly, the color of the moon, or the cheap liquid terra firma of the planet Snov. Oil covered the sand. Each wave crested false. The crest itself was oil so the crest couldn't break. Rather, the crest fell, and a little milky water leaked out of the thick sludge and slid slid up the beach. . . .

The oil is already beginning to settle around us. Around us an entire world of life in tidal pools and shallows and tide lands is slowly suffocating beneath the oil. Crabs, anemones, starfish and mussels and kiters and worms and seaweed and rockweed and grebes and loons and murres, the diving birds, are now choking on the oil that drives the tankers that carry the oil that powers the truck that drives these lines to you.

Margot Doss, John Doss, Mel, and I walked along the shore and watched a cormorant plunge again and again in a vain effort to clean itself of the fatal black stickiness. It ducked its head like a mechanical wind-up bird and plucked at its feathers. Nearby, another seabird turned bewildered among oil-paved rocks.

"Should we tell someone to bring these in?" I asked Margot.

"No. It is as likely to survive here as rescued."

In his journal, MacAdams:

In their frenzy to rid their bodies of the acid goo the birds nose-dive or duck under the surface only to come up blinded and suffocating beneath a mask of tar. Even with their entire body surfaces matted the birds don't want to swim in to man's hands. Even now, almost completely helpless and bobbing in the shallow surface barely able to swim, the birds paddle madly out to sea to drown or drop dead of heart attack exhaustion when they hear the gross human splashings as rescuers approach them with long fishing nets shouting Here's one, I got one. By the time the birds float onto the beach and are carried to the biology center their skin is almost on fire. It is boiling pink. The bird's frenzied escape attempt has raised his body temperature and the tar has blocked off the escape of the body's heat. Then, after the bird is cleaned, he loses all his feathers. The sudden helpless cold drops the bird's body temperature into shock. (At future oil slicks emergency equipment should probably include incubators.) Within forty-eight hours of oil contamination, most of these singing life forms will be dead.

Within the week, the oil spread as far north as Point Reyes and south to Half Moon Bay. Up the coast a great fight was underway to keep it out of the lagoon, a rich marine life zone. Mel and I drove up to see. North of Stinson Beach we stopped at the Audubon Canyon Ranch and got part of the story from naturalist Clarin Zumwalt.

The ranch is home to about 150 nesting pairs of egrets and herons, both endangered species. They feed in the lagoon while nesting, so Zumwalt was alarmed when news of the tanker collision reached him early that Monday morning. The tide was due to change at 11 A.M. so he had to act fast. He called Standard Oil and got a promise of a boom. Then he called Point Reyes Station for straw and headed for the mouth of the lagoon.

By the time I got there the fire department had arrived with all the gunny sacks they had for flood control. But the fantastic thing was that about a thousand kids were here—with ropes, cables, everything they could get a hold of. Weird-looking trucks with telephone poles came in; a thousand feet of cable, five hammers, two buckets of nails. They had already stretched a rope with gunny sacks across the lagoon. Now they nailed the cables to the logs. Nobody was in charge but everyone responded like magic. By the time the tide began to move in, they had a barrier up, reinforced with straw and all kinds of stuff —even a tennis net. Standard Oil came with a plastic boom but that collapsed while the kids' boom stayed. At about 3 P.M. you could see oil seeping through but depositing in the straw.

Then the straw went under the boom. So five hundred gunny sacks were filled with straw and stretched across. They did it in what seemed like two minutes. Straw and oil were still coming in but not much. I think the kids saved the day, the kids crawling out from behind the bushes at the right time.

We found these "kids" when we got to the beach. They were not really kids, of course, they were longhairs and stoners. But to many people longhairs are kids because they can't conceive of adults living that life-style.

Right now the "kids" were building a giant boom that would be really solid. They were nailing together logs and reinforcing them with a net. The net would stretch underwater to catch any oil that slipped under the logs. Though the other two booms were still in place, these folks were taking no chances. They'll go to great lengths to protect their interspecies community.

The scene on the beach made me think of a town fortifying itself, a battlefield just before the action. All able-bodied citizens seemed to have been mobilized.

All over the beach, they were working on fortifications against invader Oil. People were lugging around lumber, hammering, shoveling, kibitzing. Standard Oil had set up a catered community kitchen. People were gathered in clusters with steaming cups of coffee. Someone escorted me to "a very evolved Taurus" named Pepi, who was in charge of the new boom job.

Pepi was a muscular fellow with a small blue flower earring in his left ear, heavy black sweater, and a head that was shaved bald except for one strip of long hair along the top of his head. He gave me the Hindu greeting—slight bow of the head, with the palms together, fingertips toward the forehead. Unrolling a blueprint, he showed me how the boom would curve across the lagoon's mouth and then swirl back, catching oil or debris in a deadwater. At four o'clock, deadtide, Pepi and "all the brothers and sisters" would set it in place.

We sat on a log and talked awhile. Other people gathered around. "I don't know that this is Standard Oil's fault," someone said.

But fault wasn't the main issue. The real issue was the way we use energy. "The system is like a junkie," said Bill Beckman, who founded the *East Village Other*, a New York underground paper, and had later fled the Big City toward healthier habitats. "We're gonna have to slow people down. My suggestion is to make caffein illegal."

"Outlaw every internal combustion vehicle that carries fewer than thirty people," someone else suggested.

"Stop consuming."

Pepi was about as close to a non-consumer as anyone could be. He lived with a friend in a 1941 bread van, often parking next to friends' houses. In exchange for help with chores, he'd use the kitchen or share meals. He owned little and shared what he had. During this crisis he emerged as one of this community's leaders.

Leaving the beach, I walked to the marine station where birds were being cleaned. On the porch a boy and a girl, both about sixteen, sat with arms around each other, shivering. She was dressed in a man's jacket that was about ten sizes too big, in ill-fitting jeans, and sneakers. Red hair tumbled around her pale freckled face. The right eye was covered with a patch of surgical gauze. She'd been out here six days already, cleaning birds. The eye irritation was from the oil. The clothes were borrowed from friends. All her own were oily already.

Inside the building, pairs of children bent over birds, administering emergency treatment. First some drops in the eyes, then the bird was blindfolded so he would be less frightened. Then they swabbed him all over with mineral oil and sent him to one of the shelters where he'd be kept until he moulted and grew new feathers. Very few would survive.

A thin girl approached a boy monitoring traffic: "The Sierra Club had someone here who wants to do a movie with floodlights. I said no, it would bother the birds. They said they'd do it outside, then. I said we couldn't take the birds outside, they'd freeze. So they said it's more important for people to see this happening, even if it does bother the birds. He said most of the birds would die anyway. So I said all right because he was right." Her voice pleaded for reassurance.

"You were right," the boy replied.

The young faces were intense, bending over the stricken wild creatures. The red-haired girl was back inside, working on a murre. Even if all the birds were to die, this experience would leave its mark.

Later, I would hear an eight-year-old girl tell how she came to this place and cared for the birds. She told about it at her grandmother's house: how the little kids took the little birds and the bigger kids the bigger birds, how they wrapped them and put in the eyedrops and smeared on oil and the birds got oilier but that was all right, it was the first step to getting them clean.

The grandmother said: "I should have brought the cat, she would have cleaned those birds up." She laughed.

The little girl stared at her in disbelief.

"I should have brought the kitty," the grandmother said.

A couple of the adults in the room must have looked shocked too, because the grandmother snapped: "Well, there are *people* getting killed in Vietnam and here you are fussing about a bunch of birds."

But for that little girl the birds were real and Vietnam was not. She had felt the shivering bodies, the fluttering hearts, had looked into the wild eyes. Near tears she shouted: "I care more about the birds!"

Now this little girl's grandmother is a warm-hearted woman. But she could not see—as surely the child would—that if we cared enough about those birds, people would not be getting killed in Vietnam.

Three weeks after the oil spill and the murder, I realized, turning the key of our front door, that I had driven past the Lees' boarded up store without looking at it. Nobody had yet been apprehended. In the paper, another story of violence. Again: "The neighborhood reacted in disbelief.... Residents were stunned.... 'Never here,' they said."

All these stories read like clichés until you happen to live one. All oil spills are abstracts until your private one comes along. Instead of writing about them, perhaps, we might erect signposts:

Experience
Meditate

Of the 4300 oil-soaked birds retrieved, only about 250 lived long enough to be released with a good chance of survival. The last eleven were freed at the Richardson Bay Wildlife Sanctuary on September 7—eleven white-wing scooters with fresh new feathers.

Keeping the birds had cost thousands of dollars, much of the total put up by Standard Oil. But some valuable lessons were learned that could lead to a 50 percent survival rate in future oil spills.

"Stress is what killed most of the birds," said David Smith, a former Peace Corpsman and junior high school teacher who was one of the dedicated team who nursed the birds those seven months. "You need to get them back into water almost immediately. You have to keep them wet and warm—heated water, warm environment. You monitor skin temperature with electronic devices. With some waterfowl, you need to reintroduce certain oils and waxes into feathers. Cortical steroids also help. If you don't let the feathers get ruined, we estimate that ninety-five percent of the birds could be released in one or two weeks."

Smith is a member of the International Bird Rescue Research Center formed after the spill here. It is ready to send teams to help bird rescuers at future disasters. Within the first few months, the teams were to assist in Seattle and San Clemente.

"It's not that we're saving a bird or species of bird," Smith says. "In trying to save them you develop the knowledge and attitudes that we need to save ourselves."

At a poetry reading soon after the oil plague, Gary Snyder told how John Doss saw those liquid dinosaurs rise out of the ocean and remarked:

"It's energy, the squandering of energy, that's at the root of our problem. . . . Blake says energy is eternal delight. And that's the energy we have to live on, and until we learn that we'll be doom-bound."

The energy generated by the Bay oil epiphany was to have far-reaching consequences that were nowhere so apparent as in the tiny seacoast village on the lagoon. So astonishing, in fact, were the events in that community in the months following the disaster that I've decided it's wisest to talk about them without mentioning the village's name. These events constitute a fragile experiment. If it succeeds, it could become a model for many other communities. But publicity and a sudden population influx would very quickly destroy it.

I call this village Amanitas.

9

The Last Place

❧

But the spell can be broken. . . .
—CAMUS

This is the last place. There is nowhere else we need to go.
—LEW WELCH

The sign showing the turnoff to the village I call Amanitas keeps disappearing, to the annoyance of highway department people in charge of signs. They've even threatened, I'm told, not to replace it—to the delight of some of the community here.

Some of the Amanitas folks would be glad if the road itself disappeared, if the only way you could get to the village were on foot or bicycle. Were it possible, they'd detach the little peninsula they inhabit from the North American continent entirely and just let it drift, wherever ocean currents go.

It's an unusual community, Amanitas. Not just because it's so pretty, curling along the shore of a lagoon and perched on top of sandy cliffs that rustle softly all the time as pebbles crumble down to the beach. There are other pretty villages up and down this coast. What's special about this one is that it feels like a real community, the kind Black Elk may have meant when he talked of "a nest of many nests." Its people have gotten together to try to protect a way of life they love against a fate others accept as inevitable.

In Today-USA the simple and natural appears utopian. Life close to what nature allows seems less and less possible, except for a privileged few. Small farmers are driven off land, homeowners find they can't afford to hold out against developers. Land use is governed by a system geared to the supremacy of the profit motive. Waste is cheaper and easier than conservation. But the people of Amanitas act as though, for them, all that needn't be so. They are trying to build a self-sustaining community that produces most of what it needs, without exploiting; that shares space with diverse humans and great numbers of wild creatures.

The village is within easy driving distance from San Francisco, in a region where land prices have been steadily rising. In terms of dollars and cents, it's ideally suited for development as a second home or ex-urban haven for people who can afford to buy the best. It could be one of those "planned communities" now favored by home builders hip to the ecological sell.

But Amanitans talk, instead, about keeping the population steady, establishing community-owned farms and fishing cooperatives, keeping poor people from being forced out by high rents or unemployment. They hope to develop new jobs in agriculture even though ranches are being cut up for subdivisions and orchards chopped down for trailer parks not far away. And because they've already accomplished things here that knowledgeable people have called impossible, their plans may well turn out to be more than pipe dreams.

A few months after the big Standard Oil spill in the Golden Gateway, Amanitas—this unincorporated community of some 500 homes—forced the cancellation of an eight-million-dollar regional sewage treatment system dear to the hearts of real estate investors and developers. Then a slate of insurgents, who share the view of Cliff Humphrey that progress means not more dollars but more serenity, took over such local government as exists, namely the local public utilities district (PUD).

The people here have started to do what the People's Park story showed must be done: they're taking over control of the place where they live, for the inhabitants' benefit. They're proving that Camus was right, "that there is only an illusion of impotence, that strength of heart, intelligence and courage are enough to stop fate and sometimes reverse it. One has merely to will this, not blindly, but with a firm and reasoned will."

Greg Hewlett is one of the four radical members on PUD, elected in November, 1971. A tall, broad-shouldered man with an easy manner, sandy hair, and a red beard, he's inclined to watch and listen more than to talk, especially to reporters. He has consented to an interview only with reluctance, after I assured him I did not plan to use the name his village is best known by. Amanitas has nothing to gain and much to lose by publicity. So now we're settled in the kitchen of his house on the lagoon and he's telling me how the impossible was brought into being with energy generated by the fight against the Bay oil plague.

While we talk, the dusk deepens on the water just outside the big windows and the golden mesa, on the lagoon's other shore, fades to brown. We don't turn on any light, preferring to watch the day go out. This quiet time is precious to Greg. When he came to Amanitas four years ago, every night was like this, still and peaceful. Now there are more people and more cars, particularly on weekends. Kids and dogs can't sit in the middle of the street anymore and be sure drivers will slow down or stop until they get out of the way. But there still may be time to carry through the delicate experiment that has begun here.

Greg came here as an escapee. He had been a social worker

in Newark, program director of a settlement house in the black ghetto. One day he just couldn't go on. "It was like bandaids on real bad wounds and I just couldn't reconcile it any longer," he tells me. "I ran out. I just ran out. Didn't have anything left to give—died inside, I guess, really. So [soon after the Newark riots] my wife, two kids, two dogs, and I got into the VW bus and came west with everything we owned in it."

They headed toward the Bay area because the only friend they had in California lived in the East Bay. They rented a place in Mill Valley and Greg took a job with a contractor. Then he was laid off, so he started to explore the region. One day, driving along the coast, he turned off the main highway and happened into this little village.

Frame houses, winding streets. A wharf and a beach, a general store, post office, church, bar, two restaurants, a library, book store, real estate office. Seabirds gliding above the water. "I went home and told my wife, 'I know where we're moving,'" Greg recalls. "We didn't know a soul here."

Before long they were acquainted with many new neighbors. There were retired people from the city, old-timers who had once upon a time raised chickens and cows, commuters (though not many), and ex-urbanites. Some families came summers and weekends to second homes here. Others, also escapees from urban traumas and pressures, had settled permanently and fulltime. Greg met artists and poets and longhair gypsies who lived in trucks and vans or in shacks improvised on the beaches. It was a diverse community, speaking just of the humans.

As he settled in, though, he became increasingly aware that his neighbors were of many species. The mudflats teemed with tiny creatures and plants that attracted curlews, willets, avocets. Snowy egrets, blue herons, cormorants, grebes circled above the lagoon watching for fish caught in the shallow waters. A little colony of sandpipers commuted daily from an island off San Francisco to feed on the edge of the tide. Shellfish were abundant and some were rare—the geoduck clam, for instance, which burrows three feet under the mud and sends up a siphon for air. Raccoons, weasels, rabbits, and deer came down from the woods and meadows to drink from the creek as it flowed into the lagoon. Greg and his family had settled beside one of the richest natural wildlife preserves in northern California. In time, he came to view all its life forms, not just homo sapiens, as his neighbors.

Then those two Standard Oil tankers collided and black death drifted toward the lagoon. Greg was one of those "kids" Clarin Zumwalt said "came out of the woodwork" to save the day.

In a way, you could say that Standard Oil did a favor to Amanitas because the emergency brought together some people who, it seemed, needed to meet. They shared an awareness of the richness of their habitat and of its fragility. Now, their success in keeping most of the oil out of the lagoon and its marshes sharpened that awareness and gave them a sense of power. They decided to keep alive the communal energies generated and, for that purpose, organized into the Future Studies Center.

"We searched, consciously, for an issue," Greg says. "And we found it very quickly in the sewer."

Amanitas had a problem with sewage. Most of its homes were equipped with septic tanks which, for the most part, were adequate. About 180 homes, however, were hooked to an antiquated sewer system that dumped raw effluent into the ocean. There had been an outbreak of infectious hepatitis some months ago. County health authorities had announced that the beaches were unsafe for swimming, shellfish gathering, and water sports. The state had ordered Amanitas to stop polluting or face court action and fines. So PUD had come up with a "solution": a gigantic, enormously expensive and ecologically harmful sewage treatment system tailor-made for the developers Amanitas people had been fighting off for years.

The people of the village had so far managed to keep out highways that would speed the trip to the city and put the community within closer commuter range. They had stopped logging along the ridge above the village by lying down in front of lumber company trucks, appealing to news media, and finally winning a temporary court injunction.

When a developer proposed filling part of the lagoon for the building of a race track, they ran him off, then sought protection against others like him by creating a harbor authority. But that authority became too interested in doing something. It produced a proposal for a yacht basin and marina that would have brought little Amanitas the wonders of Today-USA's vacationland. They dissolved the authority, together with its plan.

Through this anti-progress stance, the community forfeited jobs and other economic prizes. But enough Amanitans were wise to the way that particular continuum of economic growth works: the short-term gains would have meant eventual loss of everything they cherished in their environment. Not only the birds, fish, and deer would be driven off, they themselves would be, in time. Jangly urban vibes would surround them.

Their single strongest safeguard against development had been the inadequate sewerage system. Now PUD was about to do away with it by allowing the construction of a system designed, in part, for ten times the population of the region it would serve. It would put a heavy financial burden on land owners, thereby pressing them into selling to developers. It would irreparably harm marine life. The damage would be long-term, therefore worse than anything the oil disaster might have done. A network of pipes would collect sewage from homes, carry it to cement "lagoons" to be aerated and twice chlorinated, then dump it into the ocean through an outfall pipe. So the chemically treated effluent would flow into marine life-spaces, drift into the estuarian mudflats and onto the reefs.

It was on the ground of ecological outrageousness that the Future Studies Center decided to fight the project. Besides Greg, the insurgents included Russ Riviere, a recently returned Vietnam veteran and Sanskrit scholar; Lewis MacAdams, a poet from Texas and points elsewhere; Mark Maser, the town electrician; Jack Kerr, a sanitary engineer who had resigned from PUD because he objected to the eight-million-dollar proposal; Susan Resta, a young mother; and Peter Warshall, a Harvard-graduated naturalist in the process of evolving a new synthesis of Western science and post-psychedelic vision.

They drew up a multi-faceted campaign. They would saturate their community with information about the PUD-accepted plan and alternatives. They would seek help from outside experts and try to enlist any public officials who might be helpful. They would search for what Peter called "soft spots in the system" through which they might attack the projected plan. And they would try to take over PUD in the November elections. That meant they not only would have to win the two seats up for election, they would have to unseat two incumbents by recall and replace them. It was an audacious undertaking, to put it mildly. Except for Kerr, none of the insurgents had any prior experience or interest in sewage treatment projects and their acquaintance with the political process was, by and large, minimal.

By the time they embarked on their fight, early 1971, the PUD-accepted project seemed, to many, a *fait accompli*. Surveying was about to begin. Though approval of some state and county authorities was still pending, that seemed no more than a formality.

The Future Studies people set out to convey their vision of an Amanitas "self-sufficient, in harmony with the planet, thus free," in the words of Lewis MacAdams, and to show how that vision was threatened by the PUD-approved sewer system. In this transmission, Peter Warshall was to play a key role.

"I was turned on," he told me. "Finally the information I was learning was of use in the human community. Everything I'd done before was purely for animals, really anti-human. It meant: 'Humans, keep out.'"

Before coming to Amanitas, Peter had studied monkeys in

Africa and the Caribbean; worked to save the red-footed boobie from extinction on an island off Puerto Rico; and, most recently, tried to set up a preserve for the last of the wild mustangs in Wyoming. In each instance, homo sapiens was, by and large, an enemy species. But in Amanitas the interests of humans and wildlife were interwoven. For Peter, this was a long-awaited bridge.

"My connection with the animal world came through a direct vision," he says. The statement doesn't startle because it fits with what Peter's face, especially his eyes, convey: an intense glow, as one sees occasionally in poets and lovers. "I was brought up in Brooklyn so I didn't know much about animals. One summer I was in one of those camps, Crystal Lake Camp for Boys and Girls, and my aunt had a job there teaching nature studies. One morning, mostly because I was their only nephew, she and my uncle took me out to the lake at five in the morning. The sun was just coming up; mist was coming over the cattails; it was really fantastic. We took this rowboat into the midst of the cattails and a pin-tail duck came up. To me, at that time, there existed only ducks, brown birds, and robins. But I knew this duck was a special creature. It flew up and hit the sun and I couldn't see it anymore. I kept watching but somehow it stayed in the sun. Or maybe I lost it a moment and then it was gone [he adds with the scientist's passion for accuracy]. Anyway, I never got to see it again.

"That moment was so powerful that years later, as soon as someone suggested I could study live animals I was right there. In Harvard zoology was mostly dissection. But the bridge had been made that one moment with the pin-tail duck so I jumped at a job that involved going to Africa to study baboons."

I ask him to talk about Africa a little but he says, "That was so overwhelming I can hardly remember it. I can remember coming out of my tent at full moon and seeing two hundred and fifty zebras walk by my tent, the dust kicking up so I couldn't see their legs. They were the color of the moon—black would be the landscape and white would be the stripes of the moon. Just the movement of the moon across the savannah. And I was supposed to be . . ." He laughs.

"I got the job to help someone do a census of monkey groups. So I spent an incredible amount of time counting monkeys. I wasn't asked any heavy questions so that left me the freedom to look at everything."

After six months with the monkeys, Peter returned to Harvard and was graduated with a degree in biology. The following summer, trying to earn money for further studies as a migrant laborer in southern California, he came to other meaningful connections.

"That's the first time I learned about water," he says. "I knew there was a federal law that said you weren't supposed to benefit from federally developed water on more than a hundred and sixty acres. I worked on a ranch of about five thousand acres that had water from a state pipe. But this state pipe fed from a federal one. That was my first consciousness that there was an ecology in America."

Later, a small rancher gave him a lesson in consumer economics when he asked Peter to cut down his plum trees though they were healthy and laden with ripe sugar plums.

"Some giant company had put out a plum that looked exactly like the sugar plum but matured two weeks earlier and lasted better. This company also controlled shipping. So it totally copped the market and this guy lost his buyers, just like that. He had a hundred and fifty of these beautiful plum trees, and he couldn't cut them down. So he offered me this incredible salary just so I'd do it. I couldn't believe there was nothing he could do. Maybe now he could develop an organic food market but there was no alternative then. I cut down about a hundred of them.

"Then I go back to Brooklyn and there's my mother buying plums and they look great but she notices they don't quite have the same taste. But how does she enter a protest that has any effect on orchards on the other side of America? The housewife in this country could cause the revolution toward decent eating but no city housewife knows the steps.

"It's the same thing with the sewage plant here. You learn the steps. Something goes from the toilet down the drain and to an outfall pipe. When we first started we couldn't use the word outfall pipe because people didn't know what it was. And then people understood: oh yes, that's the pipe through which all your crap falls into the ocean. Suddenly that word became real and the connection was real. The other connection was—where did all this water come from? So suddenly the town becomes aware that every flush of the toilet is five gallons of perfectly good drinking water."

Said Lewis MacAdams: "We could have fought it on the basis that it was too big or would ruin the quality of life. But although those things were true, we tried to fight it on the basis that it was jive. It was a one-way system, it had nothing to do with the forms of the earth that were real. There's no such thing as waste, for instance. Our shit is not waste. Nothing leaves the planet except a few rockets."

Future Studies people talked about the household chemicals that would wash into the ocean through the outfall. "No one knows how these things work together," said Peter. "But we do know that in San Diego they had an outfall just like this one and thirty percent of the species died off. The halibut around San Diego no longer have bright red bellies and when you pick them up in a net you get ten percent kill—simply since the outfall. Up the coast fifty miles you get perfectly good halibut.

"We do know that the ocean works in rhythmic circles and that nature hates a straight line. Most animals in the sea live close to the moon's cycle. The plankton, the smallest animals in the sea, come up and recede with the moon. This means that sometimes you have high amounts of nutrients near the surface, sometimes small amounts. An outfall will break the natural cycles of food distribution, causing year-round linear growth of a few species at the expense of others."

Sea urchins thrive on the nutrients in sewage and proliferate, in the process destroying kelp, the anchored seaweed that shelters small fish and provides breeding grounds for them among its fluttering strands. So that means fewer fish. "Like mercury in salmon, everything eventually comes back to the human species," says Peter. "We have to stop tampering with the ocean as if it were a local drain."

Thus far, the process was easy to explain. But to convey their vision, the Future Studies people had to show that the preservation of a diversity of species was essential to a community that sought self-fulfillment and the good life.

"When most people think of environment they think of a green lawn," Peter said. "But a green lawn is almost a desert, as is a pine community." There is little to be learned from a lawn or a pine grove because of the dearth of interdependent life forms. The beaches, reefs, and wild meadows, meanwhile, offer endless opportunities.

From becoming acquainted with other creatures, we see that man is tuned into but a few of nature's vibrations. Western scientists have turned up proof of this each time they have learned to tap some new energy source. When radar was developed, for instance, we learned that bats orient themselves by emitting high-frequency sound waves that humans can't hear. When infra-red rays came into medical use, we discovered that the pit viper finds its prey by picking up the infra-red radiation of warm-blooded animals.

In an article in the November, 1971, issue of *Clear Creek*, an ecology magazine, Peter wrote:

Many times, I am in awe, if not jealous, of the pit viper and the bat. . . . The more I have known the animals that are consciously sensitive to vibrations humans cannot directly appreciate, the more my imagination expands and I find a certain delight in the Earth and its creatures. Eskimos believed that the essential vibrations of human speech (what Tibetans call "seed syllables") were taught to them by the wind, the sea and the animals. They carefully and with joy imitated the sounds of the ptarmigan, walrus, ocean, and each other. Each time they searched for the chant that incorporated these sounds and rhythms, until they felt it was common to themselves and the elements and animal worlds.

And was that chant not, perhaps, that experience of oneness that we keep longing for? Perhaps the delight Peter feels in other animals' vibrations is the energy Blake said we must learn to live by.

"America has a great desire to get back to magic," Peter wrote. "To connect the frozen chicken legs to the chicken, music to animal sounds, the power of herbs to healing." Amanitas now had a chance to make such connections.

Besides the direct effects of the outfall on marine life, there were secondary consequences to be expected. Once it was in, subdividing was inevitable. Increased population would mean more cars emitting pollutants that would be absorbed by the water surface. More building would mean accelerated siltation, erosion, depletion of forest and field habitats. Eventually, the increased population would want more water. That would lead to a dam on the creek that flowed into the lagoon. Before long, people in this community wouldn't be much better off than city dwellers who tend to know only four other forms of consciousness beside the human: dogs, cats, canaries, and goldfish.

But none of this needed to happen, the Future Studies people stressed. If sewage were treated as a resource rather than as waste, it could enrich rather than impoverish their multi-species community. They proposed, instead of the PUD-approved eight-million-dollar system, a much less costly land retention project similar to many already in use in Japan and some American communities. Solids would be processed, compacted, and used as fertilizer.

Liquids would be purified in lagoons that also bred fish, then sprayed on fields or recycled.

"It isn't a matter of a hopeless situation," Peter kept telling all who'd listen. "It's a matter of perceptual shift."

But there was also the matter of the surveyors about to appear, to start work on that other system. Warshall, Hewlett & Co. studied engineer reports, law books, and procedural handbooks in search of "a soft spot in the system," as Peter put it. They held small house meetings, made door-to-door calls. "Once you get past the assumption that engineers know something you don't know, it gets a lot easier," said MacAdams. "It's a simple system." Before long, some Amanitas citizens were as well informed about outfall pipes and their effects as sanitary engineers. And the Future Studies leaders were answering questions more knowledgeably than the startled PUD members. Hundreds of letters poured into government offices. Public functionaries were invited to tour the area and hear the Future Studies point of view. And slowly, they persuaded.

To their surprise, many government people and experts were glad to help. "Time and again we'd hear: 'No community ever did this before. This has never happened before,'" Greg recalled. "The Army Corps of Engineers turned out to be most sympathetic."

"We found that every time we had a guy from HUD [Department of Housing and Urban Development] or EPA [Environmental Protection Agency] or whatever out into the community, talking with people here, we had a friend."

"Russ Riviere would say, 'Give them the vision,'" added Peter. "And if they got the vision, when they were back in their offices they were on our side. Some kept coming back."

"We need each other," added Greg. "They need our belief that we can do it. We were pretty determined."

The soft spot they needed was provided by a requirement in the National Environmental Policy Act of 1970 that environmental impact statements be submitted on federally subsidized projects. PUD's eight-million-dollar sewer depended on both state and federal aid. The engineers who had drafted it had submitted something called the environmental assessment statement, saying that no significant environmental damage was expected. But no impact statement had been filed.

The assessment statement was available for public inspection. So the Future Studies folks had a chance to comment. They sent EPA a voluminous, carefully researched criticism. This prompted that agency to ask the engineers for an impact statement. It also prompted the state water quality control board to ask EPA to postpone any action until the board could examine the merits of the case.

Both these agencies had already authorized funding but now both reconsidered. EPA's reaction was never made public because the state authority acted first.

"It was the first time that a state water quality control board decertified a sewerage plan after approving funds," Peter said.

The Future Studies people of Amanitas had won more easily than they had dared hope. The eight-million-dollar threat was no more. To start in a fresh direction, they now turned their energies to the November election campaign. Their slate of candidates consisted of a school teacher; a journalist and author specializing in China; a former Wall Street management consultant now teaching at the local school; and Greg Hewlett, former social worker. They promised to work for sounder fiscal policies, better management, limited growth, restoration of local powers that had been ceded to the county. And they pledged to turn PUD meetings into open town meetings in which many subjects could be freely discussed.

During the campaign, these candidates aired some rather startling ideas. Greg suggested, for instance, that instead of building more roads, the community might consider slowing down traffic by planting trees in the middle of existing thoroughfares. But they convinced enough voters of their qualifications for office to win both elected seats, and to fill two more by recall, unseating two of the staunchest advocates of the now-dead sewer scheme.

"It's not by any stretch of the imagination over," says Greg. "It's just begun. The pressures on the community from the outside are so intense that unless we present a united front we just won't make it. I think our young and old, straight- or curled-hair, short- or longhair people agree on the basic value of the size of the place. Some people don't like domes; others don't like lawns. But for the most part we agree on growth, cars, traffic, speed, that kind of thing."

"There seems to be a growing realization that speed means waste," I say.

"I have a theory of scale that this village fits into," says Greg. "Here the systems are manageable because when you pass down the street you know most of the people you pass. Where you don't there's a lot of fear and personal isolation.

"We tended to assume for a long time that growth was good economically and socially. We're finding that's not true anymore but it takes time to dismantle the machine." Other California communities had lately begun opting against growth. Marin County voters had just defeated an aqueduct project that would have made more growth likely by expanding the water supply. Palo Alto had discovered that development can cost a community more, even if it does bring more property taxes, than leaving open space. But often, anti-growth policies mean that poor or minority people are excluded. What about that, I ask Greg, wasn't he just building another privileged little safety island for a lucky few?

He points out that, coming straight from Newark, he can't help but be aware of such questions. But "I see that we have to determine the carrying capacity of this part of the earth in terms of human development. We're developing technology that will enable us to have more people in sensitive ways. I think we can do it here. At the same time, it's a delicate balance. Right now the poor can live here. There are maybe a hundred people on food stamps. We have maybe four hundred year-round households. I would consider it a representative community in terms of income. But if something isn't done in a positive way poor people will be excluded. Land prices are up. There are no jobs. Taxes are up."

So, to maintain the income spread and improve living standards, Greg and associates have some imaginative ideas in mind: setting up community-owned farms and other enterprises, for instance. But how?

His ideas revolve around the cultivation of public awareness of the part each person plays in the environment immediately around him, combined with the use of PUD tax- and land-acquisition powers to make the community more self-sustaining, more of a whole system.

"I think the property tax is getting beyond reason and if that's a pivotal point, we can get a lot of people behind the idea of changes," Greg says. "Now a large portion of the tax goes to subsidize water supply. We're going to try to set that on a cost per service basis, to have revenues from the sale of water pay the cost of providing it. Now the large users are subsidized: as you use more, the rates go down. We want to turn that around: raise rates as use increases. Education is critical. Most people don't know where their taxes go or how much water they use."

Once they start learning, by seeing some of it spelled out on their bi-monthly bills, for example, they are likely to be more sparing consumers. Then they might also get interested in such questions as whether it's really necessary to flush five gallons of drinking water every time you use the toilet; whether it might not be possible to set up home recycling systems that use dishwater for that instead.

If water consumption goes down and the population remains near-steady for a while, and if the new people on PUD can really find ways to affect the economies they think are possible in management, then funds would become available for purchasing land for other community uses. The process of returning to a more self-sustaining and natural system could continue.

All this is barely a beginning, but it signals a trend reversal that has to take place everywhere if the planet is to continue surviving. What made it happen in Amanitas is a fortuitous conjunction of unusual people who decided that their community was worth fighting for.

A few days after the election that put the new PUD board into office, Amanitas citizens rejected a county planning commission proposal that provided for a new shopping center, a boat harbor, turning the highway into a parkway, and recreational development along the lagoon. At the Planning Commission hearing at which this happened, one planner remarked that this community had "more activists per acre than anywhere else in the county."

A member sighed that "this commission seldom finds itself anymore before a group that doesn't like its community just the way it is."

The lagoon is a county- and state-sponsored wildlife preserve, which was being considered as a national recreation area, so suggestions were entertained about that project. Amanitans suggested that all parking lots in the vicinity be shut down and that access be by walkways or bikepaths or jitney buses only.

Their reasoning was that automobile traffic would be destructive and disturbing to the whole population, including birds, fish, shellfish, and humans. Visitors, if they came, should respect the inhabitants' need by coming quietly. But a commission member chided:

"You understand that the lagoon belongs to the people of the whole county. It's the people who put up the money."

"No," shouted MacAdams. "The lagoon belongs to the animals that inhabit it."

At this the commission member smiled. "If you want to include the shrimp, the weenie worms—fine. But I don't choose to be sentimental. It's the people who make the decisions."

"Belong?" remarked Peter. "That's a funny way to see it. The lagoon does not belong to anyone, really."

This life-centered perspective is shared, so far, by only a few. But before the oil spill and its epiphanies, it is doubtful that even that exchange would have taken place at such a meeting. I thought back to the poster I had seen in the Future Studies office at the height of the campaign, with the photograph of an oil-soaked grebe and this poem by Basho:

> *The sea*
>   *darkening . . .*
> *Voices of*
>   *wild*
>   *waterbirds*
> *Crying, whirling, white.*

And then I thought of the poem by Lew Welch, "The Song Mt. Tamalpais Sings," with its refrain:

> *This is the last place. There is nowhere else to go,*

ending:

> *This is the last place. There is nowhere else we need to go.*

It isn't Mount Tamalpais or Amanitas, of course. It's wherever we are that is the last place.

For Alvin Duskin, businessman, it was the city of San Francisco.

10

Merchandizing a New Consciousness: Alvin Duskin

"I'm only a garment manufacturer, not an economist," Alvin Duskin is saying, "but I found out very quickly that, with highrises, the more a city builds, the more it loses. It's like making a dress for ten dollars, selling it for nine dollars, and trying to make up the difference in volume."

At the wave of appreciative chuckles, Duskin smiles. He's at a microphone, surveying the thousand or so people gathered in his San Francisco factory loft in response to his latest ad.

The little reference to being "only a garment manufacturer" is the perfect cover—citizen Duskin, solid, a businessman. People automatically assume here is a man with both feet on the ground, pragmatic, no campus crazy, a man who knows the value of a dollar.

But what Alvin Duskin, garment manufacturer, is proposing, the idea he spelled out in his expensive spread in the *San Francisco Chronicle*, has nothing to do with women's wear. The ad that brought everyone down here was placed by Alvin Duskin, citizen.

MERCHANDIZING A NEW CONSCIOUSNESS

It set out the argument that his native city's charm and delight—those much-loved views of the Bay, the rows of little pastel frame houses climbing gracefully up and down hills—were being destroyed by high-rise development. The monolithic skyscrapers that had begun sprouting during the past several years in the choicest parts of town, Duskin wrote, were no bargain in any way to San Francisco. Carefully citing his sources, he proceeded to refute the widely accepted notion that bulky new buildings are essential to the city's survival because they bring in new taxes and provide more jobs. The jobs, he had discovered, go mostly to out-of-town white-collar commuters. The increased costs of municipal services, however, and the damage to the environment, must be borne by city dwellers.

So, Duskin concluded, it was time for a citizens' revolt. He had decided to lead a move for a ballot initiative that would outlaw the construction of buildings more than six stories high in the city unless voters granted specific approval. Anyone wishing to join him in this endeavor was asked to please come to a meeting at his plant this Sunday morning, October 25, 1970.

No new building more than six stories high anywhere in the city? The idea would have sounded preposterous coming from anyone else. Even from this successful businessman it was audacious, maybe unrealistic. Yet people came to the meeting. All kinds of people packed into the loft.

Duskin looks around and sees long hair and short, women in feathered hats and girls in macramé vests, men in fringed leather, army surplus wear, and business suits. There appears to be a good cross-section of the local population. And that, to him, is proof that he hit it right once again—spoke his mind and found he was speaking for a lot of people. Maybe half the citizens of San Francisco are with him. Who knows? Maybe they were all just afraid to suggest something they thought would sound unrealistic and therefore make them seem foolish—failing to realize that only their mind-set made it so.

Duskin radiates energy and competence. His stance is casually athletic, the look on his heavy-featured face is alert. He's wearing well-fitting, slightly belled navy trousers and a light blue work shirt embroidered with red suns on the collar, peacocks on the pockets, poppies on the cuffs. This light touch of the homespun places him on friendly terms with the longhairs, yet wouldn't lead anyone to mistake him for a stoner. He's the wheeler-dealer who started a small sweater store five years ago and now manufactures and sells five million dollars worth of garments each year. The way he tells it, the task is fairly simple: only 25,000 signatures are needed to put the measure on the ballot. If everyone here present collects fifty, that's already twice what's required. But the goal would be 75,000 because, he says, "the people at city hall will try to throw out as many as they can."

For those who would like to do more, he has drafted some form letters.

As he leafs through them, his patter hints he is on familiar terms with the establishment.

"Nat Owings [architect of the controversial 550-foot U.S. Steel Corporation tower proposed for the downtown waterfront] used to be a neighbor of mine at Big Sur. He lives in this marvelous A-frame over a cliff, waves washing below, birds. He's saving the environment there." Chuckles again.

"Cyril Magnin [chairman of the port commission] . . . nice guy to have lunch with . . .

"Ben Swig [owner of the Fairmont Hotel and a powerful local Democrat] will tell you he's just an interested bystander. But he's in on every important real estate deal in the city."

Familiar doesn't mean cozy, however. What's happening, Duskin says, is that this city—the last livable city in the whole USA is on its way to becoming "very much like Chicago or New York where life has all the joys of the bottom of an elevator shaft—a crowded elevator shaft where everyone has guns." And people like Owings, Magnin, and Swig are responsible for this "Manhattanization."

"Our goal is a long-range goal," Duskin declares. "We're not just in this just to stop buildings over six stories. We're gonna keep this thing going to keep this city livable. Maybe the next thing will be to ban cars from the city."

"This thing" for Duskin began in 1969 when he became a folk hero overnight—right up there along with Eric Hoffer, the longshoreman-philosopher; Saul Alinsky, the community organizer; and Ralph Nader—by personally leading a revolt against city hall and recapturing Alcatraz from Mayor Joseph Alioto, who was going to hand the island over to Texas millionaire Lamar Hunt for commercial development.

Duskin did it by running full-page ads in both the *Chronicle* and *Examiner* telling Alioto what he thought of his plan and offering to pay the $10,200 it would cost the city to hold on to the abandoned federal island for six months so the mayor could come up with something San Franciscans would like better than the space museum Hunt had in mind. Duskin's own preference, he said, was for giving the Rock back to the pelicans.

Attached to the ad were some coupons to clip and send to the mayor, San Francisco County supervisors, and the Interior Department. They were like the coupons that sell toothpaste and coffee. You clip them, take them to your dealer, and have them redeemed.

And Alcatraz was redeemed. The coupons poured in. The mayor reconsidered—but not before losing his temper at a press conference:

"Who is Alvin Duskin?" Alioto snapped. "A New York dress designer who doesn't like our designs . . . I've seen his designs and they're lousy."

That remark, more than anything, endeared Duskin to all who

thought Mayor Alioto was too high-handed. For it developed that Duskin was not a New Yorker at all but a San Franciscan, born and bred, who was turning out sweaters and dresses below Mission Street and selling to smart New York stores. So plain, plucky Alvin became the people's hero.

"What made it so funny," according to Duskin, "was that I'm a garment manufacturer. I mean, how scruffy can you get? Alioto was implying you had to be somebody to object and I was nobody, just a garment manufacturer."

Duskin's involvement with Alcatraz began when he ran into his old friend Jerry Mander, an advertising man. Mander was lunching at a North Beach restaurant with radical publisher Warren Hinckle and author Jessica Mitford. They were talking about Alcatraz and considering some kind of protest action. The Rock had strong emotional connotations for them. All of them had, more than once, been moved by the thought of the men locked up on it and wondered if they also could see the sun setting behind the Golden Gate Bridge. You couldn't watch a sunset from a San Francisco hill without seeing Alcatraz. You were compelled to think of those gray cells everytime you watched lights go on all over the city. Now that the prison was abandoned, the island was a landmark. The thought that it was to be commercially exploited was outrageous. And Hunt's plan for a space museum was totally out of keeping with the site.

While Mander, Hinckle, and Mrs. Mitford talked, Duskin walked by. Mander came up with the idea. Why not ask Alvin to run an ad appealing to the people? All right, said Duskin, why not?

A few weeks later, elated at their success, Mander and Duskin decided they had hit upon a new tactic for forcing politicians to respond to public sentiment. They agreed to try the ad-plus-coupon technique on another hot environmental issue, the California water project.

Controversy was at a peak about this vast scheme for carrying northern water to the arid south. Via the most complex system of dams, canals, pipelines, and pumps, vast amounts of fresh water that now flowed into San Francisco Bay were to be diverted to the western part of the Central Valley and the region of Los Angeles, to irrigate lands for agribusiness and make possible new subdivisions in desert areas that could not now support human life. The project would lift the water more than 2000 feet over the Tehachapi Mountains, across earthquake fault zones, and carry it in aqueducts to be stored in reservoirs until used. According to Governor Ronald Reagan, this was "the largest and most complicated engineering feat of our time." William Gianelli, director of the state department of water resources, called it "an enduring monument to man's stubborn, daring and courageous effort to tame the elements."

Forty years ago, when it was first begun, most people might have agreed, as far as the technology of the thing was concerned. (The distribution of benefits and nature of financing was another matter.) But now, in the age of rising ecological awareness, this was a perfect instance of the colossal mistake. The project's opponents called the California water project the most expensive faucet in the world. They said it was unnecessary, harmful to land and life in both north and south, a giveaway of public wealth and health for the benefit of a few exploiters.

The water to be diverted south was "surplus" or "waste water" to the project's advocates. The way they saw it, it was running uselessly down wild rivers into the Bay, occasionally flooding.

But those who opposed the project argued that fragile northern ecologies depended on this water and that fish, plant, and human communities would suffer disastrously if the flow were diminished as planned. Rivers and the Bay would become smaller and more polluted. In the south, the water would go toward the production of more cotton—even though cotton was already overproduced and federally subsidized. It would go to "make more Los Angeles," even though what that city needed was not more water or more people, but more air. It would add dollars to the landholders' and developers' pockets and smog to southern Californians' lungs.

Besides all that, the state's water authorities had recently acknowledged that they had overestimated the projected need for water. Population was not expanding as expected. Many had begun to move out of Los Angeles. Plus—what should have been the clincher—vast geothermal springs had recently been discovered under the Imperial and Mexicali valleys, capable of providing much of the Southwest with an abundant supply of distilled water and electrical power, without causing any damage to rivers—and almost no pollution.

Still the colossal project moved forward, immune to all reason. It was near-complete and soon to begin pumping the water. But a portion of it still awaited the governor's approval. There seemed to be a slight last-minute chance of persuading him to withhold it.

Duskin's second ad ran in the *Los Angeles Times*, and the *San Francisco Chronicle*. The Los Angeles spread was headed: MORE SMOG, MORE PEOPLE, MORE TRAFFIC, MORE OF EVERYTHING WE DON'T WANT. The home version was bannered: ALCATRAZ, THE BAY, WATER, AND THE IMMINENT DEATH OF CALIFORNIA.

"In order to save Alcatraz for wildlife, it is necessary to keep life in the Bay," Duskin wrote. Therefore, the California water project was most urgently relevant:

> With less fresh water flowing through the rivers and delta, the pesticides, nitrates and industrial chemicals that wash into it will have much greater destructive power than even now. They are likely to kill off millions of fish, species which eat the fish, plantlife along the shores, birds which need the plantlife, and finally, the marine plankton along California's continental shelf, which produce 70 per cent of the oxygen we breathe.
>
> It's a chain reaction. Everything needs the next thing, you see; that is the miracle of nature. We are busily destroying the chain, for-

getting that if it is disrupted, so are we. A few too many chemicals in the plankton, or the fish and birds we eat, and we can forget Alcatraz forever.

These same chemicals flow into San Francisco Bay and eventually we will have a bay as dead as Lake Erie. . . . We cannot afford any longer to give commerce and industry first say-so over the environment, not if we once get it in our heads that we are also wildlife; we are only one strand of the web of life on this planet and in order to survive we have got to save everything else.

He included maps of the water project, details explaining how much of its cost of three billion dollars or more would be borne by the state's taxpayers (even though the state kept saying that wasn't so), and a coupon to send in for a list of more complete information sources. There was also a coupon to be mailed to the governor urging that he disapprove the Peripheral Canal, the portion of the project waiting his go-ahead, and to other political figures, urging they stop the whole project.

A few days later, when the governor was asked at a press conference how many coupons he had received, he turned to his executive secretary, Edwin Meese III, for an answer. Meese was reported as saying: "They haven't been counting. We have better things to do than count silly coupons."

Reagan added: "I didn't know that dressmaking encompassed so many outside activities." So, Reagan outdid Alioto in building Duskin's image as the little man with a brave heart.

Duskin's next full-page ad was headed: SUING CALIFORNIA, and ran in the *Chronicle,* the *Los Angeles Times* and the West Coast edition of the *Wall Street Journal.* It maintained that the plan violated a number of laws and constitutional provisions and announced that suits were being prepared against the state. The response exceeded all his expectations. About $60,000 flowed in to help in the legal battle.

It was at this point that Duskin began to realize he was in

"a thing." He had a following. He was getting invitations to address meetings and conferences. He was expected to take a stand on other environmental and political issues.

All the issues were interconnected. One led right into the next.

Alcatraz had taken him to the California water project. That, in turn, led him to consider other threats to San Francisco Bay, particularly the encroachment of development beyond the shores and the construction of view-blocking high-rises.

Until recently, San Francisco was a city of small, white, or pastel buildings with roof-lines that followed the contours of the hills. Only on hilltops did you see anything much over four stories. And then hill towers were usually slender, did not intrude much on anyone's view of the Bay, and accented the natural curves of the land. Standing alone, most of the city's buildings were not particularly distinguished. The charm was in the way they all blended.

But lately, tall bulky structures had begun to intrude on the skyline, violating tradition. The trend had begun with the crescent-shaped, eighteen-story Fontana Towers apartment complex erected ten years ago at the foot of Russian Hill, rudely blocking views of the water, the Golden Gate Bridge, and the hills of Marin—like a fat man who insists on standing up in the second row of a theater during the performance. It provoked citizen anger and led to restrictive zoning along the waterfront, but a precedent had been set. The low profile along the shore was no longer inviolate. Then the Bank of America headquarters broke two more traditions by looming up downtown not only fifty-two-stories high but bulky and dark. And the Transamerica Corporation began to build a showy pyramid that *Progressive Architecture* magazine described as "insensitive, inappropriate, incongruous, inescapable and in the wrong place." Mayor Alioto observed that in time people would cherish the pyramid as a landmark.

The city appeared to be on its way toward becoming a West Coast Manhattan. Alioto was pushing for growth and dense development, speaking of progress and new beauty. Conservationists accused him of a robber-baron mentality that viewed city land as exploitable real estate rather than a common environment. But they dissipated their energy fighting particular projects rather than focusing on the whole picture. And they talked in terms of tradition, ecology, and aesthetics which seldom stood up against the promoters' promises of economic gain.

One afternoon, addressing a luncheon meeting on the subject of the water project, Duskin mentioned the high-rise issue. Afterward, an architect in the audience asked whether Duskin was aware that some doubt had been cast on the assumption that highrise development was, per se, economically beneficial to cities. Studies had shown that as population density increases, per capita costs of running the city tend to go up. San Francisco's planning chief, Allan B. Jacobs, had suggested that there might be economic reasons for opposing high rises.

Duskin's interest was piqued. He did some research and discovered enough additional facts to convince him that he had a solid pragmatic argument against those who justify all new development on the ground that it is "progress" essential to an urban center's survival.

What a lot of people didn't realize, as they marveled at the figure of this little businessman taking on city hall and the entire real estate establishment, was that Alvin Duskin was as good at moving minds as he was at selling dresses. Under cover of the garment manufacturer lived the teacher who had stumbled into the women's wear trade almost by accident.

In 1953, while working toward a doctorate in philosophy at Stanford University, Duskin taught an English course at San Francisco State College. "I was the lowest man on the totem pole in the department, so I had an eight A.M. class of double bonehead English," he told me. "I had thirty students who all came in because they had to."

Sickened by the sight of all those blank-eyed, nodding faces, Duskin one day declared that the semester was over. From that day on, nobody would have to come. He would continue to teach, though, for those who cared to continue.

The first two sessions, less than a handful of students showed up. Duskin threw away his curriculum instructions and talked about what was close to his heart—Freud, Marx, John Locke, Plato. But as word got around about the class, more kids began to show up. By the end of the semester, he could count on sixty students to be there promptly at eight, ready to take part in discussion.

His appointment expired at the end of the year and he returned to Stanford for fulltime doctoral study. But teaching that class had whetted his appetite. He wearied of Stanford, left before completing his thesis, and founded a new school. He did not believe that any established institution would long grant him the kind of freedom he had enjoyed that single semester at San Francisco State.

Ralph Waldo Emerson College, in the highlands of Carmel, was the first of the new wave of alternative universities and free U's. With no more than five faculty members, twenty-five students, and much enthusiasm, it gained a national reputation among progressive educators. Duskin taught a course on the precursors of Socrates and another on Plato. He saw parallels between the time of Athens' decline and his own time.

"The age was ending. They knew Sparta would win and that would be a triumph of regimentation and law and order and the free-swinging, drunk, marvelous society they had was finished. So here was Socrates trying to develop a heavenly city." And so here was the flower generation. Who would be the new Sparta? Forces within America? China? Nobody dozed in those classes.

But the school lacked sufficient funding and Duskin soon found he had made himself a trap—he had to expend most of his energy on hustling money and trying to keep the complex running.

MERCHANDIZING A NEW CONSCIOUSNESS

There wasn't as much time as he wished left for teaching or for his wife and children.

So Emerson College shut down in 1963, after its third year. Duskin felt he had, nevertheless, achieved something significant: "I had created a situation where kids could do some independent thinking in total freedom." Others were now trying similar ventures. Free schools were proliferating, particularly on the West Coast.

Duskin decided to take a teaching job in the East the following fall. During the summer he thought he'd make money to bail out of a $4000 debt. His father had a small knitting mill in San Francisco, so he decided to open a sweater shop in North Beach. He bought some items from his dad, designed a few himself, and had them manufactured.

To his surprise, he was soon making money—much more than he had expected. So he recharted his course.

"I realized that in a society dominated by monetary values, the thing to do is get some money," he told me. "In this way, by the time I was forty, I would never have to worry about money again."

Soon he had a small factory, and was making and selling a line of dresses. Business grew fast. Marsha Fox, whom he had hired as salesgirl, turned out to have a gift for designing. He hired Sara Urquart and Betsy Johnson and soon was selling to Joseph Magnin's, Bloomingdale's, Saks, and Macy's. His "gimmick" was plain down-to-earth sense.

His designers were told to make dresses they would like to wear rather than try to dope out the desires of the mythical consumer. The result was the sort of thing smart young girls look for but seldom find on the moderate-price racks—simple knit garments that show off a good shape without ostentation.

A fad he spotted in Italy, of wearing tiny over-shrunk sweaters, inspired him to make thin-ribbed tops that stretch to several sizes.

When he saw girls wearing his mini-dresses over jeans, he devised the pant-suit. He showed off his garments in a series of ads in the *New Yorker*, using ordinary girls in candid poses rather than models. The effect on eyes used to the extravagances of fashion photography was startling. The photos looked like fashion spoofs. But they were charming. Girls could identify with them.

Always it was Duskin's sound intuitive judgment, plain speaking, and brash self-confidence that brought out products that made dollars. Those very same qualities later helped him merchandize eco-politics.

But a six-story height limit? In San Francisco in 1971? Had self-confidence turned finally to ego-mania?

My appointment was at 10 A.M. but when I arrive, apologetic, at 10:30, Duskin's receptionist says he's still home sleeping. So I wander down two floors to see Lou Harris who's in charge of the environmentalist line.

The response to the height-limit ad has been smaller than to the others, Harris tells me. But a lot of people have volunteered time and effort, including fifteen lawyers, eight architects, three photographers, and two earthquake experts.

Harris is a soft-spoken and slow-moving young man with a trace of discontent at the edge of his voice. He used to work for the University of California, on the urban crisis and Peace Corps programs, until he wearied of bureaucratic inertia—until he freaked out.

"I was down getting my driver's license renewed," he tells me over coffee. "When I got to the picture taking I suddenly messed up my hair. As soon as I'd done that I felt free. And soon after that I just quit."

He shows me a picture of a truly wild-haired fellow. The Harris beside me is tidily groomed.

Around noon someone calls to say Duskin has come in. I go up and find him closeted with two gloomy young buyers from

MERCHANDIZING A NEW CONSCIOUSNESS

New York. "Things are slow in the retail trade," Susan Fishman, buyer for Experiment I, a chain of far-out boutiques run by Alexander's, tells me. "We've come to seek direction from the man who knows where it's at."

She's only twenty-two but her face is hidden behind a battle mask. The hair is pulled back tightly; mascara covers both sets of lashes; eye shadow and thick powder hide her skin. With her is a worried-looking young man in a tweed business suit. Duskin is in the blue workshirt and blue trousers that are his customary attire. He basks in their expectant gaze. Sometimes, very fleetingly, I get the notion his self-confidence is not quite solid. That's when he has that slightly sheepish, appealing face of a little boy who's shy and eager to charm. I've noticed that look before on certain politicians and public personalities and it's a clue to what must be complex motivations. Maybe that is the weakness that he has worked into his strength.

"We have two items—plain knickers and the knicker jumpsuit—that are selling like crazy," he says. "But one of the things most wanted is the simple, dumb dress."

He leads the buyers to a nearby room where they can see this "dumb dress" in mini, midi, and ankle lengths, made of droopy crepe and washable cotton jersey.

"This is newness and excitement; this is what Alvin Duskin means," he says in a flat voice. "The prices are moderate but on some items," half-smiling, "we have to sell a little more expensively to get an illusion of quality."

The buyers choose. Meanwhile, Duskin closets himself in another office with his treasurer. "We have a million dollars in orders we can't fill," he tells me. "We're expanding in a time the economy is contracting and it's hard to get capital and credit.

"When I started five years ago, I was supposed to be a millionaire by forty. But here I am thirty-nine and I'm still in the garment business."

We lunch with the two buyers and a delegation of sardonically smiling *Women's Wear Daily* staffers, also out from New York. Duskin offers a quote: pants going out, dresses returning.

He escorts them all out via a tour of the plant, past a floor where knitting machines move delicately, like kinetic sculptures, past some of the plant's 225 employees, and past the showroom—skipping Lou Harris's corner.

Clearly, a successful man. Yet Duskin insists he has no ego-involvement in the dress business. For him, it's simply a tool to advance his real interests, which are, very broadly, those of a teacher.

He admires Saul Alinsky, John L. Lewis, Cesar Chavez, Ralph Nader—all of them, in that same broad sense, teachers. Alinsky showed poor urban people how to organize their communities and so gain more power and freedom. Lewis did this same thing for miners. Nader showed that one man, with information and energy, can confront a giant the size of General Motors and get it to budge. More importantly, Nader "changed the consciousness of what it means to be a lawyer," says Duskin. Chavez set a new style for peaceful spiritual leadership and made a connection between labor and ecology by bringing the issue of pesticides into contract negotiations. All these men did what the teacher is supposed to do: they gave people tools to expand their potential, allowed them to experience a greater sense of freedom, showed them how they can mold their own destiny and affect their environment.

After talking with Duskin at some length, I realize that the six-story height limit is a cover within a cover. It does not matter much whether the ballot initiative passes or not. Duskin is out to show people they have more say than they think about the nature of their environment. That was the subliminal message in the ad with its coupons. Duskin is merchandizing a new consciousness.

"We can't lose," he says. "This is maybe a part of a hundred-year fight on who controls the planet."

During the months following that first meeting, the powers that be in San Francisco were compelled to deal with Alvin Duskin's outrageous proposal for a six-story height limit. Some 45,000 signatures were collected, more than enough to place the issue on the November, 1971, ballot. The merits of the idea were hotly debated before public bodies and in civic groups. A well-financed campaign against it was mounted by a group calling itself Citizens for San Francisco. In one of its counter-ads it tried to defuse Duskin's appeal by cutely patronizing: "Alvin Duskin, we think you're marvelous. But . . ."

When the required reports of campaign contributions were filed, they showed that opponents of the measure had $152,211, most of it in large sums from corporations with interests in highrise developments. Duskin's people had $17,659, mostly in small gifts from citizens. (They had also spent $28,000 to place the measure on the ballot.)

Opponents had contributions of $10,000 each from the Bank of America, the Southern Pacific Transportation Company, Milton Meyer and Company (a real estate concern based in San Francisco), the Standard Oil Company, Pacific Gas and Electric Company, and Pacific Telephone Company. Six contributions of $5000 each were recorded from more banks and corporations, a construction firm, and a giant insurance firm.

Duskin's biggest single contribution was $2000 from a lady conservationist, then $1500 from a local art patron.

The measure was defeated—partly because of a careless error: the way it had been drawn up, it would have abolished existing forty-two-foot limits in certain parts of the city while creating the city-wide seventy-two-foot limit. But it made a respectable showing: No—142,399; Yes—86,792. An idea that had seemed outrageously ridiculous when first proposed now appeared quite practicable to a sizable number of voters.

In the course of the campaign, Duskin discovered that the problem he was trying to attack with his initiative—how to keep the city livable—was more complex than it had first appeared. He wrote his supporters his later thoughts on the matter:

> You have to take back control of the place where you live. . . . It may be that the problem is not to stop high-rise alone but to stop the construction of all buildings that raise the density and bring more people into the City. How do you then improve the quality of life and the economic vitality of the City? My hunch is that the only thing that makes sense is to allow only the construction of buildings for the use of businesses that will employ the people who already live here and want to work here.

After the election Duskin let it be known he would continue to fight, unless the city fathers took steps toward his goal. He sent them a list of suggestions, including:

> an independent study of ecological and economic effects of high rises;
>
> a tax on all new buildings to defray cost of services;
>
> increasing bridge tolls and instituting tolls on highways into the city;
>
> banning cars from the best walking streets;
>
> neighborhood control of local planning for parks, buildings, zoning;
>
> a city environmental agency with power to prevent new buildings that would be harmful to the city's liveability;
>
> a law prohibiting political campaign contributions from corporations with an economic interest in the outcome—unless the city was willing to foot the bill for the opposing side.

All these ideas were aimed at the same thing: returning to the people power over their immediate environment.

And once again, in the inner sancti, politicians and their cronies bristled: who is this garment manufacturer, telling *professionals* how to run the city? Who's telling *him* how to make dresses?

"But you know," Duskin reflects, "I think I blew it. This whole last year, I blew it. The problem with everything I've done, I'm beginning to see now, is that I've seen it in terms of advertising. But the net result has been to make me into a character that's now on the verge of being institutionalized. Like Ralph Nader. People expect him to police the fish markets. That's his slot. They don't do it themselves.

"People who should be my friends, like the unions, react to me with anger because of the way I set up the scene," Duskin reflects. "I think maybe I'll go on a fast."

But Alvin, his friends protested when he dropped out of Stanford to found his own school, Alvin, be realistic.

But Alvin, others pleaded when he closed the school to go into the garment business, Alvin, not you!

But Alvin, it's suicidal, ecological allies argued when he proposed the six-story height limit. You've gone too far.

But Alvin, a fast?

Within the garment maker there lurks the teacher. Within the teacher still the student. Erik Erikson's book on Gandhi protrudes from Duskin's jacket pocket.

"I don't know," he says grinning. "I've certainly changed the consciousness of what it means to be a garment manufacturer. I've done more to change that than anyone in the world."

11

Nudging Along the Perceptual Shift: Ro-Non-So-Te

Keith Lampe can't help but be pleased by the presence of so many reporters. They're evidence he hasn't lost his touch with the media even after the past year's total withdrawal. He's launching another media number and the turnout is excellent, really. Two or three TV channels, some radio people, both city dailies and the underground press too, of course.

Surveying the newsmen sipping coffee at the San Francisco Ecology Center, Keith can see he has gauged the extent of psychic change fairly well. A few years ago on most dailies, a concept like Living Creatures Associates would have rated maybe three paragraphs knocked out by a junior rewrite man to be used as a space filler "bright." But today he knows he can expect them to listen. Once again he marvels at the rapidity of the perceptual shift.

His own transformation has been proceeding so fast it's hard to remember, actually, where he was a year ago when he left in search of sense and sanity in the back country. Past paranoia, mellowed and heightened by many hours of chanting the Vajra Guru Mantra—Keith is flying.

NUDGING ALONG THE PERCEPTUAL SHIFT

OM(YE) AH HUM VAJRA GURU PADME SIDDHI HUM

The mantra is a tool to get past ego-consciousness and connect with universal life energy. Still, he can't help but be pleased, at this moment.

His announcement for this news conference had managed to pique curiosity and make a statement at the same time. Thanks to the people at Cranium Press who do free work for the subculture on occasion. Thanks to them, he was able to send out elegant notices printed beautifully by letterpress on off-white bond. Along the top of the page was this quote from Gary Snyder, set in italics:

the most/ Revolutionary consciousness is to be found/ Among the most ruthlessly exploited classes:/ Animals, trees, water, air, grasses.

Then in capitals across the page:

LIVING CREATURES ASSOCIATES

Press Relations
On Behalf of All Lifeforms
Of the Earthly Biosphere
    Ladies and Gentlemen of the Press:
    We at Living Creatures Associates (LCA) are pleased to announce our official opening 11 A.M. Tuesday, March 9, at 710 Montgomery Street, San Francisco.

The "LCA" was a touch suggesting big business, cable addresses. The "pleased to announce . . . official opening" hinted at free drinks, coffee, and pastries. Then came the substance:

As a concept, as a perspective, we are at least three millennia overdue. The present emergencies in the biosphere are preponderantly the result of human-centered thinking—or of no thinking at all. We shall counsel and promote Habitat Thinking, the beginnings of a flexible and informal and partly intuitive rationality which will allow decisions to be made on the basis of all affected lifeforms simultaneously. Beyond anthropocentricity toward biocentricity. Lifeways.

As disasters to the biosphere increase in scope and frequency, journalists are called upon to develop the talents of poets and emerge as storytellers in the best manner of the oral traditions. . . .

If we are to communicate the feelings of these disasters effectively enough to allow people elsewhere to prepare, we shall have to experiment boldly—in the manner, for example, of the *nouvelle vague* film community fifteen years back. One way to get stronger emotional effects is to interrupt conventional expectations of time or sequence. Let a camera rest, say, twenty minutes on limpets continuously sloshed with oil. When this sort of footage makes its way onto the Cronkite Show, the beginnings of the necessary perceptual shift become possible.

Keith knows that, with the media, much hangs on finding the right style—the right cues for recognition, differentiating states of awareness. You have always to remember that people who talk about "pollution" and "environment" are in one mental place (still thinking it's possible to make separations), the people who use "holistic" tend to be in another (moving, but academics), while the "whole-earth" and "world-around" users are generally farther out (or deeper in)—perhaps with the "life-ways" and "life-realms" people.

The trick is to speak to all of them at once. There's hardly time enough for anything else. And you have to speak in a lot of ways at once, combining words, music, dance, theater.

Clothing, for instance, can be significant. For this event, he had selected a work shirt, oil-stained khakis, a roomy bush jacket, eucalyptus pod necklace—an ensemble that did not place him easily within any stereotype. He had tied his shoulder-length hair with leather string into two bunches that hung down on either side of his rather lush beard, and stuck in a single red hawk's feather at the nape of the neck.

The feather was a light touch in deference toward Indians. He had hesitated, however, before signing the announcement with his Indian name, given to him just the other day by the Mohawk poet Blue Cloud. Ro-Non-So-Te: He-Has-A-House. The press accepted even that, however, calling him "Mr. Ro-Non-So-Te" and not—as might have happened a year ago—dismissing him as a fraud because he was not a blood Indian. Things are moving that fast.

Feeling very mellow indeed, Keith waits for the cameramen to finish. They're mostly interested in the little kit fox Dr. Sterling Bunnell brought along. Then he opens with a statement of intent: Living Creatures Associates aims to represent beings on their own terms—whales as whales rather than part of a process called whaling, deer as deer rather than as aspects of fish and game. Clients will include homo sapiens, but only rarely. Emphasis will be on other life forms and on trying to show how men's interests mesh with those of other beings in a common habitat. Today there would be words in behalf of the kit foxes, the blue herons, the American egrets, the pygmy forest in Mendocino County, and the Hopi Indians.

Then, the preliminaries over, Ro-Non-So-Te, AKA Keith Lampe, steps back to allow the event to find its own course.

But first, ladies and gentlemen, we'd like to interrupt this program to give you the story of this Living Creature so far.

Mahina: Flyin' high, Daddy?
Keith: Which way is the ground?

The Epiphanies of Keith Lampe

AS TOLD TO MAHINA DREES AND RASA GUSTAITIS

Told with laughter, free of cynicism or regret.

"I was born in 1931 in Johnstown, Pennsylvania. Went to public school in Detroit, lived in Pittsburgh six years. Chose the

University of Missouri because they had a good journalism school and I wanted to be a journalist just like my pop—he was a Hearst editor; managing editor of the *Detroit Times* and then editor of the *Pittsburgh Sun-Telegraph*. I'd also heard Missouri was a good drinking school and I was just going through that adolescent speed trip, some kind of incredibly sick macho way to make up for your inability to get it together with the women.

"I was a fraternity boy. Sigma Chi. The whole thing—dashing down three flights of stairs naked on hands and knees, with the boys swatting me on the backside and occasionally missing and hitting the head. Played bridge, was trained to date in only a few sororities (Kappa, PiPhi, and Theta, with Tri Delt and DG marginal). I stayed with it four years. But a few seeds for skepticism did get implanted.

"In 1950, between sophomore and junior years, I was a police reporter for the Detroit *Free Press*. No eighteen-year-old would have had that job except for nepotism. This wasn't my father's paper, but it was all within the same little close tribe.

"That summer the police quote seized some blue movies unquote from a black neighborhood. Soon after, they called the press into the formal conference room used for departmental trials. There were all the senior inspectors and inspectors and captains and one or two lieutenants and the three or four of us from the press and we all sat down and watched those films in an atmosphere electric with perversion—in the sense of men of late middle age trying to keep their hands off their cocks. I was a touchy adolescent, not quite so nervous as the nervous system J. D. Salinger showed us in his work, but nervous.

"That summer, also, a friend gave me a draft card which indicated I was twenty-two years old although I was only eighteen. But to use it in bars in Detroit I needed a second piece of ID. The press card said I was eighteen. So a friend of my father's on the *Detroit Times* took me up to the police commissioner and told him my problem: 'Young Keith here can't get served in some of your bars around here because the press card you gave him says he's only eighteen while his draft card says he's twenty-two.' No difficulty with that. 'Have my secretary take care of it on the way out.'

"Also that summer, they gave me a magical little notebook—odd shape and color—that detectives and off-duty cops use to park illegally with. I tried it out even along fire routes and in emergency zones of hospitals and *nobody* ticketed me.

"At eighteen I had an upper-middle-class, white Anglo-Saxon Protestant upbringing. Can you imagine the sanctity of a Hearst newspaper editor's home? So of course I was surprised. That wasn't the way they played it in the newspapers. And I trusted the newspapers because my father worked for one, see?

"Then the Korean war started, halfway through my four college years. I didn't want to be drafted so I took refuge in the ROTC program, thinking that by the time I graduated the war would be over. But the years went by and there it was 1952, and they had a scheme to give me a diploma and a commission simultaneously, one in each hand.

"One or two guys I knew actually tried to flunk out but weren't able to. You had to have total mastery of the material and get everything wrong. Otherwise you'd get something right and they'd pass you. No one had that mastery—to get zero on a true-false test.

"So they got us and we went off to fight one of our country's battles, trained as forward observers. That's the most dangerous job in a war, much worse even than a platoon leader's. The forward observers were the cats with the field glasses, lookouts for artillery fire.

"In the last half of the war the lines were relatively static and it was an artillery duel. And the whole other side was looking for just a brief glint of sun in your field glasses! Just five seconds on your lens! They already had their instruments zeroed in. They knew all the impaction points, all the company headquarters.

Each side had the other totally psyched out. So it became this weird little thing of getting the forward observers as soon as you saw the sun in their field glasses.

"We heard these stories and this is what we were going toward. After they catch the glint of sunshine, all these six- and eight-inch shells come screaming in. You're not going to be able to dodge them because they're so large and they kill in such a wide area. There is no ducking.

"So I started to drink heavily—there was no dope then—and got quasi-alcoholic at age twenty-two. Before leaving for Korea in February, 1953, from San Francisco, I went out with two guys and got so drunk I had what they call a blackout. At about six-thirty that night I knew exactly where I was, all about myself and the people I was with. About two hours later I woke up with these same two people plus three women in the Papagallo Room of the Fairmont Hotel with Billy Eckstine singing "Gloomy Sunday" a few feet away and no sense of remembrance of the women—although knowing that I had been on terms of intimacy with them because of the way they related to me.

"That was a good thing for me to have happen, a nice lesson. I backed away from drinking as soon as I had a chance to . . . which wasn't until a year or two later.

"It was a choice between Japan and Korea at one point and I volunteered for Korea along with a couple of other guys, one of whom was the son of Henry Cabot Lodge.

"One day, when I was officer of the day, checking the perimeter at four A.M., I heard some shooting. So I went to the captain and he said, 'Take three men and a jeep and investigate.' Three men! To me it sounded like a major action. But I went with the three men down to the village. On the way I realized that all I had was a pistol that I hadn't even been trained to use. It was a ceremonial thing for the officer of the day, but I didn't have my carbine with me; this was my only weapon. And I didn't even know where the safety catch was. Riding down toward the shooting I was trying to recall the blackboard diagram at the university!

"And then I realized that even if I had had the carbine, I didn't really believe I could put a man in the sights and pull the trigger. Targets were one thing but to zing one into *flesh?* Wait a minute! I wanted to raise my hand but I was out of school; I had my commission and I was driving toward the shooting.

"Luckily, just before I got there the shooting stopped. This was a rear area and we had instructions never to follow into hills at night. We Americans didn't do it by day, either, actually. The dirty work was done by the Korean National Police. We were the elite, minimizing our risks. Anyway, I went back to camp with a lot to think about.

"I spent only six weeks in Korea. A couple of times we were told to pack up and we packed up and sat around trembling and drinking champagne which was a dollar twenty-five a bottle. Then the whole unit was transferred to Hokkaido. The whole Sixty-First Field Artillery Battalion, part of the Fifth Cavalry Regiment, was transferred. I was really getting flippy by this time. The contradiction between being a pacifist and a lieutenant was really a lot of pressure.

"In spring, 1954, the International News Service [Hearst's wire service] wrote a letter to the army saying they were hiring me for their Tokyo bureau. This was a lie arranged through nepotism to get me out. So I got out and then was mysteriously transferred to Paris by INS. Then, with what I had saved in the army, I took a trip around the world. I was to circle it three times within the next ten years.

"In Aden, I remember, I wandered into the native quarter and an Arab pulled a knife on me. I stood there while that blade was a few inches away from my chest. A goat started nibbling on my fraternity-boy sportscoat. And I was so narcissistically fond of that sportscoat I didn't know whether I should sacrifice it even if that meant taking the knife. That's how much of a clotheshorse I was! It was central to Sigma Chi in that time and place and the training lasted a few years past graduation. Anyway, I backed away. I guess the Arab wanted to make sure I would never enter that quarter again. And I didn't.

"When I returned to the U.S., I was a Stevensonian liberal and my ideas of what I wanted to do for a living had changed. I had wanted to be a newspaper man and was also being prepared to be a public relations executive sometime later. There was some expectation in my family that I would become the vice president in charge of public relations for General Motors because my godfather was, at that time, vice president for public relations for Buick. I was prepping for that—big house in Grosse Point or some fancy suburb of Flint, bar and billiards in the rec room, that sort of thing.

"But when I came back from my trip I was going to be a novelist. I went into the creative writing program at the University of Michigan and wrote a novel there in lieu of an MA thesis, also a few poems and short stories. The novel was a satire of the fraternity boy. I had developed an enormous hatred for myself and was working in satire to get rid of it. But I wrote it so close that some of the people reading, I think, did not even know it was a satire.

"My parents weren't all too happy about the change in my life's direction, so the tensions were pretty strong at home. My mother wanted a prestigious son, not a novelist. My father had this idealistic newsman's adherence to objectivity so he didn't try to dissuade me. But occasionally he couldn't stand it anymore and he'd say something and—coming out of all this tension—it was devastating. He was really articulate.

"After the University of Michigan, I spent a semester at Columbia. So far, by some incredible luck, I had had at Missouri a whole semester of John Neihardt reading his own poetry; and at Michigan, Austin Warren's very spiritual, intimate, creative writing seminar. Warren was a great person, though not well known. He was one of the modest fathers of the New Criticism with his book *The Theory of Literature*, written with René Wellek. Then at Columbia, eight or ten of us had a seminar with Daisetz Suzuki.

"Just before Columbia, I spent Labor Day weekend as the house guest at the marvelous oceanside home of Henry Cabot Lodge in Beverly, Massachusetts. His son, Henry Sears Lodge, was an army friend. We had this elegant weekend of boating and martinis. The Ambassador—he was ambassador to the U.N. at the time—had to cut short his weekend because of some crisis in the Mideast. But he was there the first night and he said something like, 'For the last twenty years in politics I've been trying to overcome all of the various contradictions and difficulties, and at last I've entered into nirvana.'

"It wasn't a word used much at the time, 'nirvana.' But as he was saying this, one of his hands was beating compulsively on an arm of his chair. I don't think he was aware of it. But I wondered —what kind of nirvana is *this?*

"From his nirvana I went to Suzuki's. I had developed a paperback interest in him at the University of Michigan. Also in Tillich. I went to New York partly to catch up with Tillich who was supposed to be at Union Theological Seminary. I was digging existentialism and Zen both.

"After a semester in New York—one course at Columbia, one at Union—I went to Pittsburgh to save money to go to Denmark to study Kierkegaard. I worked for the *Pittsburgh Press* on the copy desk for six months and lived with my parents way in the suburbs. I didn't have a car, so that meant getting up at four A.M. to get into the city by seven.

"But I did learn a few more things about the newspaper business. I saw a story disappear between the first and second editions because in it a Norwegian urban specialist had said Pittsburgh had a slum. And Pittsburgh didn't have any, dig?

"In 1956, I enrolled in the Danish Graduate School for Foreign Students in Copenhagen and wrote a paper with the modest title: 'Some Aspects of Lucid Thinking: With Reference to the Positions of Kierkegaard and Tillich.' I talked in it about circular logic: if logic could be visualized it would look like the playful circular flourishes of Paul Klee and not like the straight lines of Occidental logic. My adviser didn't like that too well. He wanted me to pay more attention to the Christian aspects of Kierkegaard.

"That's really a big step, to question the very logic of the thing you're born into. I was there even then. That's interesting. [Keith, 1971, is visibly pleased with this discovery about Keith, 1956.] I've always felt I was qualitatively behind all of the Buddhists because I couldn't get past the reading about it, couldn't quite get into the zendo.

"Anyway, in Copenhagen I also had an incredibly weird romance with a woman who reminded me a little of Lotte Lenya and a little of Marlene Dietrich—a romance that was painful in the manner of that play *Look Back in Anger*. Kind of vanguard neurotic. She was very beautiful and the mistress of one of the most sophisticated men in Denmark and she later became a lesbian.

"In June, 1957, I stopped seeing this woman, I went on to Paris and there actually did become a correspondent for INS. I was there eight months, in one of the prize jobs of the generation —I actually used Ernest Hemingway's typewriter a few times; it was still there. But I was placed in positions so corrupt I could not stand it.

"Ingrid Bergman was one of my favorite creatures at that time, combining the mother thing and the sex thing for me. The guy who usually covered the movie beat was up with the IRA, wading through icy creeks with gelignite bombs strapped around his waist (he died in Spain a year or two afterward, his name was

Ed Ford), so I had to cover the movie beat. I didn't want to, but I had to.

"There was this story from Bombay about Rossellini being on his way to Paris to see Sonali das Gupta. Remember those stories about his Indian mistress? So we were getting wires from New York: get Bergman's reaction.

"I didn't want to but I had to. I gave my card to her doorman. On it I'd written 'Urgent.'

"She asked me in and, with this great big smile, asked: 'Now then, *what* is so urgent?'

"It was horrible. I said, 'Well, Miss Bergman, we have this story from Bombay. . . .

"And she looked at me and said, very slowly: 'Well. I'm sure . . . if he . . . were . . . coming he would . . . let me know.'

'Thank you, Miss Bergman,' I said. And on the way to the door I turned and said, 'You sure have been patient with us of the press all these years, Miss Bergman.'

"And she said: 'Oh yes. I find I must see you *all* and answer *all* your questions because if I don't you tell *lies*.'

"So. That was the heaviest experience of all. Then there was the Camus thing. I wanted to interview him but my bureau chief said no, who's he? A month later, he won a Nobel Prize and every journalist in Paris wanted to interview him. So he tried to get rid of all of us at once at a cocktail party and interview at his publisher's, Gallimard.

"My bureau chief said, 'Ask him anything you want to, Lampe, but be sure to find out if he plans to come to the U.S. sometime soon.'

"I couldn't believe it. Such a vulgar question! How could I possibly? The bureau chief was a typical alcoholic, burned-out newsman who still had, in a superficial way, a 'heart of gold.' He was totally copped out to the system yet trying to believe he had integrity. I was starting to feel culturally different. I had some fancy questions· on existentialism that probably would have surprised him, coming from an American, but I was too embarrassed. I made myself ask him the bureau chief's question and he looked at me with raised eyebrows and said 'Évidemment, évidemment.'

"I left Paris in January or February, 1958, just before INS merged with United Press to form UPI. In retrospect I was incredibly humiliated at what I had done. We had all been into guilt in graduate school. That's what I didn't like about the New Criticism—the way it used T. S. Eliot's 'Lovesong of J. Alfred Prufrock' as a model of behavior—'Do I dare to eat a peach?' That incredible diffidence and self-pity.

"So I got into this self-pity and guilt thing about 'what they made me do.' When the ship docked in New York I was listed in the press as one of several 'prominent people' disembarking and that freaked me even more. I knew I wasn't prominent.

"So I took a job as night switchboard operator in New York and, six weeks later, went to Alaska, to work as clerk-typist on the DEW line—like a pennywhistle T. E. Lawrence into the RAF barracks!

"The idea was that I'd read a lot and write the great American novel. I took up heavy books—Heidegger's *Being and Time*, Sartre's *Being and Nothingness*. But after a year I couldn't read any books, I'd just flip through a few pages of *Life*. I couldn't concentrate.

"It was too crowded. We were all cooped in on this little island, not even permitted to go down to the Eskimo village because there were too many of us; we would overwhelm them. I never had a room of my own that whole year. I stayed in rooms of people who were in the temperate zone on vacation or business.

"The idea of the DEW line—part of the paranoia of politics—was to keep a lookout for enemy aircraft or missiles and warn Colorado Springs. I saved a thousand dollars a month—seven hundred dollars on salary, three hundred dollars on poker winnings—and typed thousands of identical forms, over and over:

work records, pay checks. After eleven and a half months I went down on vacation and never returned even though they had a big bonus if you finished your eighteen-month term.

"I came back ten thousand dollars richer but also thirty pounds heavier. Bovine in mind and body I wandered listlessly and slightly aphasiac for many months through the temperate zone. I wandered through Mexico, then down to Japan where I met Gary Snyder, Joanne Kyger, and in their company began to sense the first stirrings of a better future.

"Gary became one of my teachers. His first didacticism was to get me out of those button-down shirts, suits, and ties. He told me how Allen Ginsberg changed sartorially in the week he wrote *Howl*. He had worn neckties till then. But one night, after that poem, he walked into the San Francisco bar where the poets used to read to each other in the mid-fifties and he was totally transformed.

"I met Ginsberg in Calcutta in 1962. He and Peter Orlovsky were living in a slum hotel, wearing loin cloths, smoking opium, taking showers every couple of hours on the roof. It was terribly hot.

"I was traveling pretty comfortably all this time—wearing suits, staying in hotels. In Katmandu I rented a bicycle and that's about the farthest I got from the tourist economy that time round. The third time round was with my wife Judy, whom I'd met in Korea. She was there as the wife of an artillery lieutenant. We played tennis together at the officers' club in Seoul. When I got back to the States in '62 she was back too—and about to leave the lieutenant. She got a divorce; we returned together to Kyoto. I started a novel with the heroine based on my Copenhagen romance. On the way back to the U.S. we took the trans-Siberian railroad across Russia—four and a half days from Irkutsk to Moscow. You might find this hard to believe, but all across Siberia it was incredibly hot. We sailed from Copenhagen in August, ending my third trip around the world.

"Sometime while we were en route, there occurred the triple murder of the SNCC [Student Non-violent Coordinating Committee] workers in Mississippi. That struck deep. Maybe it broke through my neo-cortex and hit straight into my animal brain, I don't know.*

"Then as I was visiting my parents in Detroit, I saw a picture, in the old *Saturday Evening Post*, of Bob Moses of SNCC. He looked like some young contemporary Gandhi—as, by the way, one of the young black leaders in the Attica prison revolt did, from the picture in the paper the other day. The story seemed to bear this out. So I went back to New York, walked into the SNCC office and asked for voter registration. My idea was to go to Jackson and pick up where they had left off."

At this point, we conclude the first segment of Keith's recollections. We meet again a couple of weeks later at our house.

Keith has arrived elated by an encounter downtown with a fellow in a crewcut. The man had complimented him on his hawk feather and asked why he wore it. Keith explained that he was trying to learn from the Indians. The man had nodded and volunteered that when he and his son go camping with a YMCA group, they take on Indian names. He's Big Moon; his son is Little Moon. So Keith offered to arrange for a visit by a genuine Indian. And then he told the man he was trying to learn from Indians because our civilization had failed.

And the man had *nodded in agreement!* He *agreed* that American civilization had *failed!*

"I sense that something happened to that guy recently that

---

* Keith's reference is to the theory that man has evolved three brains, each complete and enveloping the one preceding: the reptile brain (limbic node), concerned with survival; the mammal brain (cortex), capable of love; and the new brain (neo-cortex), containing man's spiritual energy.

was as deep as what happened to me in 1964 after that SNCC murder. That's how I could get into this close conversation with him. A year ago he would have terrified me because he would have looked like a redneck to me, like someone who'd shoot me out of his pickup truck with a shotgun. And now I can get close with him and get him to agree that we have to bring Indians forward because they are the only models we have of successful living within the natural cycles of this place and that our thing failed, simply failed. I said it to him in a gentle way, not trying to lay any anger in it. When he sees I'm not personally angry at him he agrees. He's been trained enough in American common sense to *see* it's failed.

"I think large numbers of Americans, average people, are now going through the kind of things that I went through in 1964. There are incredibly deep psychic changes among average people, coming off environmental news. They too, maybe, are freaked back into the mammal brain in the same way.

"When I went to SNCC in New York I was very new to the idea of idealism and the Movement. My romantic notion was that I'd pick up exactly where those three guys had left off in their street-to-street voter registration. If they stopped at 15 Magnolia Lane, I'd pick up at 17 Magnolia Lane.

"But when they found out I was a journalist, they wanted me to do press relations. So I spent only one day in Jackson, then was shipped to Atlanta to fill in for Julian Bond on press relations, together with another guy named Francis Mitchell.

"I was really naïve, having been out of the country so long and getting the news just through *Time* Magazine, mostly. Now here I was, being awakened at four thirty A.M. to do the press relations on the latest atrocity in McComb, Mississippi. I'd get terrified phone calls from these towns like McComb: 'Can you get some police officers to come and scare these people away? They've got us surrounded. Try, please, to get the police to come down. Can't you call them and imitate a journalist?'

"So that's where I started my imitations of overground journalism—speaking in their style—which was useful later in the anti-war movement. I'd pretend to be this powerful network newsman getting angry on the telephone at the police. It was the only trick I could offer.

"In the summer, 1965, there was this thing in Washington called the Assembly of Unrepresented People, sponsored by the Committee for Non-violent Action. It started on Hiroshima Day and ended on Nagasaki Day. Bob Moses (he later changed his name to Bob Parris) was one of the architects of it, also Dave Dellinger, Staughton Lynd, and Bob Ockene, whom I didn't know then but who was soon to become my best friend.

"That gathering was seminal to the formation of the Movement on the East Coast because someone thought to get those attending to sign their names and addresses on a huge scroll. Out of that came a mailing list. And that was how, months later, I got a notice in the mail that some veterans were starting a group against the war.

"The first meeting was in fall of 1965. At that time I was working as editor of two book clubs—Behavioral Science Book Service and the Library of Urban Affairs.

"It was a weird job, dealing with psychoanalysts, psychiatrists, psychologists, a few sociologists, and anthropologists. I was shocked to learn how archaic their reading tastes were. Most of them were still reading those basic Freudian texts, and were closed to any kind of healthy innovation. I had to write these glossy 'reviews' that weren't really reviews at all, only sales pitches. The decision had already been made to offer the book and so you didn't pan it. The idea was to sell a lot of copies.

"Anyway, the job was just too dishonest so I lasted only four months in it. It was during this time that I met Bob Ockene. He was editor at Bobbs-Merrill and he called me up one day and invited me for lunch the next day, to discuss some books he thought the club might offer. That same evening I went to the first meeting of the veterans and we started, some thirty or forty of us, a group called Veterans and Reservists to End the War in Vietnam.

"I walked out of that meeting with Myron Shapiro, who, at that time, was editor of the Mid-century Book Club. At the door, someone offered to share a cab up the East Side with me. I got in and there in the back seat was another passenger. He introduced himself and turned out to be the fellow who had called me from Bobbs-Merrill just a few hours ago.

"By the time the next day's luncheon rolled around we didn't talk about books much at all. We talked about the war and how to resist it, about the power of a group of veterans. Ockene had been in Korea too, though after the war.

"So that was my entrance into the Movement, really. The SNCC episode was too brief to count. We burned discharge papers and did a lot of other things. And we were listened to because we were veterans. We got a niche in the media as a reasonable voice.

"Between the start of the veterans' peace group and the Chicago convention in 1968, I was arrested seven times. The first was on Hiroshima Day, 1966, when a dozen of us tried to get into an elevator in midtown Manhattan to complain to the Dow Chemical Company people about napalm. Another time about sixty of us—including A. J. Muste and my wife Judy—were arrested for blocking an entrance to an induction center in Manhattan. The next one was for trying to board a U.S. destroyer in the Hudson River as part of a protest. Then in Washington, six weeks before the march on the Pentagon in 1967, for throwing leaflets in the Senate gallery complaining about war and racism.

"I remember I was nervous. I tried to throw the leaflets very slowly and gently, like the Pope giving a blessing, to make sure they [the guards] saw that they were only leaflets. I knew they were armed and dangerous. We struck it lucky on that one. We thought we might be charged with a felony but it turned out we'd hit an incredible loophole: the penalty for disorderly conduct on federal property was a maximum fifty-dollar fine. That came from the time when the federal government was held in much suspicion, I guess.

"The fifth arrest was at the Pentagon; the others were during Stop the Draft Week in Manhattan.

"At the Pentagon we were held for a long time in this van. It was totally dark and so crowded we had to stand. The temperature was, I'd say, in the 130s. I was fortunate to have the luxury of being able to see outside through a little airhole. I would have been hysterical without it, I think. But other people didn't even have that, yet their calm was so beautiful. They gradually stopped talking to conserve energy and oxygen and began to breathe shallowly. Occasionally we'd pound on the door.

"That experience frightened me but it also made me admire the kind of people I was in with. It was Bob Ockene who saw beyond—that there were many of these people, and that they needed some form of expression. Bob Ockene was one of the original architects of Yippie. History tends to credit five people—Ed Sanders, Paul Krassner, Abbie Hoffman, Jerry Rubin, and me. But that's an oversimplification—characteristic of how inaccurate and oversimplified history is even when it is well-intentioned and written by relatively bright people.

"Bob Ockene was one of the earliest spirits of the thing. He stayed out of it partly out of a real modesty and partly because he already considered himself as something of an infiltrator, needing something of a cover to keep going effectively at Bobbs-Merrill. He was bringing out effective books like the *Marihuana Papers, LSD and Psychotherapy*, a volume by Dave Dellinger, Barbara Deming's *Prison Notes*, something by Carl Oglesby of SDS. He and Allen Ginsberg both must be credited as founders of Yippie.

"Bob was also one of the first to become disappointed with Yippie. He felt the first action was superb—a satire on the pre-dawn raid at the Stony Brook campus of New York State University. They'd actually raided the dorms, pulled students out of bed, searched the place.

"So we got Country Joe, a couple of the Fugs, a few other musicians, and went off toward Stony Brook at four A.M. It was still winter, and cold. The other side was doing its comicbook thing, trailing with plain-clothesmen. At one point, on this deserted road on Long Island, the light changed to amber as our first car went through a crossing. I wanted to see what the plain-clothes people behind us would do so I went through just as the light turned to red. Sure enough, the car behind just kept going. Right on through.

"They had about forty policemen at the front gate of the campus, so we set up outside and did some music. A couple of hundred students joined us and we had a very festive atmosphere from dawn till about noon when people got tired and went home. Someone who was on the Stony Brook faculty at the time said that event had a seminal influence on the place and that even now there are certain nice qualities than can be traced back—if you're careful—to that infusion of energy. It was an action rooted in reality, dealing effectively with a pre-dawn dope raid by satirizing it. But Bob Ockene felt that later actions were too much media presentations. They were still good, I thought, but Ockene was such a beautiful purist.

"I don't think he knew yet that he had leukemia. He died of it in December, 1969. I got the news he was dying while I was in Colorado, at Libré [community] and got to New York in time to see him. He recognized me, I think, but he couldn't say much. He just kept repeating, every half-hour or so: 'Afterwards/ all together/ each other.' Over and over, for about five or six hours. It was his final vision of a total human community in unity. Now it's become the minimum. We have no choice.

"At the time Yippie began, I was teaching English as a foreign language in Queens College. But as I got more and more into the movement, my activity in the streets felt more relevant. Before leaving in early 1968, I let my hair grow. And the liberal faculty members, who had been tolerant of my arrests, started getting nervous about the hair. They probably all have long hair themselves now.

"That year, 1968, was the incredible Yippie roller coaster into Chicago. Martin Luther King and Robert Kennedy murdered, all the burning cities—it was quite a roller coaster to ride. We wanted, in Chicago, to create a festival of life as an antidote to the festival of death sponsored by Mayor Daley. But all of us had forebodings.

"I won't go into the Chicago experience. It's been described by David Lewis Stein, an overground journalist, in *Living the Revolution* [Bobbs-Merrill]. Afterward, I came out here, as you know. I couldn't stand to stay in New York anymore. Also, I had decided that the situation had gotten too serious for laughter."

"You've come full circle, then, back to where you were with the Yippies, haven't you? Now you're saying it's so serious we'd *better* sing and dance and laugh."

"In a sense, yes—but the humor now is different—it's no longer reactionary—not so much *against*. Now what I see is something like the blockbuster humor of Mae West and W. C. Fields and Groucho Marx. Mae West saying: 'Are you packing a rod there, in your pants, big boy, or are you just glad to see me?' Nothing to do with politics per se. Or Groucho, pulling out his watch, holding on to a man's wrist: 'Either this man is dead or my watch has stopped.'

"I'm thinking now more and more in terms of physics, as helping to provide an infusion of energy. It's essential to stay high now because everyone is so close to panic. The fear is so great. You can hear it in the newscasters' voices. Sterling Bunnell seems to have the same field theory. He said the other day: 'Well, we just have to keep ourselves going at ever higher levels of energy input-output.' Something like that.

"The other big difference between then and now is that of the guys I was with in the police van at the Pentagon, more people now have the stamina, more can remain clear through the quanta of persecution and pressure all of us have to put up with. The quanta is higher now too. So that's where yoga and meditation and chanting come in. Remember the Weatherpeople, in one of their messages, were talking of 'the yoga of alertness'?

"As a fraternity boy I was a comedian, I remember. So the latest thing to me now is to fill out chant and dance with humor."

But wait a minute, how did we get from Chicago to Groucho Marx? Where does Living Creatures fit in? Isn't that where this story started?

Keith has flipped on the radio to KSAN and the room is now full of rock music. Keith and Mahina are dancing, their hair flying, arms flailing, entranced, non-verbal. Keith's next book, he told me, will be *Beyond the Verbal*. Or perhaps (books kill trees) he'll start radio station KAWW (pronounced like a crow's kaw), featuring news from Living Creatures Associates. Or perhaps he'll do Om-ah-Hum, the *inner* magazine of body, speech, and mind, with chant and dance. Anyway, I'll try to fill in the rest.

Further Epiphanies:

FROM BURPEE SEEDS TO SEED SYLLABLES

Keith, Judy, and little Issa came to Berkeley after the Chicago convention and Keith started doing occasional pieces for the *Berkeley Barb*. One afternoon, when he was on his way to some protest demonstration, Gary Snyder persuaded him to go to the Sierra Club's Wilderness Conference instead. The eco-doom information he picked up there fit right into his Chicago-generated paranoia, expanding it to planetary proportions. Keith decided to start a radical ecology newsletter, the *Earth Read-Out*. He mailed it to people he thought would be interested and to the underground press. It ran as a column in several little papers. In it, he began to talk about going "beyond humanism" and crossing the "species barrier."

In May, 1970, more than a year and some twenty issues of the *Read-Out* later, the Lampes and three other families decided to leave "typewriter ecology" for the real stuff of life by moving out into the country. They left for the Sangre de Cristo Mountains in the Southwest to purchase land and start farming.

I received three more *Read-Outs,* postmarked Las Vegas, New Mexico. They told of troubles in making the transition from city to rural life. There was tension, Keith wrote, between two types of longhairs—the survival-oriented and the apocalyptic. "One kind of person will wish to continue to take chances even on the edge of the abyss; the other will struggle to live all the way into old age despite actuarial possibilities." He left no doubt as to his own inclinations: "The central contradiction in the longevity trip is that in the process of stretching your life as far as it will go you risk becoming so boring no one wants to grow old with you."

He tried for a generous perspective:

The difficulties encountered in attempting to create one's own culture in a short space of time are staggering—and understandably, the early answers are regressive. At present in the Southwest the most popular regressive answer involves an attempt to imitate the nineteenth century American small-farm-on-the-frontier trip: skirts down to the ground for the women (preposterous waste of fabric & implications of flesh shame, etc.) glorification of big families, mawkish attitudes toward children and pets and a very plain—drab, really—style. It will take shaman-poets to pull it all together and provide a progressive answer.

The third issue hinted that boredom was turning to restlessness. Keith had queried some of the shaman-poets on whether they thought the "centralist Nixon regime may coopt the ecology movement."

Allen Ginsberg thought not: "Present ruling establishment Visible Nixon Invisible white magicians down to NY Times middle class diagnose neither extremity of ill, nor moral social economic structural pathology of police state capitalism & so will not be able to understand or mobilize communal medicine radical enough to arrest much less cure the ill."

Abbie Hoffman thought not: "Earth Day was a fuckin bore—because so many establishment types supported it."

Gary Snyder's reply showed he did not see the question as relevant:

> The Movement has fallen into the hands of Romantic Adventurists and Left Opportunists. The Establishment is like a mired Mammoth, still very strong. On both sides there are disoriented individuals who are secretly happy to have what they think is a license to kill. The real changes will begin when the people of America—black and white together—begin to feel the pressures of the ecological crisis mounting and pullulating right in their own homes and minds, and not until then. Perhaps the 1980s.

(Within a few months, Snyder's new poem "Spel" would appear, printed as broadside, taking off from this observation.)

Keith had answered his own question with another:

"Two years ago genocide was the largest horror most of us could imagine—and we prepared to die resisting it. Now most of us lucky enough to have time/energy for quiet thinking see genocide as a characteristic of a larger biocidal situation. What, besides preparing to die and preparing to live, must we do to resist biocide?"

An acquaintance returning from the Southwest reported seeing Keith striding around, in dark glasses, his head down, scowling. It was hard for me to visualize him as farmer.

So I should not have been surprised when he turned up again, in mid-October, 1970, in San Francisco. He was sun-burned, and had grown a lush beard. His attire was counter-culture, country-style: workshirt, aggressor pants (durable khakis with many deep pockets on legs and hips), logging boots, a buckskin knife in hand-made sheath and, rather incongruously, a brand new white ten-gallon hat.

The hat was a prop, he said, to ease his way through territory hostile toward longhairs. He hoped it might suggest the Texas rancher. Three years ago, in Chicago, while he was doing press relations for the Yippies, he had carried around a tennis racket and found it helped deflect police. Just a tennis player passing through on his way to the courts.

Was he serious? Nobody, but nobody, looking at Keith, could mistake him for an eccentric member of mainstream USA. It wasn't just the hair. It was—well . . . *everything* about him.

Leaving the hat on the hall table, he came in for lunch. He seemed more relaxed than when I had last seen him, but also distracted. It was hard, he said, to get used to doing four things at once again after five months of one thing at a time. He had not realized how discontinuous and jangly the city was. Also, the fear level had risen. The situation seemed to have grown so explosive that he was beginning to think it might be a mistake to add to the fear in any way. What was needed now, perhaps, was some plain survival information to help people stay calm and in touch while preparing to die. Maybe all angry rhetoric should be laid aside for a while.

Mm, I said. It seemed to me Keith had a tendency to make broad generalizations about the state of the nation based on his own momentary state of mind. That day, the papers carried a story about that explosion in the brownstone in New York's Greenwich Village in which two young people were killed, apparently by bombs they had been making. Keith knew them both. He reflected that most of his friends were now either dead or in jail.

He had tried to prepare for his own death during these past five months, living amid the incredible doomed beauty of the Southwest, its fragile ecology about to be sacrificed to soot-spewing power plants that would feed air-conditioners in Los Angeles and Phoenix.

NUDGING ALONG THE PERCEPTUAL SHIFT

The *Read-Out* family had bought 300 acres 7400 feet up the slope of a mountain. It was good farming land, with an extraordinarily good supply of stream water. They had laid in a vegetable garden and managed to raise squash, tomatoes, a few green peppers, corn, an abundant crop of peas.

Keith had few of the skills needed for life on the land. His biggest contribution to the community, he felt, was a strong right arm developed by pitching baseball in his fraternity-boy years and playing tennis in Korea. So he chopped a lot of wood and dug a lot of holes, and thought a great deal about the near-certainty (or so it seemed) that civilization would collapse in twenty years at the most.

Twenty years. After that, the few surviving humans would probably live as nomads. Eco-consciousness had now evolved into its fourth phase: "from conservation to literal-sentimental ecology to hard-science ecology to magic, mysticism, meditation, esthetics and preparations for death."

Frightening—if you saw the situation in a Western time perspective. But if you could relate to Eastern metaphysics, everything changed. "Vedantic metaphysics can be a help in getting accustomed to an earlier-than-expected death," Keith offered in one of the last *Read-Outs*. And the transition to the appropriate state of mind was probably more easily made on the land than in noisy cities.

The women were the ones who had it the hardest in New Mexico. They had to put up with being whitey in a brown world, hippie in a straight world, and chickie in a man's world, in Judy's words. They, in fact, had asked Keith to look around, while he was on the Coast, for possibilities of resettling in more congenial surroundings; somewhere up north, perhaps.

There had been no trouble with the immediate neighbors. But in the next canyon, at the Kingdom of Heaven Commune, a girl had been raped and a young man murdered. That was an open commune. It accepted everyone and it therefore had turned into a crash pad for a lot of kids who had no sense of the place; who thought nothing of bathing nude or walking around with a hole in the fly within sight of people to whom public nudity was an inflammatory outrage.

After that murder, everyone on Keith's farm slept with guns next to the bed. They were afraid that the thirty vigilantes who had attacked the Kingdom of Heaven would attack them next. The police were also in the area. They had found pot while investigating the rape and murder. So Keith's farm family, being draft resisters and people with multiple arrest records as well as longhairs, were nervous. So nervous, the family split.

Steve Beckwitt wanted to take down a bright-colored tepee because it might signal "hippie" to the vigilantes. The rest of them had agreed. But when the time came to actually do the thing, they couldn't. Keith remembered the "Four Changes": "There is no need to survive." So the tepee stayed but the Beckwitts went.

"I find," Keith said, "that I'm paying more and more attention to style. I guess you'd call it style. This morning, for instance, I had to go see an editor whom I don't know, at a semi-hip publishing house. I thought for a long time whether to wear a hat or not. Finally decided not to. When I read I seem to notice style more than what someone is trying to say. It's as though the *sound* of it counted more than the words."

He collected his hat and went off. From that day on, we were friends. Our paths no longer crisscrossed. They now ran parallel.

He called a few days later to deliver what I would come to know as his news broadcasts. As counter-culture newsman, he not only carries bulletins to the overground media, he transmits orally from house to house within his tribe—of which Mel and I begin to be members.

He's been up north, talked with various counter-culture shamans, arranged for some soothing survival pieces for the *Read-Out*: an article on vasectomies by someone who just had one; a letter

NUDGING ALONG THE PERCEPTUAL SHIFT

from Peter Coyote, Digger, to country neighbors; a few poems by a Mohawk poet, Peter Blue Cloud. The big news is his meeting with Blue Cloud. It happened in the Free Bakery in Oakland. The Indian walked up to him, put a hand on his shoulder, and looked into his eyes: Keith had never seen him before. Later, he would tell Keith: "Something told me I should speak with you."

They went into a bar together and then to an Indian fish fry, which, Keith said, turned out to be "some kind of Valhalla." The men called each other's names and ran down each other's bravery and fine qualities, the way their grandfathers had probably done before battle. And they talked of taking up arms in the spring.

It seemed that the Indian militants felt that desperate, said Keith. Of course they would be massacred. But even so, he now felt called to stand with them. So he would go back to the farm for what time was left. He'd recommend the family stay put for the interim. In the spring he'd be back.

"Mm," I said. Indian uprisings couldn't have been more remote from my realities. I was about to take a bath, about to go out to dinner and the movies. Indian uprisings were movie stuff. The Alcatraz episode had provided final proof that there were no more Indians left capable of any real confrontation. The Indians had invaded the island and settled down in the abandoned federal prison. Nobody could believe it was for real, at first. Real Indians! Delighted San Franciscans packed boats full of children, blankets, and food and sailed across to see. But the federal government simply ignored the whole thing. So the rebellion just sort of faded away, though no set-up could have been more favorable. So what was Keith talking about now?

Less than three weeks later, he called again. He was at the airport and did we have a bed for the night. He and Judy had split after seven years together.

He stayed two days and seemed to be taking his pain extraordinarily well. He even managed to laugh at himself a little. On the third day he rolled up his sleeping bag and headed toward the ocean. The sleeping bag, a few items of clothing and some books and papers were now his only possessions.

We did not hear from him for a few days. Then he came by on an afternoon with Margot Patterson Doss, who writes a walking column in the *San Francisco Chronicle*. Every Sunday she describes a walk you can take and what to watch for en route. It's an innocent sort of column, on the surface. But she has used it well—to get billboards removed, highway projects stopped, new parks built, and expose odd deals between real estate interests and the city. All this by simply scheduling the right walk at the right time, with the right instructions.

Mayor Joseph L. Alioto once sat in the studio of KQED-TV, waiting to go on the air to answer citizen questions, when he happened to look into a set and see a walk of Margot's being broadcast on the local news show. She led the viewer through Fort Mason, a choice piece of land on the waterfront that the army was about to relinquish. On the city's master plan it appeared as a park. However, the head of the Parks and Recreation Commission, of all people, had recommended that it be privately developed. Odd—on the surface. Not so odd when it was pointed out that he was Walter Shorenstein, president, also, of the Milton Meyer Company, a giant real estate concern. Alioto had appointed a real estate man as guardian of citizens' park interests. But the way it all came together in Margot's little walk made the mayor so mad he stomped right into the studio and exploded on camera.

Most of the time Margot stays behind the scenes in conservation battles. Several years ago, for instance, four women in Santa Cruz asked her help in fighting a highway that was planned to run through an old part of town and the brand-new university campus. She asked each of the women to produce a dime. When they did she told them they had now paid their dues as members of a new organization, which they must name. One woman was to be president, one vice president, one secretary, one treasurer. She gave the dimes to the treasurer. "Now you're a pressure group," she told them. "You can start protesting and expect to get into the newspaper." The highway project was defeated. Margot Doss's name was never publicly associated with the issue.

She looks as innocuous as her column too—at first glance. Slender, of medium age, with curly brown hair, and plain round glasses. But at second glance you notice that casual sort of elegance, the sensuality in the lines of her mouth, the alert amused look in her eyes, and you know she's capable of surprises. She is, in fact, a wise and witty lady, known for her lively literary dinner parties at which her very special plum pudding never fails to lift spirits to mellow heights.

Keith has been staying with Margot and her husband John, who recently left a successful pediatrics practice to become a community medicine man and poet on the coast. Some say he's now something of a shaman.

Thanks to the Dosses, Keith has revived. He talks about a girl named Suzanna who goes around making people dance. When she meets a man who's too sad to dance she stays with him until he's dancing again. Apocalyptic bliss.

"Keith was talking such old man talk that we figured the best thing to do would be to throw him with a beautiful girl," Margot explained, her eyes twinkling.

Tomorrow, said Keith, he would go, with John Doss and poet Joanne Kyger, to look for Blue Cloud. He wants to know if the confrontation *has* to be this spring. He's hoping it might be a little later, maybe as late as next year.

"Well," he said, a couple of days later, "seems there's more time than I expected. Blue Cloud has slowed down quite a bit."

They found him in a farm house in the Sierra foothills. They drove there stoned on seed syllables, playing some "guerrilla cassettes" Keith happened to have—tapes of Buddhist chanting by Tibetan monks, Allen Ginsberg, Gary Snyder, and Masa.

Keith is upset, by the way, at not having heard from Gary since he sent him a letter after that first meeting with Blue Cloud. Maybe, he thought, Gary was irked because he had sent a carbon of the letter to Ginsberg. Maybe Gary thought transmissions should be made more slowly—his own letters came beautifully inked on small sheets of bond. Maybe Gary was even moving toward a time when it would all come by word of mouth. The newsmen would simply go around, telling their stories.

In Barbados, a friend of mine told me, villages are built with little houses all in a row along a single street. During the day, everyone rolls up the screens between them and you can look down the line and see what's going on in each one. Certain women carry news from village to village and house to house, making no separation between public and private. So and so has troubles with her daughter. Coconuts are plentiful on the other side.

These women sit down and exchange such information. So people find out what they need to know and share in each other's lives at the same time. Now Keith, sitting down on my couch, is like those women.

Playing the cassettes and chanting along, Keith, Joanne, and John Doss drove through the valley and into the mountains. They picked up a black hitchhiker and he too joined in. But when he asked where they were from, Keith suddenly felt that old threat of invasion. If they named a town, he thought, everyone would rush to get there right away. So he said Marin County and the man left it at that.

Blue Cloud was staying with a bunch of longhaired pacifists. He had been there two weeks and already he was—well, he really wasn't doing anything, he was . . . well, enjoying himself.

Above the fireplace, with the flames licking up at it, these pacifist kids had a highway sign that said: SLOW. Not STOP with THE WAR magic-marked in; not DETOUR, just SLOW. And they had cooled out Blue Cloud to the point where he didn't even mention the coming war with the government. One of these blond kids even said, "You know, when Blue Cloud came here he was sort of militant but we think we've turned him around."

He didn't seem to want to talk about anything, really. He gave only about two minutes to business and then picked up a guitar and started to sing and to get drunk on the Red Mountain wine they had brought along as a gift. During those two minutes he told Keith only that there would be a meeting of Indian leaders on December 23 and that in a few days he'd introduce Keith to Richard Oakes, the Mohawk who led the Alcatraz occupation.

Later he came out of the Drunken Indian act just once more, to tell Keith to look up Sun Bear, who put out *Many Smokes*, a newspaper in Reno. The rest of the time . . . well . . . it had to be said: Blue Cloud didn't have himself quite together. There was that moment with the knife. Someone said something that made Blue Cloud mad and he pulled this knife on one of the kids and started yelling about motherfucking honkies. Keith was sitting down with one of Blue Cloud's poems in his hands. He went through the alternatives—should he shout, step forward, and try to interfere?—and decided that if he could only concentrate all his energy into the poems and not send any of it out there into the room, then Blue Cloud would not stab the kid. He forced himself not to look. After a while he heard the knife drop to the floor. But the tension was still there. The blond kid and Blue Cloud still stood facing each other. Keith wanted desperately to know whether the knife tip had stuck in the floor or whether the knife had just dropped—it was a test of whether Blue Cloud was competent or clumsy. He didn't look up. But he knew from the sound that the knife had dropped.

Then Denise, Blue Cloud's wife, said from where she lay on the couch: "Give me that, Blue Cloud." And Blue Cloud picked up the knife and gave it to her.

"You can't have it back until you learn what a gift is," she said.

And Blue Cloud said: "OK, very strong Pomo. Ok."

Later, Blue Cloud explained to Joanne that he had pulled "a Hemingway number."

Joanne had said: "Oh. I don't like Hemingway."

That set him off again: "You guys ain't Indians. You're a bunch of honkies!"

"Well man, I can't help it," said Joanne.

"Don't pretend you're Indians," said Blue Cloud.

"Sometimes I think I'm a pelican," said John Doss.

"Sometimes I think I'm just a pile of shit," said Joanne. That made Blue Cloud laugh and, relieved, Joanne laughed with him.

But now Denise was angry. She thrust the knife out, giving it back to Blue Cloud: "It's not anymore a gift," she said.

"What's a gift?" asked Joanne.

They sat by the fire and read Blue Cloud's poems, about "Children deformed by man-made tools," and "children forever broken," and "I'm bleeding my history through your universities,/ I'm bleeding through your government walls." Songs and laments they were, in a strong voice.

But Blue Cloud himself, meanwhile, drunkenly strummed a guitar and sang "Ramona," and "He's in the Jailhouse Now."

"Get out of the jailhouse, Blue Cloud," said Joanne, speaking for them all.

Well, it seemed clear to Keith: Blue Cloud didn't have it all together. He was disappointed and puzzled, but also relieved that now "there's a whole summer ahead that I hadn't even planned on."

Could it be, I wondered, that there never was a plan for a spring shootout? Could Blue Cloud have simply read in Keith's eyes, that night they met, that he wanted someone to tell him what to die for and had simply spoken the lines expected?

And was it possible, likewise, that the Mohawk had read what he thought was a message in the gift of Red Mountain wine and become the Drunken Indian on cue, almost by way of politeness?

Or—try a more intriguing possibility: that he was testing the trio of honkey poets. If they could see past his Drunken Indian act they could understand the Indian's condition.

Of course it was more than possible that all was just as it appeared. Maybe Blue Cloud was just relishing the visit of these three people from honkeyland and making fun of their expectations. To each his own reality. I decided I wanted to hear Joanne and John's version.

What I had in mind was a sort of Rashomon—the same story seen by three or four people. But the meeting with Joanne runs its own course. We're invited to dinner at the house of friends, in the village where she lives. Afterward we sit, mellow, together in a room with a fire—Keith, Mel, Terpsichore Suzanna, Margot Doss, some others, Joanne, and me. Joanne is formidable. She laughs a lot, weaves incredible word pictures, and makes you see with her eyes. I'm so overwhelmed I fumble on some expository paragraph of question.

"Could we just get together and trip out on it," she asks, "or does it have to be a straight prose sort of thing?"

I'm anxious to get the words and the facts. The information. Her face grays. "Let's take a rest," she says. "Why don't you just let the tape run. It's trusting your mind to make the connections; trusting it to govern itself."

Government. We both slither into the grayness of endless tiled halls with fluorescent lights and the echoes of secretaries' heels tapping, fingers tapping keys, hurried unseeing passage of bent-shouldered officers of the underdepartment.

"It all comes out of living here," says Joanne. On the Coast, next to the sheer cliffs that drop into the Pacific, at the foot of a sloping mesa, on a little peninsula often covered with fog, with few telephones and fewer television sets.

"I was, in my writing, trying to feel myself in a place—what it feels like to be in a place. Trying to sense what my roots are—

European culture plus a mixture of the East? I've lived in both places. But I'm here, on this ground. So I thought—who knows this ground really well? The Indians did. We aren't using those land instincts and that's why we're fucking it up.

"I read Peter Blue Cloud in the *Earth Read-Out* and I thought: 'Here's a voice that's trying to tell some story about what the land is about. And mixed on top is a very reactionary voice against the white man, like a lot of the politics Keith has been in —reacting against the establishment. I was on a very big high just then and Blue Cloud's voice came in. You know, people who live here start looking like Indians after a while. I've seen the same thing in Big Sur."

At this point we're interrupted by the arrival of two friends who are returning from a walk in the hills with some magnificent *amanitas muscaria* mushrooms—red-topped with white spots; white stemmed, glowing, and poisonous. They place them on the hooked rug in the center of the room. We look at them and sense their damp earth fragrance. There's some discussion about ways to eat amanitas.

I recall that as a child in Lithuania, I saw these mushrooms used in farm kitchens to kill flies. They were also associated in folk tales with dwarves and goblins but I never even wondered why until now.

"Poison things sometimes open up to be other things," says Joanne. "You see, Indian isn't outside. It's in the way people look at mushrooms.

"I felt when I was out there, with Blue Cloud, that he was suffering real pain," she says. "He says his heart is in a steel box under the ground. As the earth suffers he suffers. So he tries to cover up. He takes this persona of the Drunken Indian and he sings English songs like 'Ramona.' And a girl there—she has a face that was very old though she is also very young—sings a long peyote song for her father with a lot of suffering in it about what happened to her people. Then she says: 'This is a terrible weeping cry' and she goes into an Indian chant that is *beautiful*. But she calls it *weeping*. And then she says, 'I want to return to my land' and she looks up and becomes like a Joan Baez on a horse, her hair in the wind—a young American girl *enjoying* it. She recognizes in her spirit she's kind of an American. It's like Blue Cloud saying, 'We can all understand in the same spirit.' And talking about race again. Can he trust the spirit enough to know it's going to be strong enough so he can let go his particular race and come alive right now, so the earth can be taken care of and lived on?"

At one point, Joanne says Blue Cloud was "directing this incredible diatribe against the white man for having killed him and his people and killed the earth. So he's sitting there and telling me this and all of a sudden there was this flash: 'Are you talking to *me*? Is that how you feel about me? Who are you talking to? Was he telling me I killed him? I'd be killing myself. He can't put me on the other side of that fence."

"And I think he knew that too," says Keith. "You kept saying, 'Get out of jail, Blue Cloud.'"

"Well, he's not in jail yet," says Joanne. "Those blues came out of a real place. Don't put them on before you even get there."

"There's a sense in which he's been in jail from the beginning," says Keith.

"But that's the one he has to get over," says Joanne. "I wanted to hear his true voice. At one point he knew who he was—an Indian and a very strong man. Then he flipped into the Drunken Indian again, singing those English songs. I guess I hoped he would be a shaman—a voice that would speak to people."

Later, Blue Cloud would come to visit the village and read a poem he had just written, remembering what Joanne said, "They're trying to jail the ocean." He would not talk to me about the visit of the three poets.

Now Joanne and I stare at the poisonous, vision-inducing mushrooms. Conversation has died down in the room. Somebody puts on a tape we made yesterday at the ranch, of Nanao Sakaki chanting.

"The Indians are so close to nature there is no shadow in their eyes," Nanao said. "But they drink Coca-Cola."

Nanao's chant fills the space.

That visit to Blue Cloud had begun with chanting.

"Chanting—original language, I sit down to chant in the desert and always someone come sit beside me—coyote, rattlesnake, scorpion, lizard—always somebody. And he chanting too!"

Nanao is visiting from Japan, where he is the leader of an unorthodox ashram on a tiny volcanic island. His people live a rigorous life, subsisting on fishing and sweet potatoes, one of the few plants that will grow in the island's soil. A boat visits once a month if the weather isn't too bad. Every year, some of the grass houses are blown away by typhoons. Nanao sits on the edge of the volcano, looking down into it, chanting.

"There is no past, there is no future," Nanao said. "So what happened?

"What time is it?" asks Nanao, sitting across our kitchen table.

"A quarter past five. Exactly."

"So late? A quarter past five?" says Nanao. "The sun goes up; it goes down. There is no time."

Time stretched elastic in and out. Keith laughingly suggests there's no reason we shouldn't all live to a ripe old age.

The ranch was ready and waiting for somebody like—indeed for—Nanao to come and sit, straight-backed in lotus on his round black pillow, looking out at the fog drifting across the mountain. He ends his meditation with the ringing of a little bell. "In the city, air is bad. Sounds too loud. Here much different—clear." Then the long, full-voiced chant. Little Usha chants along.

We've come up to the ranch not knowing whether we'd still find Nanao here. His goings are unpredictable. But the living

NUDGING ALONG THE PERCEPTUAL SHIFT

room's sudden spare neatness was the answer. All the sitting cushions in a single tidy pile. In the stove a tiny fire, perfectly banked. Keith stepped outside and let out a long whoop that echoed twice in the valleys and ended in a chant floating up out of the oak grove below the house. Nanao came out of the grove, a slim figure with small beard, in black and green checked woodsman's jacket, jeans, and soft leather boots.

"Before chanting I hope to offer some Japanese green tea."
He pours it from a tiny brown pot into doll-sized tea cups.
"Just enough. Not to drink. Sip. Tea service original LSD. People have forgotten."

We sip and hold the tea on our tongues. First it's sour-sharp, then gradually it softens. We sit crosslegged on the worn rug in the cabin, watching raindrops waver down the panes of the many-paned windows. Gray windblown oaks outside. The iron-belly stove glows. Usha has fallen asleep. Nanao's chant fills the room with deep peaceful joy sounds. Since he's been here we have given each other full attention and treated each other with regard.

Nanao has never been inside a Buddhist temple. "Too middle class. *My* teacher is ocean."

"You go to yoga class?" he asks me. "Why? Your baby is your teacher. Baby work hard so we can play." And he laughs.

Keith chants with Nanao. He has a good full voice, excellent for a TV or radio newsman. Nanao tells him to go to visit Tarthang Tulku, Rinpoche, a Tibetan lama residing in Berkeley, and to ask to be taught chanting.

Keith follows Nanao's advice.

OM (YE) AH HUM VAJRA GURU PADME SIDDHI HUM

A few weeks later Keith tries to chant one afternoon and can't. His mind is clogged with anger at David Brower, head of Friends of the Earth, with whom he has just had an exchange of letters. He accused Brower of playing along with the prevailing value system through "studio book politics"—printing expensive volumes with pictures of trees at the expense of living trees. Brower responded with the suggestion that Keith's back-country excursion had been an escape from certain realities.

So Keith's mind is full of static, his chest is tight, his throat constricted. He can't chant. And then it comes to him: anger and chanting are incompatible.

Every day Keith chants for at least a couple of hours. At home. After writing or any other kind of work. Driving. Whenever he feels afraid or angry. He begins to talk of becoming a mendicant chanter moving from town to town to help people lift off from fear and anger and see past various mind-walls.

Then those two tankers collide spilling torrents of oil into the Bay and, like nearly everyone he knows, Keith looks for the spot where he can be most helpful. He finds his niche at KSAN, rapping about moving from ecology to epiphany, morality to neurality, from objects to states of mind, from street protest to neuropolitics. He tries to speak slowly, using words in a way that is close to chanting.

It's out of that KSAN experience, and of the chanting, and the days after the oil spill Keith spent helping out with bird rescue efforts, that the idea for Living Creatures developed.

A taped conversation between Keith and Blue Cloud, done at Joanne Kyger's house:

Keith: One problem I haven't been able to resolve. I think the last time I saw you I told you I was tempted to change my name in certain contexts to Laughing Eagle and you said why not. In this press relations firm I'm tempted to move into something like . . . maybe Lightning Eagle because there's something coming out of Buddhism right now that's also very strong.

Blue Cloud: What kind of names do Buddhists have?

Keith: Well, Gary Snyder laid on me a vajra which is like a lightning bolt. He laid it on me because I'm into that chant, in a way.

Blue Cloud: Lightning Eagle? You're taking on two of the strongest connotations available with our people. I wouldn't recommend it. Something might happen to you.

Keith: I see. Well, I'm afraid something *is* going to happen, man, I've had . . .

Blue Cloud: Don't be afraid of something happening.

Keith: Well, I've used the wrong word. I've had a lot of suggestions in the last months that I've got to do a lot of very severe things and go out as far as I can. That chanting, I do that chanting twenty to thirty minutes a day and it helps me a lot. I'm not fearless but I feel less fear than most people around me and I'm able to give because of that. Maybe Lightning Eagle would . . .

Blue Cloud: I've got a name for you: Ro-Non-So-Te.

Keith: What's that?

Blue Cloud: He-Has-A-House.

Keith: He-Has-A-House. I like that. Goddamn! [He laughs, astonished, happy.] Maybe you understand how *nice* that is to hear.

Blue Cloud: I'll write it down. Here. Ro-Non-So-Te.

Keith: Oh, Wow. Ro-Non-So-Te. Ro-Non-So-Te. Is that right?

Blue Cloud: Perfect. I understand it. He has a house.

Keith: That's so beautiful to me. It gives me a lot more confidence.

Blue Cloud: I give you chief's name. I don't know if it was by mistake or what.

Keith: You want me to wait then?

Blue Cloud: No, that's your name. To break it down further,

He-Has-A-Long-House and the long house has six families in it or so, mostly of opposing clans.

Keith: Ro-Non-So-Te.

Blue Cloud and Keith: Ro-Non-So-Te.

Blue Cloud: Ro-Non-So-Te.

Keith: Ro-Non-So-Te.

Ro-Non-So-Te steps away from the microphone yielding to ecologist Sterling Bunnell, who holds in his arms a brown furry animal the size of a large cat, with big ears and round dark eyes. This San Joaquin kit fox will be extinct within the next five years as the California Water Project brings irrigation to the desert in the western part of the Central Valley, says Bunnell. About 90 percent of its habitat will be destroyed.

It's already threatened by pesticides and hunters. The pesticides are dropped from planes to kill rodents. The kit fox eats the rodents and dies too. The hunters shoot it because it's extremely tame and unsuspecting and does not know to stay away from guns. Yet it is a harmless animal that could be much more useful than chemical pesticides as rodent controller, were it given a chance to live and do its natural thing.

The kit fox could be saved, Bunnell says, if refuges for it were established among the irrigated fields. These could be no more than forty square acres in size and could serve the double purpose of also harboring wild bees which, says Bunnell, are much better pollinators than domestic ones. "So the diversity would be beneficial to man. But when we let short-term economic criteria determine what we do, we can't avoid destruction of our environment...."

"This is one of the loveliest creatures on earth," he concludes, while the little fox sits tamely on his arm. "It would be a particular tragedy if it were lost simply because no one cared."

The next speaker is Clarin Zumwalt, naturalist at the Audubon Canyon Ranch near Stinson Beach. He tells of the plight of the American egret which now has a hard time hatching young because its eggs have become thin-shelled and break easily. Yolks have been found to contain high concentrations of DDT which keeps calcium from forming in shells.

So the kit fox and the egret may be doomed to extinction because of a short-sighted drive for more production without regard to environmental cost. So also the Hopi Indians. Jack Loeffler, of the Central Clearing House in Santa Fe, New Mexico, talks of the way sacred Hopi lands in the Southwest are to be mined to fuel power plants that will feed electricity to urban centers as far away as Los Angeles. The plants are being built in the desert partly because they will emit pollutants way beyond what most cities will allow in their vicinity. The first of these plants is already in operation. Its plume of smoke was the last sign of man the astronauts saw on their way to the moon.

"We now have to weigh the life and death of the Southwest against Los Angeles's possible electricity needs," he says. Part of that life are the Hopi. "Their whole tradition is oriented toward a sense of balance with nature. They regard themselves as stewards. But the Hopi tradition will fail. They cannot cope with what is happening in their back yard."

LCA never was an organization. It was a media number, a way to transmit a point of view. Each of Keith's press conferences was a variation on one theme: the need for a shift toward life-centeredness. Each included more music than the one before. The first one ended with ballads delivered by a sweet-voiced young man with mellow guitar. The second began with a bust-through rock session by a group called One, led by Reality. At the third, Allen Ginsberg tinkled a tiny bell. Each of these events was more than a press conference. It was media theater.

In an elegant loft looking out upon Washington Square Park, two blond mountain lions, representing another vanishing species, lie panting on the polished oak floor, surrounded by tastefully framed prints and antique furniture. They have been brought here by a man trying to dramatize a bill to protect them pending before the state legislature. He has them chained to his wrist, like courier pouches. But they're alive and they're scared.

Coyote, of Indians of All Tribes, walks in with Blue Cloud. He looks at the lions. His face twists. He turns and walks out.

The lions are photographed and led away. Focus shifts to a herpetologist who has a plea in behalf of an animal hardly anyone has even heard of: the San Francisco garter snake. Karl Switek speaks of it with affection and sadness.

"It's difficult to get legislation for a snake," he says. There is laughter. "It's a loser." He smiles but then looks anxious. He tries to describe the beauty of this particular serpent. It's many-colored, striped green-bluish, yellow, black, red, and blue, with an orange-red head and bluish-gray belly.

A TV man interrupts: "What's the purpose of a snake? What does it do? Why do you want to save garter snakes?"

(Later, I ask that question of my nine-year-old nephew. He tries to find acceptable reasons:

"It eats harmful bugs?"

"Would you save it, if it were up to you?" I ask.

"Sure!"

"Why?"

"It has a right to live," he answers without hesitation.)

The herpetologist hits it directly: "It's just part of nature; it's here. If you're saying what good is a snake, I'm sure somebody else is saying, what good is a butterfly or a grasshopper. It has no food value, it . . ."

"What is the purpose of a man?" someone offers. Switek smiles gratefully.

Then Coyote steps up and takes the microphone.

"I came here initially to talk about this bill to preserve the last three wild rivers in California—the Klamath, the Eel, and the Trinity. Our ceremonies revolve around those rivers and the salmon. . . .

"I wanted to speak after those mountain lions because when they came in here—when I saw those chains I felt those chains. These are our brothers. Out of respect for them I went into the back room and turned my back. You made a spectacle of them, taking pictures of them chained." His voice is full of emotion.

"There is no shame in this state of California where they'll fly the state flag of the grizzly bear and there's not one in the state of the thousands that were roaming here at one time.

"The nation flies the flag of an eagle and you can hardly see them anymore. Maybe we should readopt a national bird, gluttons that we are. Something that has no respect. Something ignorant.

"It sounded funny to some people to hear this man talking about the San Francisco garter snake. But what we're talking about is life, all life. There are balances for all these things. If the rivers will be destroyed not only salmon will be destroyed but many other things. One of the main things is the Indian. We have an advantage over those poor animals that were chained here a while ago because we've learned your language and we can speak to you at your own level. We speak for our own survival. But I would like to have it known that I'm gonna speak on behalf of the mountain lion because he can't speak English, and in behalf of the forest and other species because they have thoughts and spirits like me."

Coyote walks away, having unexpectedly delivered the message Keith had tried to convey through Switek and the lion man. The herpetologist had not been able to do it because he fit into a mindslot without subjecting the Western value system to question. He was a specialist. It was his *job* to care about snakes. *His* job, not other people's. But when the Indian spoke, it was out of a wholly different frame of reference. He was undeniably life-centered.

"I have learned something," Keith told him.

Keith moved on. As usual, he seemed weird to many "serious" and "realistic" people. He pared his personal needs to almost bare subsistence. He took to walking barefoot and he lost his buckskin knife. The police took it from him one night. They stopped and searched him after a rock concert, told him it was a fraction of an inch longer than legal, and arrested him for its possession. Keith's ninth arrest. The value of the tool was, for him, largely sentimental for he had not used it except for cutting cheese and bread at picnics. So he did not try to reclaim it after the charge was dismissed.

For a while a more prosperous Living Creature sponsored Keith and his press agency with a $40-a-week subsistence grant, part of which he sometimes passed on to Blue Cloud. Then he supported himself with a weekly column in *Crawdaddy* magazine ($30) until he decided he could no longer accept profit from something that involved killing trees. He decided he could survive on donations for chanting and dancing for people.

"We have been sacrificing the sentient-beings trees to the nonsentient-nonbeings *words* and that's the weirdest most superstitious most self-destructive fetish of *all*," he explained to his readers.

Awright! Let's slow it down! . . .
These days "drop out" means find some other hustle less destructive of the biosphere & after that find still another even less destructive etc etc till finally we *have* slowed the thing down.
"Lest" somebody feel that my act is futile, let me remind you that just 5–6 years ago very few people were ready to inconvenience themselves to provide an anti-war example (e.g., sit-ins, draftcard or dischargepaper burnings, draft refusal, desertion), yet the small number of examples in fact when combined with the inherent truth of the anti-war position has led us finally now to the moment at which the heads of the Catholic Church in the U.S. publicly turn against the war. [Several bishops had in recent months taken a stand against the war.] There is good reason to believe that a few strong stands taken

NUDGING ALONG THE PERCEPTUAL SHIFT

this year & next combined with the inherent truth etc may cause the head of that church (in the name of St. Francis of Assisi?) to turn against the sacrifice of trees for human profit by 1977 or 1978.

Awright. Keith continued to chant everyday, developing a style of his own, full of wild animal-like sounds. He looked more and more like a wild creature. His press releases began to look like poetry. By 1972, LCA was more and more a state of mind, less and less a tangible entity.

BULLETIN FROM LCA TO THE PEOPLES OF TURTLE ISLAND:

Living Creatures Associates Loves You.

We Are Presently Working On

A Crystal Radio Set
  which will pick up
    only

Seedsyllables—

Not words!

And Then Om

A Diamond Set
  which will
    pick up
      only

Small Birds.

       —ro-non-so-te

I recall what Bucky Fuller said when I told him about Living Creatures Associates: "A nice manifest of man's consciousness. Their effectiveness approximately zero." So it might appear if the results had to be spelled out on the application form of some foundation. But the Western notion of cause and effect, we have learned, is a misleading simplification of natural process. Keith the artist (He-Has-A-House), with his original media poetry works, was living out the fourth of the "Four Changes":

> Since it doesn't seem practical or even desirable to think that direct bloody force will achieve much, it would be best to consider this a continuing "revolution of consciousness" which will be won not by guns but by seizing the key images, myths, archetypes, eschatologies, and ecstasies so that life won't seem worth living unless one's on the transforming energy's side. By taking over "science and technology" and releasing its real possibilities and powers in the service of this planet—which, after all, produced us and it.

Our own heads is where it starts.

12

Holy Ground

We Americans need now more than ever before—and indeed more than we know—to imagine who and what we are with respect to the earth and sky. I am talking about an act of the imagination essentially, and the concept of an American land ethic. . . .

    Once in his life a man ought to concentrate his mind upon the remembered earth, I believe. He ought to give himself up to a particular landscape in his experience, to look at it from as many angles as he can, to wonder about it, to dwell upon it.

N. SCOTT MOMADAY

Focus on Grace Cathedral. First, in wide-angle lens, take in all of Nob Hill, where Gold Rush barons built mansions and saw them collapse in the great 1906 earthquake and fire. Now hotels, apartments, and halls have replaced them, but still this is the pinnacle of wealth and status in San Francisco.

The castle-like Fairmont and Mark Hopkins hotels vie for visiting notables and big-business spenders, each with a penthouse where tourists can drink and watch sunsets over the city as the white fog drifts in through the Golden Gate.

West of the Mark Hopkins, so discreet it's barely noticed by the casual passerby, a gray stone mansion, once the James C. Flood home, now the exclusive Pacific Union Club with lowered silk shades. Then the hedged serenity of Huntington Park where you can listen to the soothing trickle of a cherub-garlanded marble fountain, to the clatter of cable-cars and the forty-four bells of the cathedral carillon. This is "that corner of San Francisco which is forever England," someone once quipped.

The cathedral close occupies the square block west of the park, its Gothic design faithful to Europe, brought across to the New World along with bone china cups, hats, guns, and corsets. The Crocker family—railroad money—gave the land. William F. Nichols, the Episcopal bishop of California at the turn of the century, envisioned "a great Gothic edifice whose gold cross could be seen by the ships at sea," it is recorded in a guidebook. So it was raised, a bulwark of Christianity, among the heathen of an untamed continent, facing the yellow hordes across the sea, offering grace to those who would accept its terms. Fortress for the faith that sees man as the only creature on earth cast in God's image.

But forget the time scale that sets the beginning of American history at 1492 and refocus. People lived here long before Columbus and the Conquistadores. They knew this land as Turtle Island and themselves as its stewards. They built no monuments and never thought it their task to tame nature. Their role, as they knew it, was to act so that the earth would continue to nourish all its creatures. For this they sent prayers in all the directions for the great family of beings.

Now the Cathedral is a foreign intrusion, a dead weight crushing the hill.

A Zen Buddhist master, touring America for the first time, was heard remarking: "This is a very old continent."

Set your mind to infinity and move out till the whole earth appears as a ball in the void. Move in slowly, taking in cloud masses and ocean currents, the smoke plumes from the power plants destroying the Hopis' sacred Black Mesa, the last herds of whales, the last pelicans, porpoises dying in gigantic tuna nets as they are cranked into factory ships, wolves machine-gunned from airplanes flying low over the tundra, life extinguished in Vietnam by bombs that drop from above cloud cover. Then once again zero in on Grace Cathedral and step inside.

The great space overwhelms. "When you're there you know you're there, but you can never occupy it," someone said. "You can't ever find its center or ever see it all." Stained-glass windows cast multi-colored light patterns on the stone floor, reminding that over the ages men kept having the same ecstatic vision. The great rose window above the eastern main entrance was done by an artist in Chartres according to the motif of St. Francis' "Canticle of the Sun." It is a universal mandala.

On the autumn equinox, 1971, some people gathered in the pre-dawn darkness around the baptismal font, under the rose window, to begin a twenty-four-hour event "to recognize the existence and rights of the Great Family of Creatures, Plants, Land, Water, Air and Space which sustain us and of which we are a part." Nothing quite like it had ever before transpired in this sanctuary.

A few votive lights flickering at the foot of the font illuminated figures seated in a circle and others standing in shadows beyond. Maybe fifty people in all, gathered for a water ritual.

Within a few days, Governor Ronald Reagan would activate the California water project, sending torrents of water from northern rivers through pumps, tunnels, aqueducts, and over mountains toward the dry south. He would praise the people who took part in building the vast complex, one of the most colossal engineering feats of all time.

Many of the people in the cathedral this morning fought hard against the project on the grounds that it would cause irreparable harm to human and other beings and deplete the life-support system. They lobbied, made speeches, demonstrated, filed lawsuits, tried to show how this was another step in the land-grab that began with the early settlement of the West by Europeans. They talked much about water as a resource that must be used wisely for everyone's sake. But this morning, around the font, water was a sacrament.

Exactly at 6:48, sunrise, the Right Reverend Bishop E. Kilmer Myers began the liturgy for the living waters. He spoke of "that precious fluid which is the source of life for all creatures" and he invited others to speak.

First Dr. Paul Taylor, professor emeritus of economics at the University of California, who has given much of his life to the struggle for a just distribution of water and against government policies that subsidize the few at the expense of the many. His passion and perseverance for justice have made him a hero to many younger ecology activists. Now he stands up to reaffirm his faith that the struggle will go on.

A schoolgirl speaks next, lovely golden-haired Michele Osborne, just sixteen. She talks about being scared of the future because of what she sees happening to the earth.

Then Scott Newhall, former editor of the *San Francisco Chronicle*, talks about childhood recollections of watching life in a now-threatened lagoon. And Alvin Duskin, the feisty defender of San Francisco and the Bay, with words on water as a miracle and a sacred trust. Last Brother Jeremy, Franciscan monk, tells how Saint Francis, this city's patron, talked of "Sister Water, most chaste, most clear."

The windows are beginning to glow with daylight when Gary Snyder rises to read his "Prayer for the Great Family," written after a Mohawk prayer. It gives thanks for the earth, plants, air, creatures, water, the sun, the sky. Its refrain, "In our minds, so be it," sounds as the prayer of all of us here, who are beginning to realize that only when water is once again a miracle, a sacred trust, and a sister can we find true harmony with nature. Perhaps only then will the ecologists win their fights.

Some have brought water as an offering. One by one they step up to pour it into the font. I wish we had brought some from the spring at our ranch. Mel and I married by drinking some of the bubbly mineral water and sharing it with friends. The spring is our holy place, though we don't really talk of it that way.

One by one, people dip their fingers into the font and touch the forehead and heart of another person, "deputizing" him to help in the task of liberating California water for the use of all beings. They step up reverently, the way I used to step to the altar rail to receive holy communion years ago. The priest would place the wafer on my tongue, I'd bow my head, rise, and walk back to the pew to kneel, swallow, bury my face in my hands, and enter the beautiful garden of Jesus. Nothing had ever been so magic to me in my whole life. I was a Catholic convert at thirteen, instructed in the faith by a loving nun during many afternoons in a convent garden. My first communion was in the convent chapel, with ethereal voices chanting in the choir, an abundance of incense and flowers.

Then we moved away from the convent. In urban American churches the priests mumbled the Mass automatically and many people came late and left early, just checking in so they wouldn't be charged with mortal sin for skipping Sunday Mass. I began to notice how so much of the Church was set up like a bank so you collected credit in heaven for every novena or communion. The garden of Jesus closed.

Of course I missed it. Many years later, on Big Sur, I heard of a Catholic hermitage high up the mountain. So one Sunday morning I drove up the road, winding on the rim of the world between earth and fog-hidden ocean. Surely here I would find the reverence I remembered, I thought. But it wasn't there. Not in the way the hermitage was built, with no regard for the setting or purpose. Not in the way the hermits moved in the chapel nor in the crafts they offered for sale in their gift shop. And I knew, irrevocably, that these rituals were now corrupt.

Among the psychedelic folks I was beginning to meet on Big Sur, however, religious reverence was part of everyday life. New rituals were being created to reaffirm the vision of cosmic union and brotherhood glimpsed with LSD and other mind-altering substances. These rituals were essential to the nourishment of that vision and the cultural transformation it implied.

"It may be that some of the difficulties at the Altamont Rock Festival transpired because the organizers didn't take time to make the proper preparations," Gary Snyder wrote in the November, 1970, *Earth Read-Out*.

Such would be: formally asking the local Earth-Spirit for permission to use his space; requesting indulgence of the grass, insect and bird beings whose homes and bodies would be trampled on; expressing gratitude to the sky and air spirits and all living beings for their presence; beginning the gathering with a blowing of conches, and mantras and spells of love and peace; ending it with a prayer of thanks. Such was all done at the Gathering of the Tribes—the first Be-in—in Golden Gate Park.

The Altamont Rock Festival climaxed in a killing. The hippie high was over. But now here, at the font, is a continuance of the interrupted beginning. This new communion now includes not only young people and psychedelic graduates but also professors, editors, politicians, older people who have no interest or experience in drugs.

I go up to the front. Dipping my fingers, I am elated and grateful for something lost that has been restored.

The sponsors of the vigil intended that for its duration, the cathedral be open to all kinds of people and activities, as was the custom in medieval times, when cathedrals were not just houses of worship. Pilgrims used to sleep and eat in the aisles. Lovers met in the shadows. Public meetings were held and lawsuits argued there. The mayor of Strasbourg used his pew as his office. At Chartres, wine merchants had stalls in the nave. Dogs, cats, and pet falcons were admitted.

Therefore, for this occasion, the great gilded bronze doors

(replicas of Lorenzo Ghiberti's "Doors of Paradise" at the Baptistry in Florence) were opened to admit people who, for the most part, would never have considered attending regular Sunday worship.

Throughout the day musicians strolled about; craftsmen peddled their work; people worked on a giant banner to be carried in an evening procession. Some gathered in the choir to try to rewrite the U.S. Constitution to recognize the existence and rights of the Great Family, as Cliff Humphrey had done when he rewrote the Declaration of Independence into the Declaration of Interdependence. A brief ceremony was held during which the Senate roll was called from the pulpits and each senator was assigned a totem protectorate, becoming symbolic godparent to some species or region. (No record exists of how the senators received the news. The ceremony was in the nature of an incantation.)

At sunset the cathedral filled to capacity. Gary Snyder and Allen Ginsberg, chanting the sacred syllable OM from the altar steps, began the "sensorium." The great stone spaces filled with recorded bird calls, the howling of wolves, images of woods, seashores, animals, and trees projected onto the walls, and then with the mysterious haunting song of the humpbacked whale. In the gathering dusk, the Gothic arches became the ribs of the whale. We were inside the whale—Jonah's whale, Captain Ahab's whale, the great being of regions we have not explored, whom we are about to destroy but whom we have not learned to know.

Later some outraged Episcopalians would decry such "profane employments of this sacred house," protest the use of the cathedral for an event in which "animistic symbols and pagan cultic practices predominated." The Very Reverend C. Julian Bartlett, dean of the cathedral, would defend the vigil. But even he was, at moments, unnerved by the events of those twenty-four hours.

And no wonder. Christianity, as it spread through the West, is "the most anthropocentric religion the world has seen," to quote Lynn White, Jr., professor of history at the University of California, Los Angeles.

Pre-Christian times were full of gods and spirits, he points out. Every place and creature had its protector. Before a man dammed a creek, killed a boar, or chopped down a tree he knew it was wise to placate the relevant spirit. His attitude toward nature was therefore respectful.

But to the Christians, all this was idolatry. For the glory of the Lord they proceeded to chop down sacred groves and kill the buffalo. Christian priests taught that God spoke through nature: the ant was a sermon against laziness; fire was a way to visualize the soul's longing. But God was not *in* nature. He was above it. Man's duty was to overcome his own nature rather than find harmony with it.

White says that Christian attitudes are still basic to Western thinking, even if the theology is rejected. "We continue today to live, as we have lived for about 1700 years, very largely in a context of Christian axioms." Therefore, to find our way to natural harmony, we must either rethink the old religion or seek a new one.

In D. H. Lawrence's *The Plumed Serpent,* the people of a Mexican village remove Christianity from the church and restore their old earth religion. They prepare for the event for some weeks, weaving colorful serapes and readying a boat. One Sunday morning they enter the church and carry out the dry, painted, wooden Jesus martyred on the Cross, the Jesus with his bleeding Sacred Heart, the tormented Virgin, the saints and martyrs. Very respectfully they carry them all out to the boat, lay them down, and take them to a rocky island in the middle of a lake. There they bid them farewell and set them afire. Then they bring into the church Quetzalcoatl, the Aztec god who is bird and snake together, "whose hair is white with fanning the fires of life."

Something like that was happening in Grace Cathedral during the autumn equinox. God was again recognized as being present in all nature. Particular respects were paid to the spirits of the locality. Distinctions between sacred and profane were abolished. The whole round world was holy ground.

Each episode during those twenty-four hours was like another sprinkle of holy water on that recognition. Some hours after the sensorium, Alcatraz was consecrated as watershed cathedral in a ritual acknowledging the significance the Rock had assumed for many of us during the nineteen months of its occupation by the Indians of All Tribes.

When it first happened, it seemed unreal. Everyone was used to sit-ins, demonstrations, and protests. But by Indians? It seemed like a James Fenimore Cooper tale, modernized. Many San Franciscans were delighted and rushed to help out with food and other supplies. As the occupation continued, we got used to it. After a while we almost forgot about it.

One morning, after the story had long ceased being front-page news, I happened to turn my radio to KPFA and heard a rebroadcast from Alcatraz. Someone was reading recollections of an Indian childhood: how children played games without competing; how they weren't taught but learned by watching, trying, listening; how they roamed the landscape.

As I listened I pictured children free in the sun. It was early morning; I was eating breakfast; sun was streaming in through the dining-room window. Then came the shock:

"We're broadcasting under unusual conditions tonight," the voice said (this was a rebroadcast from the previous evening) "because we have no lights. A fuse must have blown somewhere and this is the only cell in this cell block that's being used right now."

So, from the sunny room and the image of wind-blown little Indians, I was dropped into a dark prison cell. But what the man on the radio described was just the sort of thing we had talked about, the sort of education we'd like to give our daughter. Maybe instead of sending her to a school that looked like a jail we could send her to Adam on his mountain and then to some Indian family.

I decided to visit Alcatraz to ask about the possibility of setting up some kind of children's exchange program. But for all kinds of sad reasons, the Indians proved inaccessible then. I never did make it to the island and I never caught another broadcast from there.

The Indians asked that Alcatraz be returned to them, to become a cultural and study center. The federal government offered to make it a national park, with Indian rangers and Indian monuments.

That, the Indians replied, "is a thing very few of us can imagine. Each of our tribes identifies with mountains, rivers, valleys, deserts, and other natural landmarks; these are the only monuments we need or want."

In the end, federal authorities dealt with the occupation of Alcatraz the way they have traditionally dealt with Indians. They ignored their existence until, in despair, their community began to disintegrate. Rumors of dissension caused the Indians to refuse access to outsiders. The little daughter of Richard Oakes, the young Mohawk who had led the invasion, was killed in a fall down a stairway. Oakes was critically injured during a fight in a bar. The number of occupants dwindled. Finally, on July 11, 1971, federal marshals evicted those who still remained.

And yet, for those who could hear it, there still lived a voice —the voice Keith Lampe, Joanne Kyger, and John Doss went to seek during that visit to Blue Cloud.

It was the voice of the land, and this event in the Cathedral was an attempt to tune in to that voice. Tired, defeated, broken, the voice of Richard Oakes read the last proposal of the Indians of All Tribes to the Citizens of the United States regarding Alcatraz, urging:

1. That the deed to the island of Alcatraz be given to Indians of All Tribes, with the stipulation that Indians of All Tribes act as guardians of this island, in the name of the Great Spirit, and for the benefit of all men and women who respect our earth mother.

2. That work begin immediately to level all man-made structures (excepting the lighthouse and necessary generators) so that nature can once more return to this island.

3. That the stone and concrete be made into blocks for a seawall as a protective barrier for the return of fish, sea otters, sea lions, and other creatures of the sea and air who would take shelter here.

4. That the steel bars and plates be given to children's playgrounds and parks across this land, to be made into forms and structures which the children can climb upon and enjoy.

5. That because we lost a young sister here, and because this island has been cleansed and declared sacred ground by many of our traditional leaders, it be allowed to remain as such forever.

6. That one small round house be erected, to be used once yearly, each time by representatives of a different tribe, in a ceremony of earth renewal and purification to re-dedicate it to all who love and respect our earth.

Let this proposal be acted upon immediately! Let this be a first step toward sane policies and practices regarding nature and our environment. Let us set an example that all nations of this earth can approve and accept. We must restore all that has been destroyed by greed and ignorance.

Yes, of course. But who was listening? By the time Oakes stood up to read, the crowd in the cathedral had dwindled. And in the places where decisions are made, did anyone hear?

I began to feel depressed. Was this event anything more than wishful fantasy, an evasion of harsh realities, the self-indulgence of a few trippers?

Allen Ginsberg sat down at the foot of the baptismal font with his harmonium and started a Buddhist chant. Lately, he had been using fewer words at poetry readings, in keeping with the "Four Changes": "Power is in the seed syllables of mantras." Such poems as he did read were in the nature of mantras.

He had hardly begun when a tall man in a sheepskin vest stood up directly in front of him and cut in with a drunken oration to the refrain that "Jesus lives." Ginsberg did not stop. Nobody moved to hush the interruptor. The oration continued to the chant and turned into a lament, ending "Love me mama, please love me please" as the man sank down and the sound of the harmonium continued.

Everything that was happening seemed to fit together. Even the drunk. Even that kid retrieving the bent Coke can from the font. Even the bizarre scene that was evolving.

It began slowly, with a white-faced figure slipping into the space behind the altar and starting to dance. Then more figures, costumed in feathers and robes, painted and otherwise decorated, joined in. A big bearded fellow with painted lips and eyes came waltzing out from the back and around the great altar, clad only in some frilly white curtains draped to suggest a wedding gown. He did a pas de deux with more than a suggestion of eroticism with a Mephistophelean fellow in black satin vestment of priest celebrating the Mass for the Dead. Flinging a black and red satin cloth, the "priest" stalked and stomped and postured while the bearded bride twirled, leaped, and writhed on the floor. This was a Black Mass. A scene out of Fellini's *Satyricon*. The sick effusion of a decaying culture.

By the time Gary Snyder took over, a few hours before dawn, with readings of Indian tales of the supernatural, people were sprawled asleep in front of the bishop's chair and behind columns. Someone was smoking grass in one of the front pews. A church official, passing through, trembled with visible outrage. Life, such as it was, had been invited to come in and manifest itself within the sanctuary. And it had.

The celebrants ended with a dawn breakfast in the park. They left no visible traces. But an after-image remained, changing the cathedral and those of us who were there.

"Somewhere deep in every American heart lies a rebellion against the old parenthood of Europe," D. H. Lawrence wrote in his *Studies in Classic American Literature*, published in 1923.

"Yet no American feels he has completely escaped its mastery."

The early settlers founded their new society on Thou Shalt Nots rather than affirmations of shared belief, Lawrence wrote, because most of them came here to get away from something rather than in search of something. Therefore, "American consciousness so far has been a false dawn. The negative ideal of democracy. But underneath, and contrary to this open ideal," he saw "the first hints and revelations of IT. IT, the American whole soul."

This new soul found voice in the writings of some of the early European-Americans: Nathaniel Hawthorne, James Fenimore Cooper, Walt Whitman, Herman Melville. But later generations came to view these classics as, more or less, children's books, wrote Lawrence. "Why?—Out of fear. The world fears a new experience more than it fears anything. Because a new experience displaces so many old experiences. And it is like trying to use muscles that have perhaps never been used, or that have been going stiff for ages. It hurts horribly."

In the 1970s, many young people again had ears for Whitman, Melville, and for Indian stories. Old forms of religion, imported from Europe, were sinking under their load of Thou Shalt Nots, while a fresh religious spirit was growing. Grace Cathedral was deep in debt, low in membership, out of touch with much of the new movement. But during the Vigil for the Great Family, it was an instrument for the new voice.

The sponsors of the autumn equinox event (anonymous) knew that one way people immunize themselves against new experiences is by wrapping them around personalities. They had seen that happen during the Trips Festival of January, 1966, when the acid culture came out for its first big public celebration. The intent of that event's sponsors had been to offer an LSD trip simulation by means of sound, light, and music. But the focus fell on Ken Kesey, Stewart Brand, and Bill Graham and much of the potential impact of the experience was deflected. The anonymous sponsors of the Cathedral Vigil had worked with Kesey, Brand, and Graham, back then, but in the background.

The Trips Festival marked a beginning of the hippie era, as the Altamont Rock Festival marked its demise. The hippie high self-destructed, for psychedelics proved to be a flickering energy source. Like fossil fuels, they were limited and could take you only so far. Few trippers had the stamina to proceed further on their own. So some came down into heroin and amphetamine addiction, others fled into the back country in search of simplicity. Some joined cults and became followers of assorted gurus and messiahs. Many grasped for non-drug spiritual technologies and tried to build some of the Eastern mind/body disciplines into their daily lives. The counter-culture the hippies were part of did not die. It diversified and expanded, continuing what Gary Snyder, in a 1967 essay, called "the Great Subculture which runs underground all through history." Based on trust in man's nature, it "transmits a community style of life, with an ecstatically positive vision of spiritual and physical love." But it is subversive to civilization, and therefore is usually suppressed. The anonymous sponsors of the vigil, who are close to Gary Snyder, continued to design events and environments conducive to psychic change.

The Vigil for the Great Family could be described as art, religion, a festival. Any description at all, however, presents the problem familiar to all wordsmiths, word magicians, and word technicians: it affixes boundaries, values, and shapes to events. It defines what happened and thereby distorts it. For in nature, all boundaries are permeable and shapes change constantly.

"To carry an accurate story," one of the sponsors suggested, "you'd have to leave half the pages blank. For the rest you'd have to think of the earth as seen from the moon and see how well man shows up. Then your words would have to be set so that man has the right proportion. The vocabulary would have to include the operating earth, of which man would be perhaps ten words out of a thousand."

HOLY GROUND

Focus once more on Grace Cathedral, its tower piercing the sky, presaging the phallic rockets America's favorite holy men would shoot outward. Time to make plans to get out. Planet getting dangerous. Put up the sign: Condemned. Europeanoid Americans, having plundered across the continent, see no more frontiers here and seek new ones in space. Never got into the land.

The Hopis' kiva is the exact opposite of the Gothic cathedral. It nestles within the earth. A small hole in the floor leads down into the previous underworld, from which the people emerged. A ladder to a roof opening leads to the world above. The priests do not dress in rich garments and they do not stand above others. They go barefoot and stand on the lowest level, closest to the center of the earth.

Male and female. Yin and yang. When they come together, do they balance and create new life?

The Hopis, someone said, are our native Tibetans. No need to seek for gurus in the Himalayas. But the circle of the Hopis' life-hoop is broken. We know only their legends.

Deep in the Grand Canyon, Nanao Sakaki, one of the new teachers, sits in lotus and chants with a coyote, one of the few still alive. To the Indians, the coyote had deep meaning, for in him many attributes of life met. To European-Americans he is a predator, to be killed.

Lil Lectric Lulu bends over the peacock-feathered mandala she's making. "It's easier to change your perception than your reality," she says.

(W)rap-up

The turning goes on and on. Many had the same cosmic vision as the people on the swami circuit and those on the awareness circuit and Keith and John Doss. My friend Dawson knows, after his night of acid ecstasy, that he's God's messenger, sent to tell the rest of humanity it must repent, follow the law, stomp on evil, turn to good.

After he saw the vast universal latticework, after he moved from plane to plane, Dawson began to drop out—but not quite beyond safety's reach. He gave up most but not all of his medical practice. He threw some stoney parties in his big expensive suburban house full of artifacts and cushions and Oriental rugs and lit aquaria. Stoneys sat in front of the big fireplace staring into the flames, pseudo-heads pretended to be stoned so they wouldn't have to talk to anybody. It was all very Chekhovian, just-before-the-revolution.

During the first few months after his cosmic glimpse, Dawson read Eastern mystics. Then he turned back to the Judeo-Christian tradition becoming—or so he thought, anyway—one of its new voices, speaking to the confused stoney world. Now he wants me to comment on something he's writing.

"Writing books is self-indulgence and a waste of trees," I say, almost finished with mine. I read his free-form treatise, see him trapped in his self, trying to break out of his ego-loneliness, trying to recapture that flickering moment of oneness.

Drugs can get you there but they can't keep you there, says the poet Robert Bly, who's been studying with a Tibetan lama. To stay there takes patient work.

Dawson Adam Keith John-Doss Mel I all had that same vision. It's hard to turn from ego-centeredness to man-centeredness, harder still to break through into life-centeredness.

To become greater, man must now become smaller, Gary Snyder remarked in 1969, having come to that conclusion via wilderness and Buddhism. We cannot afford our present standard of living, says Jay W. Forrester, having fed miles of world-around data into computers at the Massachusetts Institute of Technology and examined the readouts. Then Snyder moved out to the Sierra foothills to learn more from the wilderness. Forrester suggested we follow a deliberate anti-growth policy but did not say how.

There is agreement on the situation. The choice, if any, lies in the way the shift comes about. (That's assuming, of course, we don't extinguish ourselves by inaction or blow ourselves up by mistake.) Change can be imposed by a central authority or can evolve from personal transformations that compel power structures to respond. We can move from individual freedom to the total state, as in Huxley's and Orwell's nightmares, or we can move from ego-centeredness to life-centeredness as free people expanding toward our potential.

Cliff Humphrey, Keith Lampe, and others plead that we reshape our idea of progress so it comes to be measured—for ourselves personally and for our society—not in terms of dollars and bathrooms but in greater serenity, tranquility, and reverence for life. Admittedly, forecasts of attempts at central solutions seem more realistic. But I don't know of any central authority I'm willing to trust with the welfare of all living creatures, or even just myself. I do know that goals are largely illusions and that the only reality is what's happening right now. I'll put my faith in the process that seems most in keeping with natural harmony. When we look to goals and forget the process, we disconnect from nature. Then we get out of synch, out of scale, out of tune. We get megalo-agribusiness-slurban America.

Many people are now trying to get reconnected. The physical movement out into the country, to the bread-baking, down-home existence, is only one part of that effort. Interest in health foods, yoga, ecology, body language, meditation, Indians are some other parts, all growing from the same yearning.

It's lonely, being cut off from the rest of the earth family of species. Lonelier than David Riesman said it was in *The Lonely Crowd*. Lonelier than Colin Wilson, voice of the alienated man of the 1950s, described in *The Outsider*. Lonely unto death. But now more and more people are discovering that true freedom and fulfillment grow through acceptance of nature within and without ourselves, and of existence in context.

So we start wherever we are. Our heads, our house, our friends, our town. Unplugging ourselves from machines (in San Francisco, the telephone operators are actually *human*. You can exchange jokes with them), reconnecting with life. That way, we come to see the possibilities inherent in a shift of perspective, as Buckminster Fuller, for one, is trying to get us to do.

Everyone starts in a different place. Important to remember that universe, though uni-vers (toward one), is non-simultaneous. Some will take a stand on the war; some will try to keep ghetto children from dying of lead in peeling paint; some will try to save the San Joaquin kit fox, perhaps. Laying out priorities only leads to wasteful misunderstandings. All that is part of one wholly interlocking round.

(W) RAP-UP

But isn't it too late for all that? Is there enough give in our systems? People's Park seemed to indicate no. Amanitas is a tentative yes. Both are only minuscule seeds in the wind, of course. But in a most profound way they are relevant to the ghettos of Newark and Chicago (think of it in terms of Fuller's geometry)—just as Keith Lampe, bizarre though he may appear to the Dayton wife-mother, is relevant to her. Because he marched for peace in the 1960s, she is ready to march now.

The odds may be for death. The war continues. The abstracting, continues. Soon we will be so automated we will not see whom and how we kill. Frightened people disoriented by speed and inhuman scale, lost in a shrinking world, shrinking in an expanding world, keep on building walls and the fear keeps rising. With that, trust in the democratic process dies.

"Seems to me there are so many more gods and goddesses of destruction than of life," I remarked to Joanne.

"Oh no, you mustn't think that," she said. "That's giving them power. If I thought that, it would be not believing my own existence."

Chogyam Trungpa, Rinpoche, says that each person has a characteristic which is the tool with which he can make his path to Enlightenment. For one man it may be a gift of music; for another it may be a great violence or a great laziness.

So with society. Within what is now destroying us lies the way to fuller life.

We turn off the highway among redwoods and stop. Soft pine floor, reddish brown. A slope toward a stream. We walk down and are quietly enclosed by the majestic tree giants, included in their embrace of stream and rocks. Usha is one year and three weeks old. I take off her shoes and she coos, leading me by my right index finger into the clear water shimmering across little round stones. We walk across at a shallow spot and continue around a bend where there's a pool deep enough for a dip. Mel has already taken off his clothes and is going in. He emerges laughing, sparkling drops bouncing off him in the sun. Usha trembles with desire to follow. I take off my clothes too, go in with her. The water is cold and she cries out just once, then paddles, kicks, blows, eager to swim. Tara meanwhile, already eight and with plenty of civilized overlay, makes a big production out of getting into the cold water, squeals, grimaces, and dances about, asking to be coaxed and congratulated. Here among the tree giants, the Indian children still glide in like fishes and emerge brown, glistening with shining eyes. Tara is so self-consciously busy chattering she doesn't see them.

Usha, wading, stops suddenly, still holding my finger, bends from the waist, and puts her face against the mirror surface. Tongue darts out, cups, pulls in. She never saw anyone do this. This is a human being drinking. This is how a human drinks.

I've forgotten the highway so completely I don't think of the fact that we're standing there with no clothes on until Mel says something about getting dressed.

On the way back to the car Mel picks up a shred of paper. It's some kind of receipt with the word "Veterans" on it. Nearby I find a crumpled appointment slip from an infectious disease center in Los Angeles. Near that is a bail bondsman's receipt.

These tree giants with the sun streaks coming through (see them in your local Boise Cascade Company brochure), Mel as Pan, these cliffs covered with reddening blueberries—fantasy games in a palace garden. Years ago I ran along a forest path in New Hampshire toward a swim under a waterfall and nothing else existed. Now in the midst of such joy there is the sense of its death. This is a visit to a past that is bound to vanish as completely as the Indian children who splashed here before us.

The latest thing in modern living, I'm told, are those "totally planned communities" around Los Angeles, like Heather, which is meant for young middle-income families. About fifteen minutes

(W)RAP-UP

from Los Angeles International Airport, you turn off the freeway, turn into a curving drive lined with townhouses that look like they were put up by retrained set builders after long careers at Metro-Goldwyn-Mayer. Stop opposite a fake waterfall; cross a fake creek bordered with fake rocks; enter the little world of Heather.

Ah, dear Walt Disney, how your spirit lives on; this is your kind of oasis. Birds in trees that rustle in the soft breeze. From little round boxes, canned melodies. Little homes, snug as a bug, each with a patio, each with tiny lawn. Everything slightly too small and close together, cozy for Mickey Mouse people. Lawns watered automatically, all the latest in labor-saving devices, everything completely arranged.

At the pretty little playground, languid mothers lounge on the swings while watching their tinies climb monkey-bars and cement horses. Oh yes, they love it here at Heather. No need to go anywhere else. The pool is here, the tennis courts, and there are plenty of like-minded people to talk with. Besides, husbands take the cars off to work and you can't really go anywhere around here without wheels.

Stop inside a model townhouse, color-coordinated (yes, you have a choice of colors, said the rental agent, but there's no way you can replace existing carpeting with Oriental rugs you own); climb the stairs. What is that strange humming sound?

Stop at the window of what would be the children's room. Over there—armored warbugs run atop the elevated freeway. In Los Angeles the freeway is omni-present. It is to Los Angelinos what the New Hampshire woods once were to me—the total experience. When you're on the freeway, nothing else exists. You're immersed in the now. It's speed yoga. Escape. Inescapable. Just as Heather is inescapable with its domesticated everythings, its total planning enclosing mind/body. No room for wildlife in either one. And yet *we* are wildlife and confined to zoos we grow ill.

If we're to continue to ride Spaceship Earth and be nourished by Mother Earth we'll have to recognize our wildness, we'll have to shift our attention off freeways and onto free and high ways; off fossil fuel energy and onto Blake's energy of eternal delight.

To get there, we'll have to accept the bird, the snake and the child as teachers.

Dear Tara and baby Usha, may I tell you a story?

When I was a child I lived in a town (it no longer exists) where the miller's old father told stories to children every day after school. We'd sit on sacks of wheat and rye. He'd wait for us to become quiet, puffing his pipe. When we were very still, so still we could hear the brown mouse nibble on spilled grain in some corner, he'd begin.

One day he said, "There came a time when man inherited the Earth. I'll tell you how it happened.

"Before that time, Earth was home to many different creatures—whales and wolves, deer, horses, ants, nightingales, coo-coos, redwood trees, and many more I've never heard of. For every man who lived on earth, there must have been ten thousand other creatures.

"They lived together, not always in peace. Some ate others; some were eaten. Wolves ate caribou; praying mantises ate aphids. Beetles ate ants; caterpillars ate leaves. Man ate grass, fish, meat, fruit, and vegetables. For a long time, that's the way it was on Earth.

"Then man began to figure: This is a mess, there is too much going on, it must be cleaned up. All those creatures eat stuff people could be eating. What use is that? Man saw no use. So he began to change the way it was.

"He poisoned the beetle, shot the wolf, trapped the coyote, and poisoned the ant. Accidentally, not meaning to, he killed a lot of others. Soon, he said, there will be no more waste. Everything that's left will be orderly and useful."

The miller's old father stopped talking a minute, and I re-

(W)RAP-UP

membered I'd heard people say he'd been useless all his life, sitting around telling stories while his brothers worked for a living. Then he went on.

"Man went on cleaning up the Earth until it became very tidy. There were no more wild animals howling through the nights. No more foxes stealing chickens. No more bugs biting. No more useless kangaroos. No more fish. The Earth was clean. Everything that was left was useful. Man looked around and he saw that he had inherited the Earth."

That was a story the miller's father told us when we were small. When he finished we sat very still because we were scared. We listened to the brown mouse nibble, the useless brown mouse.

"It was only a story," one of the bigger boys said.

About the Author

Rasa Gustaitis, one of the nation's most humane and graceful journalists, is the author of the hardcover and paperback success *Turning On*.